A Theory of
Party Competition

A Theory of
Party Competition

DAVID ROBERTSON
University of Essex

JOHN WILEY & SONS

London · New York · Sydney · Toronto

Library of Congress Cataloguing in Publication Data:

Robertson, David Bruce.
A theory of party competition.

1. Political parties. 2. Democracy. I. Title.

JF2051.R6   329'.001   74-23542

ISBN 0 471 72737 7

Set on Linotron Filmsetter and printed in Great Britain ·
by J. W. Arrowsmith Ltd., Bristol BS3 2NT.

For Cherry

Preface

Officially I am a political theorist. One publisher's representative, knowing this, expressed surprise at seeing my office full of computer printout. My colleagues, knowing that I play with statistics find it more or less normal that I should run an M.A. course in Empirical Political Theory, but sometimes wonder what I'm doing lecturing on Aristotle, or the political philosophy of the Enlightenment. Although all three activities surprise me somewhat at times too, I have never really understood why they should be seen as incompatible.

If this book has any value, it is probably as an exercise in reintegration of these three sides of political enquiry. Aristotle collected constitutions, and was certainly an empirical researcher, without finding it impossible to write the Nichomachean Ethics. The Enlightenment Philosophers all turned their hand to scientific activity. At what point, exactly, political philosophy came to be seen as unconnected with empirical political research I am not sure. That it will not survive if it continues to be so divorced I am sure.

Accordingly this book can be read in at least three ways: as the development of empirical theoretical models of party competition, as an empirical investigation into the socio economic correlates of ideological change, or as a rather odd inquiry into democratic philosophy. If it serves in any of those ways, I shall be delighted. If readers manage not to ask such questions but read it as a gestalt, I shall be still happier.

To whom do I most owe thanks? I had never quite believed in those long and fullsome acknowledgements that authors engage in in prefaces until starting this. It really is true, though, that people beyond counting have contributed, perhaps unknowingly, perhaps without my knowledge, to the thinking and analysis that I have carried on for too long and in several institutions.

Let me thank generally all those in Nuffield College, in the University of Essex, and in the Department of Political Science at the University of Wisconsin-Madison, who have helped, encouraged, and made me welcome over the last few years. Some names just have to be singled out. In Nuffield, Brian Barry above all is responsible for this book ever being started. He has read whatever I have thrust on him, and given, as he has to so many political scientists penetrating, helpful, and kind criticism. Without him I would never have known that a whole area of political theory existed, let alone had the courage to try my hand at it. In that College also David Butler has helped and supported admirably. Keith Hope showed me how to work computers, and eased my nervous entry into the world of statistics. Much of the work was done with his programmes.

At Wisconsin I owe a great debt to Charles W. Anderson, whose conversation has helped me work out many problems about the nature of government and policy making. In all, Wisconsin provided much needed time, stimulating colleagues, and even interesting students, at a crucial time.

In my own University I must particularly thank Ian Budge, James Alt, and Ivor Crewe for their criticism, help and enthusiasm, and Kenneth Macdonald who completed my statistical education in his idiosyncratic way. I hope he can forgive my statistical immoralities. He is no more to blame for them than anyone else is to blame for my theoretical or empirical methodology, or indeed anything in this book. They do all share any credit there may be in it.

David Robertson,
Wivenhoe, July 1974

Table of Contents

CHAPTER 1

Party Competition and Democratic Theory

To talk, today, about democracy, is to talk about a system of competing political parties. Unless one chooses to reject the representative model that has been the staple of the theory and practice of democracy since the French Revolution, one must come to terms with political parties. In modern industrial society there is no definition of democratic politics that is very far from Schumpeter's that democracy is that institutional arrangement in which alternative governments, competing elites, offer themselves for selection by an electorate whose sole political function is to choose, lock, stock and barrel, one of these teams every few years.

Democratic theory is terribly vague, about the ends to be gained, about the justification for that preference, and above all about the expected working and detailed behaviour patterns that should characterise this process of party competition. About all that could be said is that it expects rational men to select one team of leaders, on the basis of their expected performance in office, to govern in the public interest. Because most of our representative, as opposed to our participatory, democratic theory was written before the twentieth century, it is fitted only for a situation in which the role of government itself is limited and unimportant. We have, in fact, no clear idea about what governments do, no real characterisation of what rough sort of action to expect from them. Nor have we, as a result, any very clear notion of the role of a political party, the standards on which they should be judged by the electorate, or the grounds on which they should appeal in influencing that judgment.

Worse than, though following from, this lack of prescription, is a nearly complete lack of knowledge about reality. If one does not know what a party ought to say, to win votes, one certainly is unlikely to have found out how in fact they go about this. Where one is ignorant of what is necessary before a mode of political behaviour, here party competition, can be expected to produce the result one desires, it is unsurprising that one does not know whether the necessary is performed.

This work attempts to examine one narrow but vital aspect of party competition, the policies suggested by parties, against the background of their need to win elections. Our concern is to show how parties compete for votes by offering and issuing different 'messages' to the electorate. For this to be useful, indeed before it can be performed in an intelligible fashion or even chosen as a research project, one has to have a model of the requirements, normative and prudential, implied by democracy. One has to know what is not acceptable behaviour, what determinants of this message are contrary to effective democracy, before one can be interested in the project or know what to look for. There is a powerful analogy with economic theory. To posit that a competitive market is a good thing requires a definition of the desired outcome of an economic system. It also requires a theory, or model, that stipulates the necessary behaviour of the firm. Economists could not practise their profession without the idea that firms must be profit maximisers, that supernormal profits, Giffin goods, or a depressed marginal propensity to save, might be unfortunate things. There exist today the Monopolies Commission and the anti-trust division of the Justice Department, because economists did more than state that economic competition was a good thing. They did more in that they allied to their normative theory (that maximal satisfaction at the cheapest cost of any desire was desirable) two other theories. One was empirical, a predictive and generalisable theory of how economic actors would respond to various stimuli. The other was the 'model', essentially a constitution, a laying down of what, given *homo economicus* as portrayed in the empirical theory, was necessary to ensure the aim of the normative theory.

Political theory used to be like this. The value of the *Leviathan* is that it is a combination of normative aim, empirical generalisation, and institutional prescription. Our aim here is no more than to help democratic theory towards being such a political theory. To this end we shall try in this chapter to fill in some of the gaps occasioned by the absence of a 'model', in the above sense, in democratic theory. Much will have to be stated and assumed, the arguments in defence taken for granted, for shortage of space. So many are the omissions of democratic theory that these points of faith are many.

The sections that follow cover:

Section 0. The meaning of party competition
Section 1. Governing as solving problems
Section 2. The aim of democracy; the public interest
Section 3. Competition for power as 'presenting a case'
Section 4. Democratic requirements of party propaganda
Section 5. Summary, and outline of the remainder of the book

It must be borne in mind that, throughout this, we assume that democracy does consist in an electorate voting for one of a set of rival 'alternative governments'. More vital still, it is necessary to remember that we take the phrase 'party competition', and the belief in its desirability and feasability, to carry many implications. These are discussed, to set the scene, in the first section, Section 0. The numeral is intended to indicate the minimum necessity of the following assumptions. Though they may be rejected as either untrue or unpleasant, we insist that to do so is to throw away the idea of competitive democracy, and thus to leave a choice only of the still vaguer democracy of participation or of some more or less than democratic form of government.

Section 0. The Meaning of Party Competition

There is an extensive literature in political science addressed to some version of the question, 'Why has the Labour party (or the German Social Democratic party, or many others) been so moderate, or "betrayed its membership" when in office?'. The answers given, whether in Miliband's *Parliamentary Socialism* [1972] or Michel's *Political Parties* [1966], have been various and could be said to have missed the mark. For the relevant question is not why, given that it is a competitive party, has it been moderate, but why it became one at all. A party which is committed to, and organised for, competitive electoral politics, must accept two principles.

One is that office is to be won, and lost, inside a system, as a result of its electoral attraction, over and over again. This leads to the second principle, which is that to win an election is only to have the right to govern for a limited period, with the high probability and not just the distant possibility, of losing the subsequent election. It is in effect to accept one rather than another of two possible views on the nature of governing.

Crudely, governing can be seen either as an architectonic activity, the building of an entire new social reality, or as a 'pragmatic' activity, the maintenance of an existing social reality, the solving of problems within this, and perhaps the gradual and incremental improvement of this along non-contentious grounds. It follows almost trivially that a competitive party has to accept the latter. We define here a competitive party as one which (a) is not in permanent opposition or permanent office; and (b) accepts the legitimacy of its major opponent and of the constitutional system. From (a) it follows that the party cannot be certain of the next election result, and from (b) that it will resign from office if defeated and will not try to undermine the legitimacy of a government formed by its opponent.

A society with two roughly balanced parties, each committed to a radically different definition of society, cannot survive long; once one such architectonic party has won office and started to implement its design, democracy can be assured only if the opponents are prepared to accept the new version. If they are not, and win the election, and repeal major legislation, the strains are too high to sustain alternating governments. Indeed the government can hardly accept the legitimacy of its own defeat if it is to be replaced by one that will dismantle all it has done. Even if revolution does not follow, alternating erection and repeal of major social institutions is not a process that can be regarded as an effective way of making social decisions. It is, in fact, hard to find more than a few major acts of repeal in twentieth century political history of Britain and America.

Those seen as extremists, the French Communist party with its insistence on abolishing Parliament if elected, or Stafford Cripps in the thirties insisting that the first action of a Labour government should be to pass an enabling act suspending the constitution, are simply more realistic. They do not wish to act inside the consensus, and realise that this means they cannot be competitive politicians.

This does not mean that competition between parties for votes cannot affect the consensus, that competitive democracies must be static. There occur from time to time major shifts in what one could call, following Kuhn, a 'Political Paradigm', when individual acts or entire programmes are implemented after the election of a party and which set the framework for ensuing years of 'normal politics'. But these have to happen either after the new initiative has been fairly well accepted by all major parties, or after an electoral result so decisive that opponents of the government realise that they cannot win again unless they accept the new paradigms.

The creation of the British Welfare State between 1945 and 1950 was such a shift. Except for two pieces of nationalisation, none of it has been repealed. Its origin was the coalition government of the war, and the coalition plans contained in the Education Act of 1944 and the Beveridge Report of the same period. Nor was there any major repeal of the New Deal machinery after Truman's defeat in 1952.

The explanation of these major and rare paradigm shifts may be contained inside the theory of competitive democracy, but one is not offered seriously here. If the rule that competitive politics is 'normal', paradigm-based governing, as hinted above and to be outlined below, is accepted, our concern is to study this 'normal politics'.

Another and more usual way of describing the politics with which we are concerned, and which we claim is the stuff of competitive democracy, is to call it the politics of problem solving. This is certainly how politicians seem to see it, and the language of political journalism is largely bound up with the ideas of 'problems' and 'solutions'. Unfortunately, common as such a view may be, it has not been well analysed, or been the focus for research or theory in politics. Mainly it raises problems, about what constitutes a 'problem', how they get to be problems, what counts as an adequate or good solution. Much as these worry us we shall skate lightly over such terribly wide lacunae, concentrating on sketching answers only to those questions that cannot at all be bypassed.

Section 1. Governing as Solving Problems

Social problems inhabit an illusive terrain somewhere between illusion and objective reality. They must be defined, obviously enough, in terms of human values and expectations, and equally obviously they owe their existence to both real conditions and human perception. All four of these elements must enter, and except for the 'reality' aspect they are only too open to manipulation and control by man, and must raise behavioural problems in a democracy.

A problem exists where some aspect of reality is not fitting with our values or desires, and where we either expect there to be a fit, or believe that it is both possible and proper to change the world to make it accord with our desires. The belief in possibility or the expectation must be there. No matter how much we might yearn for the moon, there could not be a political problem of space flight without the technology of rocketry. At the same time there needs to be consciousness, knowledge, awareness, before there exists a problem. Did we not keep statistics on traffic deaths a million people might die on the roads, we might be perfectly able to enforce safe speed limits, and have a morality which would lead us to do that, and yet there would be no 'problem' of road safety. Finally objective reality must be there, for we wish to, in our language we do, keep special abuse for those who whip up frenzy on a false problem.

In a competitive democracy political parties have to identify and offer solutions to social problems, and the governing of the state, the making of social decisions, consists ultimately in the electorate accepting one or other list of problems-and-solutions. Competitive democracy rests or falls on the extent party competitions for votes can guarantee that: (a) amongst the lists offered is at least one in keeping with the public interest; and (b) that voters are at least likely, to choose that one. That is itself a tremendous load to expect the system to bear, even before we turn the coin over. For each problem has to have a solution offered for it, and we then require of party competition that it is efficient in ensuring that the party with the best solutions is the one that gets elected.

Let us see briefly where competition might go wrong, taking first the several elements in the definition of a problem.

(i) A problem exists where conditions do not fit desires. Whose desires? One comes to this first because it is only at this point that our analysis is close to what has become the standard mode of political science analysis of democracy. This standard mode, whether carried out by one opposed to Western democracies on the grounds that they are shams, say an elite theorist or a marxist, or a proponent, probably a pluralist, is to see governing as satisfying demands. It is entirely a distributive activity. Questions are then raised about whose demands get satisfied, and how the national cake, or the 'stream of utility flowing from the government' is distributed (Downs, 1957; Dahl, 1967). We do not deny the accuracy of this characterisation, so much as find it confusing and potentially misleading. To think in terms of demand satisfaction without the framework of problems-and-solutions, without any background concept of governing, is either to abstract too much, or to produce an all-embracing characterisation that is too simplified to provide help in analysis. We feel also, though it would take too long here to prove, that it is to take far too little notice of what politicians themselves think they are doing. Still, the obvious question does arise—does competitive politics function so as to raise the concerns of some to the status of 'problems' and ignore too often some other sectors?

Without a definition of the public interest this cannot yet be answered, but it can be identified, and the source of the difficulty pointed to—it is that in some areas of policy, primarily the provision of social services, stratification of society leads to there being political problems not felt by all. The intellectual construct of a homogenous society can remove this theoretical difficulty, but others remain.

(ii) For even if a problem is one for everybody in society, it may not form part of any party's list of problems. The problem may not be perceived by the electorate, out of ignorance, and thus parties may prefer not to mention it. Or, if perceived (there are, after all, other sources of information open to the electorate) may still not be mentioned. It is not too hard to imagine a case where each party would be prepared to stay quiet about some problem as long as the other did likewise.

Imagine, for instance, that there was an increasing amount of drunkenness in Britain which was not only hurting those directly affected, but indirectly everyone else by damaging our economic efficiency and straining the health service. It is possible that neither party would wish to take it up, the Conservatives for fear of upsetting brewing interests, the Labour party because it was committed to a 'permissive' society.

(iii) Even the seemingly innocuous element, the feasibility of solving some problem, does not escape possible connection with the logic of party competition. Mistaken beliefs about how to solve some social problem on the part of politicians could lead to a party suggesting to the electorate that it could remove some inconvenience of life when it could not, and thus disorienting politics for some time. Probably worse would be a situation where politicians believed that an unpleasant choice would have to be made by the electorate were they to opt to solve a certain problem, and that rather than offer this, and have them reject the party for so doing, it would be better not to suggest the possibility of solution at all, removing even the chance to choose.

So many of these conceivable breakdowns in the transmission belt of competitive politics stem from what we are forced to call the 'logic of party competition' that it is surprising this has not been studied. The 'logic' is determined by two facts. One is that, if we place our faith in the competition for votes, for office, such a force can lead away from, as well as towards, a democratically satisfactory setting of party platforms. The reason this has been ignored is in no small part because of our demand maximisation model of governing. It is a tautology that if governments are free to divide up the national cake any which way, and parties are chosen according to the division they suggest, then the one that is supported by 51% of the population satisfies the national interest better than the minority party. If the world is as much more complex as we believe, the tautology vanishes and it is entirely contingent whether one can rely on competition. All that is needed is the possibility of a situation where one can gain more votes by omitting important problems, or offering inadequate solutions, than by offering a programme that would be in the public interest to show this contingency. The possibility of such a situation is too obvious to make it worth space offering an example at this point.

Of course the mere possibility, the contingent nature of the link between programme offered and public interest, need neither be very worrying, nor a subject worth researching. Research becomes worthwhile, and the question a worrying one, only when one suggests that it is conceivable that competitive politics might systematically break that linkage, or, at best, might in no way systematically make it.

This becomes more plausible when one considers the other basic determinant of the logic, which is that elections are fought by two political parties, one of whom is the government and one the opposition. (For convenience we assume a two party system throughout; all that we say can be generalised to multiparty systems without too much difficulty.) Analytically we can divorce the existence or importance of a problem from its solution, but in a special way this cannot be done when looking from the viewpoint of the party electoral strategist. For when the voter judges the solutions offered to problems he is not capable, often, of technical appraisal of policy itself, but instead has to reply on a judgment about the general competence of the parties as alternative governments. This, though partly informed by opinion about the personal qualities of the men in question, has very largely to be based on their records in office in the past.

A crude sketch of a logic of party competition forces itself on our attention given those facts. Can one risk, as the opposition party, drawing to the public notice a problem area in which the government has been rather successful? As the government, will one mention a problem that one has not, oneself, been able to solve yet? Will one be honest about the feasibility of solving certain welfare problems, which are dependent on a flourishing economy, if one is in opposition and the government has presided over an economic boom?

Farther than that we may not go in this section, for the working out of the logic of competition, and the necessary requirements on competitive behaviour if it is to be satisfactory, need more ground clearance. In the next section we take up briefly one stumbling block, that of the public interest. For this is the normative theory which, by defining the ends towards which party competition must work, gives us our ability to examine it. Then we shall go on to examine in more detail the nature of electoral campaigning in the rational model of democracy.

So far we have done no more than show how the existence of party competition is dependent on a view of governing, and alternative governments, that implies a 'problem-solving', 'normal politics', conception, and that this in turn focuses attention on the logic of 'problem-identification and solution-offering' by parties aiming at winning elections.

Lest this all be thought unduly esoteric, lest it be assumed that the identification of problems by politicians is totally consensual and rigorously based on reality, we direct readers' attention to Figure 1, in closing this section.

8

The Salience of Unemployment as an issue

= Conservative
Party

= Labour
Party

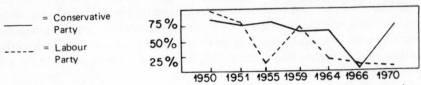

There is in this case an enormous discrepancy in the importance the two parties attach to unemployment in the years 1955, 1964, and 1970.

The Salience of Education as an issue

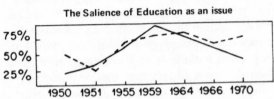

On education there seems to be rather good correlation between the two parties, although it is not easy to imagine the reasons for the discrepancies in 1950 and 1970.

The Salience of Housing as an issue

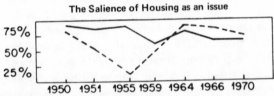

Since 1964 housing appears to have been viewed much the same by both the parties, but this was certainly not true in the earlier period.

The Salience of Nationalisation as an issue

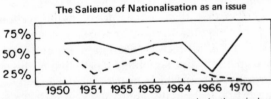

Not surprisingly, nationalisation seems always to have loomed more strongly in the minds of Conservatives than of Labour candidates.

The National Health Service as an issue

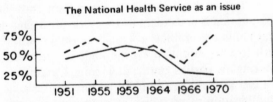

Again, there is very little relationship between the shifts in salience of the issue to the two parties.

Figure 1. The Salience of Issues 1950–1970. As demonstrated by number of candidates mentioning them in election addresses (from Butler and Pinto–Duschinski (1971))

Section 2. The Aim of Democracy: The Public Interest

Theories of democracy are somewhat silent on the question of the aim of this form of government. They certainly include restrictions on legitimate governmental activity, and various democratic testaments, the constitution of the United States, for example, contain additional values that are to be protected and assured. So the consent of the people, perhaps the approval of a majority, are deemed necessary for legitimacy in any democracy, and particular rights, to freedom, due process, equality of political say and enfranchisement, freedom from discrimination in a legal sense, are usually protected. But these are limits to action, or minimum constitutional requirements, and do little to say what should, rather than what should not, be done by a government. This shortcoming of democratic theory stems, as we have suggested already, from the time in which the essentials of democracy developed, a time when the government was not expected to be involved in daily regulation and support of all aspects of social and economic life. It is not just that democratic theory, being the work of liberals, has in the past been, economically, *laissez-faire*. For there is little feeling left that the government ought not to be involved in anything much more than peace-keeping abroad and law and order at home, yet there is a nearly complete absence of any general criteria, because there was no belief that government, or any other human agency, could hope to regulate and solve human problems.

What criteria we do have are summed up in the idea that the government ought to work 'in the public interest'. In many policy areas, and often the most important ones, this has a fairly precise meaning. The archetype is a military or other external threat to the nation, and the modern equivalent is a similar economic threat that is external, a fall in the balance of payments, a sudden world-wide fuel or food shortage. Characteristic of such problems is that they affect everyone in the society, and usually in a substantially equal way.

This is true of other good candidates for the public interest. Criminal law, and many aspects of company law, consumer law, and the regulation of contracts, for instance, are in the domain of the public interest because the capacity of a person to be hurt by activities in these arenas is not dependent on their social position. Anyone can be murdered during a crime wave, anyone can be hurt financially by sharp trading practices, just as a military invasion or an economic collapse do not have different consequences for people according to their social status. Another way of putting it is that these are principally aggregative matters, where some quantity, security against threat by enemy or whoever, can be increased for society as a whole. Yet another conception is that the public interest is clear in these cases because they concern public goods, that is, goods whose nature it is that consumption of them by one does not decrease the stock left for others. Finally they owe their obviousness as public interest matters to the fact that there exists no legitimate opposing interest.

This is the key, for where government policy concerns distributive matters, where only some people, identified by personal characteristics, benefit, where the goods are not 'public' in nature but specific, limited in quantity, the public interest requires a balancing of group interests that may involve a conflict between two equally legitimate interests. This affects the 'problem-and-solution' mode of governing in two ways, for not only may 'problems' that only affect some become political problems, but the costs involved in solving them have to be distributed in some manner or other.

Perhaps all such difficulties reduce in the end to questions about the legitimacy of some group or other, the extent to which a particular body of men are seen to be rightfully objects in the political arena. Recent examples of group conflict in which the public interest has been invoked, or where groups are singled out for special concern are illuminating. During the dock strike in Britain in 1970 it was argued by the government, and probably widely felt by the public, that the crippling of the national economy by a specific industrial group was illegitimate, because it went against the public interest, and was so declared by the newly created National Industrial Relations Court. The public has a right, apparently, over the economic interests of the members of one union. That this is at least officially an established principle was demonstrated by the wording of the Industrial Relations Act of 1970, which allowed to the court, the right to forbid for a time any strike which would be against the national interest, though this was not defined. In this case then the cost of economic production is rightly to be borne by the dockers in their getting lower wages than they felt entitled to.

Somewhat similar cases have been dealt with legislatively in a different way. The Prices and Incomes policies of the last three British governments have always included special clauses allowing the lowest paid workers to receive higher wage rises than others, thus accepting as legitimate, a group identity and a special claim. There are many examples of groups accepted as legitimate over the century, and by no means always on grounds of 'fairness', as most liberal democratic theorists would have. It was, for instance, official Conservative policy in the years after the First World War that ex-servicemen should receive preference in getting Civil Service jobs, an acceptance of group claims that can only be defended on 'desert' grounds, not on grounds of fairness, or equality of utility maximisation.

Political ethics in the United States allows for rather more group interests. There is first the idea that any group has some legitimate interests that may be put, subject (presumably, it is not spelled out) to a quasi-Lockeian requirement that as much and as good be left over. At the same time other groups are singled out, blacks and Native Americans, for 'affirmative action', that is, for advantageously unequal treatment.

There seems no way of deducing from the ideal of democracy itself what does constitute a legitimate group interest. At most one could argue that democracy is inherently egalitarian to some degree, as it denies the special right of any one group to rule, and thus the state may not be used to improve one group's fortunes over others consistently. That, and a broadening that has taken place in the idea of 'natural rights' to include the right to some minimum of housing, food, clothing, and medical care, and to those goods, principally education, that are prerequisites to compete in society, may serve to limit the group interests that are allowable.

Each society will have its own cultural definition of acceptable group interests, and the extent to which even these can be pushed will always be limited by the 'public good' aspect of public interest. Thus no private interest can be pushed to the point that it damages the public interest in the sense of creating a harm that applies to everyone, or may apply to anyone regardless of their group membership.

This last point is shown in the British and American treatment of economic regulation in monopoly and restrictive practices cases. The British Restrictive Practices Court has the duty to forbid any action in restraint of trade that cannot be shown to be in the public interest. This is to take some aggregate measure, economic well-being generally, and to exclude private interests on the part of some industrial sector in every case where they cannot be shown to further the general interest. It is, noticeably, much sterner than the equivalent labour legislation, which only forbids, and then most tentatively, action in restraint of trade (strike action) where it can positively be shown to damage the same aggregate interest. The point is that a trade union is seen generally as a legitimate group, that may on occasion have to be restricted, and a firm as one that does not have a generally legitimate case.

The relatively legitimacy of groups varies not only culturally, but inside cultures ideologically. It was a commonplace of Conservative thought, and still is of populism, that no group identity at all is legitimate, but such an escape is possible only where the ideology in question in fact identifies some entity other than the aggregate of living humans, as the rightful beneficiary of government.

If we cannot possibly lay down rules for the acceptability of groups in competitive democracy, we can nonetheless see how vital they are. For only some group interests can be legitimate, and the 'public good' conception of public interest must always prevail. Thus party competition in a democracy must not serve, if the aim of the system is to be achieved, to distort the public interest either by inadequately identifying and solving public good problems, or by raising to the status of public political problem that which is the private concern of some who may not legitimately make a demand on the public.

One has to take care over this issue because, of course, social groups are the essence of competitive politics, the social bases of parties and party loyality, and thus represent one of the greatest dangers to the democratic process. The dilemma of a leading politician in a Western democracy has always followed from this, and represents it nicely—he is, as party leader, usually a representative of a particular section of society, and as a Cabinet member once elected, part of the government of the whole population.

Having now drawn in the most perfunctory outline the normative aim of democracy, against which the function of government as the solver of problems is put, we can turn to consider the machinery of party democracy itself, the process of regular selection of governments. How should this be carried out, how is it carried out, what has to be true of the machinery of competition if the process can be relied on to serve its purpose?

Section 3. Competition for Power as 'Presenting a Case'

Perhaps the most researched question in political science is about the determinants of the act of voting. Mainly it has been, as most of social science research, dictated by the 'thing-attribute' mode of explanation, in which the voter is seen as an entity whose actions are to be explained by characteristics, class, education, colour or whatever, that can be predicated of him. In contrast, we shall treat voting, as is required by democratic theory, in 'event-sequence' terms. Doing this means seeing the voting decision as resulting from a decision made at a set time on the basis of past events, which may be the voter's experiences of governments and their messages to him. Obviously attributes are important, as colouring his perception of events, and even dictating in part which events he experiences. They are more important still in that one of them, his personal political morality, determines the choice made on the basis of the events. But of all these elements, only the message is in the party's control fully. We have therefore no choice but to concentrate on this, and to some extent the element over which a party has a lesser degree of control, its record in office, which represents part of the sequence of events experienced by the voter.

The voter obviously has to be seen as a decision maker, and in the context of policy making literature he has a terribly difficult job to do. Observing a society with many problems he has to select one from a very narrow range of policy sets, which, once chosen, cannot be altered for several years. He cannot construct policy sets, cannot combine them, but must choose from them. Worse still, he cannot set the problems which are to be dealt with, but must choose one alternative which represents both a list of problems and suggested solutions. This is all difficult enough, but only touches on the gravity of the situation, because we have not yet considered the information resources on which he can act.

First, he is informed of what social problems exist in four ways: (a) his own experience, which may be very limited; (b) by 'experts', which here means almost exclusively the mass media, which offers only very selective and partisan aid; (c) by the opposition parties; and (d) by the government, which is a competitor. Secondly he has access to the records in office of the competitors. This represents, at most, information on the general ability of a team of men to solve similar problems, or information about the general efficacy of an approach to problem solving which is reduced to a few broad principles. This information again comes to him in the four ways mentioned above. Finally he is given, during the campaign, a chance to hear each competitor making a case why he, and not the opponents, should be elected.

We shall summarily ignore from this point sources of information other than of a personal, or party, produced nature. We have little systematic knowledge about the efficacy of these other sources, except as transmitters of the parties' own messages. It may be unfair, but our own impression is that they are of negligible importance. But we ignore them here only because the question of providing adequate mass media information for the voter is far too complex for this study, and is not, what we must concentrate on here, in the control of the party or the voter.

Having said that, the voter's position as a decision maker can be seen as very strange, for his information about (a) what problems need solving; and (b) which policy set is best comes from the policy sets themselves. It is as though a civil servant was restricted, when making a decision, to talking only to the exponents of rival policies, and to having to accept their word that the situation was one he should be spending time on at all. In such a situation the 'cases made' by the rival exponents take on a crucial importance. It is common enough, in writing about modern democracy, to point out the limited range of alternatives offered by a two or three party system. This however is not obviously very important. In the fields of relatively technical, incremental policies, a wide range of alternative solutions, or of problems, can only contain many which are wrong, and increase rather than decrease, the difficulty of voting. What is less often pointed to is that the alternatives that are offered are so shadowy and uncertain, reliant for their very existence in the voter's perception, on the conflicting interpretations of men who have a personal interest in the outcome.

One needs only to read through a collection of campaign speeches, like those of 1970 in Britain, or of 1972 in America, to realize how unsure one could be not only of which party's policy was best, but what they even were. This comes not only from the vagueness and apparent internal contradictions in one party's presentation of its own case, but from the rival's interpretation of that case and the inconsistency of their two accounts of the state of the world.

For example, an intelligent, public-spirited and rational voter in Birmingham in 1970 might well have believed that a vital question was whether or not an incomes freeze would be introduced by the next government. What was the Labour party policy on this matter? According to them, they would not do such a thing, and yet Mr. Heath dedicated most of a long speech that would have been well reported in the area warning his audience that this is precisely what Labour would do if elected. How was the Birmingham voter to decide, if he cared about this issue? More generally, what was the economic situation in the summer of 1970? Favourable, or approaching a crisis? Any non-economist who wished to assess the parties rival programmes against this background could be forgiven for immense uncertainty.

The same examples could be drawn from the Presidential election in 1972, but consider these instead. If you feared communist military might, you would not wish to vote for a policy of immediately and drastically cutting the defense budget by 60 billion dollars. Did Mr. McGovern advocate this? So many were the different versions of his defense plans broadcast by his supporters and those of Mr. Nixon that it was virtually impossible to know what one would have been voting for by November. The same might have been said about the welfare policies, and even today it is impossible to know which version of different accounts of the general state of the war in Vietnam, against which any policies for ending it had to be judged, was accurate.

Such examples only give an impressionistic account of the importance of the 'cases' in elections. Like their similar common law traditions, the two party electoral system countries of the West operate on an 'adversary' rather than an 'inquisitorial' basis in politics. Elections, unlike courts, have two missing aspects. They do not have judges to instruct the jury and control the testimony, and they do not have electoral codes of conduct or professional bodies to discipline the presenters of the briefs. Were our purpose here to advocate the creation of new institutions in democracies, we should push this analogy further, for the rules of evidence and the conception of barristers as officers of the court could be most fruitful in suggesting how better to organise our political advocacy. However we can be concerned here only to examine what might go wrong in the process of electoral politics as it now exists.

The examples above illustrate, in fact, only one side of the problem of the 'case made', which is the need for accurate portrayals of policy and of the situation against which they are offered. The other question is the legitimacy of the case. This covers the appeal to voters on grounds that ought not to be introduced at all, and is divisible into two sub-sections. On the one hand, there are certain arguments that might be thought to sway the voter but of which he ought to take no notice, for to decide on the basis of them would be irrational, and possibly unfair. For instance, it ought to be irrelevant to a voter's decision that one of the candidates for office is black, homosexual, had committed adultery, or is Catholic, yet one might sway audiences by mentioning this. Equally one ought not to try to win votes by advertising those same facts about oneself. A candidate who, when visiting a factory mainly staffed by the descendants of Irish immigrants, in the United States, makes speeches packed with Catholic symbols to establish the sheer fact of co-religionism, is introducing factors that are irrelevant, but powerful. He is attempting to subvert the rationality of the electorate.

The other subdivision follows in a sense from this, but has more to do with the tentative definition of the public interest in the preceeding section. We have argued that the public interest may take account of some special group interests, but not others, and that all group interests must be restrained at some point by the 'public good' aspect of the public interest. This indicates another aspect of legitimate 'cases', which is that one may not win votes by offering policies, or taking notice of group related problems, if this is contrary to the public good, even in the long run. Yet one can easily hope to win votes by promising, say, that the problems of mid Western farmers or Midlands car workers will be given great attention, even when to do so will damage the economy or unfairly penalise some other more 'deserving' group.

One has to be careful here, because pork-barrel politics of this type has a certain legitimacy, in a more refined version, as pluralist democratic theory, and because the moral right of various groups to be taken note of is, in part, shown by the readiness of parties to advocate their interests. It is necessary to point out that while the representation of group interests may be normally acceptable, democratic theory in a modern society is only tangentially concerned with representation. It is a central tenet of this work that party competition is about the selection of governments first, and only secondarily, if at all, about the representation of anyone. It is rather likely that these two aspects of democratic elections, that they are both the selection of governments and the election of Parliaments, are less compatible than has hitherto been accepted.

There are, of course, two levels at which competitive politics can be assured of, or prevented from, realising the public interest, in as much as one could hope for the required behaviour on the part of either parties or voters. If voters resolutely refuse to be swayed by non-rational arguments, and to listen to anyone who promises to raise their private worries to the status of public concerns where this is not justified, if, in short, voters all have a democratic morality, then we need worry less about the messages parties put out, for no illegitimate case will be listened to. Equally, if political parties refuse to make arguments, or offer promises, that contradict the requirements of democracy, then voters have no choice but to select a government on the proper grounds. Restraint on one part or the other may seem adequate, but actually the role of the party is still central.

It is central because of the aspect we first mentioned, the need for accurate information. The best intentioned voters in the world cannot choose properly, given distorted messages. Indeed if both parties in a two party system insist on offering programmes that violate canons of legitimate argument in both of the senses above, voters have no alternative but to take up what cues, whether about the irrelevant personal characteristics of candidates, or the likelihood of group interests being served, are presented. In fact much political science has been concerned with leadership restraint, and phenomena like the stability of democratic states have been shown to rely much more on leadership, particularly on consensus between rival leaders than on voters. While we do not wish to endorse it, the findings on the 'authoritarian personality' (Adorno 1964) and the arguments of democratic elitists like Kornhauser [1959] all speak to the primacy of leadership behaviour in democracies.

The importance of the party in competitive politics, and the centrality we assign here to the party's public argument for its own election are, it must be admitted, very much dependent on an as yet unstated assumption. This is that the party competitive arena is far from being perfectly competitive, and is indeed an oligopoly. (Or an oligopsony—it is never clear whether an economic theory of democracy should treat parties as buyers or sellers.) Briefly, we assume that it is very hard indeed to set up another, or a new, party, so that an electorate not very satisfied with the alternatives offered cannot switch its support to a new entrant. In the short run anyway, and most probably in the long run, there will be no new entrants. The empirical strength of this assumption is hard to assess, and we go in to it very briefly in Chapter 2.

Having argued for the vital importance of the parties' 'case' we turn, in the next section, to indicating examples of the requirements of these cases that democratic theory must impose. The ways in which the 'logic of competition' may cause these requirements to be unfulfilled is the principal enquiry of this work.

Section 4. Democratic Requirements of Party Propaganda

It is common to talk of the 'rules of the game' when discussing party politics. These are usually restricted to forbidding overt tampering with the electoral process, as in bribery or coercion, or the flouting of 'one man, one vote' rules as epitomised in the slogan 'vote early, vote often'. They can be broadened, and in places have been, to cover other ways in which electoral politics may need to be restricted, formally or otherwise.

There also exist, in most democracies, laws governing campaign expenditure and access to some forms of mass media. These are not usually very effective, but their existence reflects an awareness that the outcome of an election may be 'unfair', and presumably therefore 'incorrect' unless the 'market' is controlled in some way. What we argue is that while it is hardly likely to be possible to institute rules or controls over party propaganda, the proper functioning of a democracy may be as much dependent on the observation by parties, when setting their programmes, of certain restraints as it is on the absence of bribery. We must here try to sketch such necessary constraints and requirements.

These can be divided into three categories, as party propaganda itself seems to have three elements, the description of the background, the actual policies offered, and the arguments in their favour, or in favour of the party as a government.

(A) *The Parties' Descriptions of the Background*

We use this somewhat ambiguous phrase to cover a variety of types of information. Any election campaigning must start by painting a description of the state of society, which serves both to indicate what are the most urgent problems and tasks facing the new government, and to limit the expectations the electorate ought to have for the future. Thus at a time of economic crisis, each party has to inform the people of the precariousness of the economy, pointing out that the next government must solve, say, the balance of payments and inflation problems, and, in stressing these priorities, bring the people to accept that it will not, immediately, be possible to cut taxes, build hospitals, unfreeze wages, or whatever.

The importance of the political parties in providing such information is buttressed by the fact that one of them actually is the government, and even the opposition represents the only alternative pool of expertise and talent in governing. Clearly we must require that such a portrayal of the conditions of society be as accurate as possible. Disagreements may still occur, arising from genuine differences in economic philosophy, for instance. But any tendency to interpret reality in a way favourable to the fortunes of one party is contrary to inevitable requirements. So complex is this issue that parties need to exercise considerable restraint in their selection of economic and social indicators. As an example, in a period of high inflation, partly caused by internal wage bargains and partly by international terms of trade, the electorate needs to be presented with a portrayal of the economy which neither overstresses the uncontrollable external factors, nor places all the blame on internal matters that the government could be expected to do something about.

What one requires in this area obviously has to fall a lot short of the canons of academic marshalling of evidence. Yet we can be fairly clear that any systematic tendency to interpret the economy inconsistently with the major economic indicators is damaging to the functioning of democracy. We use economic matters as examples here only for convenience, as all we have to say applies equally well to any policy field. It is historically true that in post-war Britain the economy has been of overwhelming importance in party propaganda.

(B) *Policy Determination*

There is a somewhat confusing vagueness of the proper relationship in democratic politics between the popularity of any policy with the electorate and the propriety of a party's offering it to them. There is a body of opinion, stemming perhaps from elitist theorists like Mosca, via Schumpeter, and culminating in the economic theorists of democracy like Anthony Downs, which holds that parties will, and ought, to modify their policies until they have an electorally successful package. To hold onto a policy that the voters clearly do not like, or to adopt one that, for any reason, is going to lose you votes, is seen as not only foolhardy, but devoid of value, because a properly functioning democracy is one in which the government automatically puts into operation those policies that please a majority of the electorate. In contrast there is the idea of a party, popular amongst much of the Labour party in Britain in the fifties and sixties, in which it is seen as its duty to advocate an ideologically pure programme regardless of its popularity until such time as the electorate comes to its senses and accepts it.

The power of the former model comes from the belief, discussed earlier, that governing should be seen as an activity of distributing utility to supporters, rather than the more complex characterisation we suggest of problem solving. If utility distribution, with no hindrances imagined to any distribution pattern, is or should be the essence of electoral politics, then of course it follows that parties must determine their policies entirely on grounds of electoral expediency. The power of the other model, of the 'sincere' party, also comes from a characterisation of competitive politics that we argue against, that in which governing is seen as deliberately architectonic, in which electoral victory is the prelude to the making over of a new social reality. With such a faith, there is no virtue at all, and indeed no expediency, in modifying policy to increase popularity.

The problem solving characterisation requires a more subtle and flexible relationship between electoral popularity and policy, and one exceedingly difficult to stipulate.

If one talks at all about government as problem solving, then one cannot avoid the idea that there are, in varying degrees, correct answers, or at least more or less successful policies, for solving these problems. Because one is prepared to accept at the same time that the salience of problems must depend on the relative costs of solving them, and that ultimately only the electorate can decide this salience, this does not lead to some Platonic position. So a set of policies of which the electorate flatly refuses to approve probably ought not to be advocated, at least by a major party. Policies that do work, a general approach to a problem area that is popular, equally deserve the support of all major parties. This leads us to believe that successful and acceptable policies do, and should, have a dominance, such that they are the stock in trade of all parties. They should be advocated, and a party ought not to refrain from recommending them because this is not electorally expedient. For although we normally think of electoral expediency preventing the offering of unpopular policies, it may equally work the other way.

This comes about largely because of the importance of a party's record in office. Suppose that an area, health policy, is one in which a major party at some time thoroughly established itself, created a popular and successful policy, which was opposed by, and not in keeping with the ideology of, its opponent. In such a situation it is extremely hard for the opposition to act competitively. If it too advocated the successful health policy, it does nothing more than reaffirm its rival's success, while being unlikely to win votes, for the electorate has no reason to think it would be particularly competent at, or keen on, operating a policy that it has opposed in the past. If one does like a national health service, why vote for any party other than the one that created and maintained it against opposition? It might well, therefore, suit the opposition to advocate some other policy for health, on which it would have its own predominance, while trying to convert the electorate away from national health.

If competition for votes is to be relied on as a decision applying mechanism, it must be seen that electoral expediency can cut in many ways at once. For one has to take note of the way in which competitive behaviour might not consist of offering popular and successful policies, as above, and also consider what happens when competitive behaviour is unnecessary. For we can only rely on electoral competition if we assume that a situation cannot arise where a party is free to ignore electoral expediency, at least in part. Remembering that a party policy will contain numerous items, covering several problem areas, consider the following hypothetical example. A political party might, partly because of the popularity of some of its policies, and partly because of the appalling record of its opponent, be a tremendously strong candidate to win an election. But there are other problems in society, in which a sub group, loyal supporters of the strong candidate, have a definite interest, though a minority one which could not, by itself, win an election. What is to stop the strong party from offering a programme that amounts, in many ways, to blackmail, which effectively says, 'you have to vote for me because you know very well you can't risk my opponent, so you'll have to accept these minority interest policies as a part of the bargain'?

In short party platforms are required to be sensitive to the popularity and success of policies, whether or not that is a competitive strategy, and to reflect majority interests even when that is to be unnecessarily competitive. One must require, further, that the set of policies of all the major parties react in some systematic way to objective conditions. It ought not to be the case that a change in, for example, economic conditions, is met by one party remaining in a previously consensual, popular, policy position, while another deviates suddenly and sharply from this. Either the existing policy is working, in which case it should be generally accepted, or it is a failure and ought to be generally abandoned. Yet there is a pattern of such sharp change in policy position, as we show in a later chapter.

It is obviously not possible to spell out in detail, and in abstract, what precisely ought to be the common determinants of policy. The point is that the concepts of policy success, and policy popularity, require behaviour that need not at all follow from competition for votes. We shall try in later chapters to fill out this rough sketch of democracy's requirements further.

There is one final requirement that we need to mention briefly. No chance exists of voters choosing a correct or suitable policy set if those offered them are inconsistent. Now whether or not consistency is so obviously a requirement for effective government that it always exists in the programme of the party as a whole is hard to say. There are too many ways in which policies can be inconsistent, logically, emotionally, and financially, to expect that they will be able to avoid it completely. Certainly inconsistency could be electorally very attractive. In a society factionalised by class, or divided into social groups, it may well be virtually impossible to put together a set of policies that can appeal to a majority of voters, none of which contradict each other.

For us to say here that consistency is another requirement of democracy is, at the same time, trivially obvious and begging a host of questions. There is, though, a special aspect of consistency that is less trivial. Most electoral systems divide the voters into constituencies, from each of which candidates are elected. The selection of the government itself is at second hand, depending on the number of candidates elected from each party. There is no reason to suppose, and the reverse is usually true, that each constituency is a microcosm of society. Which means that in many constituencies, the policy set that is a winner in the country as a whole, is a sure loser. As long as candidates faithfully reflect central party doctrine, many will be sure to lose, but the policy of the elected government will be consistent. However if they deviate from central party policy so as to stand some chance of winning in their own constituencies, a series of individually rational voting decisions may produce collectively inconsistent government commitments. Alternatively some majority version of government policy is applied, and the link between voting for candidates and selecting policy is broken, at least for some voters in some constituencies. We cannot go into this at length here, but it is clear that democratic theory requires as little as possible of policy deviation amongst party candidates. This requirement is not only incompatible with a faith in competitive politics as a mechanism, but in addition makes still less compatible the dual function of elections, mentioned earlier, as government selection and representation devices.

(C) *Encouraging Voter Rationality*

The third aspect of the 'case' is the sort of arguments a party can use either in defense of its policies, or just of its leaders as a governing team. Democratic theory has always been seen as dependent on the hypothesis of the 'rational voter' a *'homo politicus'* resembling somewhat *'homo economicus'*. Other aspects of his character have at times been seen as vital, so that Rousseau insisted on a certain moral element, while Marxists oppose western democracy on the grounds that, voters being ideologically manipulated and suffering from false consciousness, they could not possibly make a free, or moral, choice. No one, however, has put forward a defense of democracy itself that did not require 'rationality' in some form or other.

For this reason the research findings of survey researchers, from Berelson in 1948 to Butler and Stokes in 1969 have often been seen as invalidating some of the major democratic assumptions. Whether they do so or not, we discuss in various places in Chapters 2 and 3 and 6. What must concern us here is the opposite side of the coin, which is whether the campaign messages poured out by political parties either encourage, or even permit, rational voting.

There are two requirements, one positive, one negative. The negative one we have touched on already. Politicians probably could, and clearly ought not, to pander to the baser, or less rational elements of human nature. They could attract votes by playing on group, religious, colour or ethnic, loyalty or hatred. They could make their claim on an unsupportable and untestable 'natural right to govern' or superior capability, which in a country with a strong deferential tradition might be most effective. They could frighten the people with ogres (the Communist menace) that are not real, but which have very powerful emotional or symbolic content. They could, if in office at the time, try to confuse people between support for the institution and office, and support for the actual incumbents. Such examples could be multiplied endlessly, are all familiar enough, and hardly need labouring. It is not too surprising that where politicians specialise in using such a symbolic approach to winning votes, surveys should show that such symbols are important in the voter's mind. They are crude examples, and the game can be played more subtly, in a way hard to distinguish from legitimate pleading.

For instance, it is obviously acceptable that politicians should comment on the record in office of their opponents. At some stage however the reference to some past evil or incompetence, still emotionally important to, and capable of swinging, voters, becomes irrational. How appropriate now, would it be for a Labour leader to forcibly remind people that the Conservatives are the party of Munich, for a Democrat to remind Southerners of the Republican party's record in the 'war between the states'?

We have no precise canons, again, but to offer, insistently, information, cues, and symbols that would be ignored by a hypothetical perfectly rational man, is at best irrelevant, and, more probably, dangerous to the functioning of democracy.

CHAPTER 2

A Predictive Theory of Competitive Democracy

A.1. Introduction

If democratic theory posits, as a mechanism for social decision making, competition for votes between parties, it implies a predictive theory containing those elements. In general, as democratic theory is based on the idea of a rational, calculating voter and his interaction with politicians, who are either ambitious of office or desirous of power, it invites a theory of a special sort. The type of theory, like economic theory, which is invited is one that stresses strategic considerations, that analyses the likely outcome of the intermix of separately chosen rational strategies by actors with limited choice and highly imperfect information, bound by agreed rules. Such theories have another aspect, their abstraction of important elements of the real world into a simplified account, or model, that highlights only those structural parts necessary to give an intelligible prediction in the world, and only those motivational determinants of human action that are assumed by the theory.

To create such a theory is a totally deductive enterprise, though one that can be carried on with an eye to realism in assumptions. If the predictions it makes can be tested, and turn out to be inaccurate, it must be rejected or modified, but if they are merely unpleasant, and cannot be shown to rest on assumptions which are untrue, then the normative theory from which the model is derived may be the one requiring modification. What is clear is that unpleasant facts and normative recommendations themselves can never meet. If we require, normatively, the satisfaction of the public interest by means of competitive democracy, and find that in such democracies it is not satisfied, we have no grounds for rejecting, on that alone, the normative prescription. But moral theory, as is democracy, can be rejected on empirical evidence, about the intermix of human nature and the prescribed institutions. For that one needs a predictive theory of democracy, and in this case we need a predictive theory of party competitive democracy. One exists already, that of Anthony Downs in *An Economic Theory of Democracy* (1957), and this is both the inspiration of, and the starting point for, our theory here. It is briefly surveyed in the next section. The section following, A.3, points out a few basic weaknesses of

Downs, and the rest of this chapter consists in modifying the essential Downsian model to take account of these and in deriving predictions about the outcome of party competition which seem most obvious and important.

Whether the predictive theory we use can be regarded as following from Downs, and thus as an extension of his work, or better viewed as a critique of him is not for us to say. Our impression is that while what we have to say could not have been begun without his previous work, the relation it bears to this original is vague. The prime reason for this is that to talk of pointing out 'weaknesses' in Downs' model is unfair and inaccurate (though terminologically convenient). For the changes we make are not necessitated by logical mistakes of his, or, to any significant extent, evidence of the empirical wrongness of his assumptions. Rather they stem from our view, in Chapter 1, about the inadequacy of the pure 'stream of utility' conception of government, our preference for a 'problem-solving' conception, and also from a desire to make the model less simple, less abstract, and more faithful to democratic constitutions and politics as they are. As such they are not fair criticisms of Downs, for we nowhere argue extensively for the alternative mode, and because it is not clear that Downs wished his model to yield precise predictions about the actual world of current democracies. Perhaps it is safer to say that our theory has taken the central idea from Downs, and has used what else of his model is available, to draw out the implications of a normative theory of democracy that he himself neither advocates nor mentions.

The final preliminary statement needed here is to beg a question that has been put against all work remotely like Downs', and to which we have alluded briefly above. Our theory, normative and predictive, gives pride of place to the ancient assumption, criticised throughout time, of the rationality of the voter, and of citizens generally.

This is, nowadays, contested, sometimes fiercely, by sociologists and some political scientists. We do not have the space to discuss it fully, even in the limited context of the decision to vote. What little we have to say about the question is contained in Appendix 2, and some data bearing on it are presented in Appendix 3. Throughout this chapter rationality of the voter and of party leaders is assumed, except where we specifically relax that assumption. We mean by it what Downs meant, to the extent that he is clear about the definition, and what has been assumed about it by proponents of the assumption and opponents, inside the political science community in the last thirty years. This is that rationality is a 'means-end' relationship between a man's goals and his behaviour, so that an irrational man is one who acts in a way contrary to the goal he claims he has, being aware of the counter productive nature of the act. We assume, remember, that voters are rational, not just, the weaker thesis, that they are not irrational. Another way of saying this is that they are purposive, goal-oriented actors, and that voting is not a purely 'affective' gesture, though we leave open to some extent what the goal must be.

This topic is not only endless, but too attractive, and we must exercise restraint; all other arguments on rationality are reserved for the appendix.

We will say here though that there are three reasons for assuming rationality. The first is that classical democratic theory does so, and it is to the modern version of this tradition that the work relates. The second is that, if human nature is to be predictable at all, if constitutions are to be drawn on the basis of it, it can be claimed this is only possible to the extent that man is rational, a strategic creature whose strategies others may compute. The third reason is one seldom pointed to. Democratic theory rests on rationality not only for its credibility, but for its desirability. To paraphrase a famous political theorist who disliked political science, the normative character of democratic thought is so closely allied to the belief in the rationality of man that political scientists who prefer democracy to other systems while believing in man's essential irrationality 'prefer a generous liberalism to consistency'. (Strauss, 1962.)

A.2. The existing paradigm; Downs' Economic Theory of Democracy

There exists in the massive literature of political science one major book and a small collection of articles on the subject of party competition. They stem from the publication in 1957 of one of the most exciting, and one of the few creative attempts at political theory written in this century. The book is Anthony Downs' *An Economic Theory of Democracy*. The articles appear in a wide range of journals. A very good collection appears in Riker and Ordeshook *Positive Political Theory* (1973), which has in addition a fairly comprehensive bibliography. Critical treatments and bibliographies are to be found in Barry (1970) and Budge and Farlie (1975).

Downs attempts to deal with most of the questions we have already raised by the analytic tools, and many of the assumptions, of economic theory and welfare economics. The articles that followed, by a quite small group of men, some of them, like Downs, economists, and others mathematicians, have sought to amplify, correct, expand or generalise various of his ideas.

The aspects of his work with which we are concerned can be presented tersely as a few basic axioms and deductions. This obviously does not do justice to it, but we are not here involved in a deliberate critique. We are using Downs' formulation as a convenient framework, and one more elegant than we could hope to write ourselves.

I. Only the following actors inhabit the political scene:
   (a) Voters
   (b) Parties
   (c) Governments

II. Governments are successful parties. That is, at fixed intervals an election is held. Voters then decide between rival parties. The one which gains the most votes becomes the government.

III. (a) Voters see elections as government selecting mechanisms. (That is, they do not think in terms of electing a local delegate or ambassador, or as expressing preference in some political beauty contest—they are answering the question, 'Which of X . . . Z should be the next government?').

(b) They make this decision to maximise their own utility. Each voter can expect that who controls the government has a direct and measurable effect on his own life, and he will select the party which he believes most likely to maximise his own stream of utility from government.

(c) In so doing the voter takes note of: (i) the policies which the parties espouse (or, more generally, their ideologies); (ii) their records in the past, so as to measure both their 'reliability' (the extent to which their previous behaviour is a guide to later behaviour) and their 'responsibility' (the extent to which their promises are a good guide to subsequent behaviour).

(d) Parties produce not only detailed policies, but general 'ideologies', as vague as possible to attract as many people as possible. These are used as 'short cuts' to deciding which party to vote for by those who find the cost of voting on 'policies' too high because of the difficulty of collecting and collating information.

IV. The 'party' in this theory is to be seen as:
   (a) One completely united coalition of men with no internal policy conflicts.
   (b) Concerned only to get elected, at any cost in terms of policy output.

The party is, in short, like the economic firm, consisting of entrepreneurs who care only about profit and are indifferent about the product they make as long as there is more demand for it than for any other. It is assumed that the direct reward of office, which can be gained only by election is the sole motivation for members of the party, and that their only route to these is by creating a policy platform (and/or ideology) which will attract more voters than any other.

(c) Thus it is deduced that parties will change their policies in the pursuit of maximising electoral success.

It should be mentioned at this point that there is considerable theoretical ambiguity as to whether parties seek to maximise votes, to gain simple pluralities, or to maximise electoral victories over time. This may be a result of Downs' incomplete definition of the party. If so, it should be removed by our own version of theory below.

V. The next series of points are not essential to the Downsian model, but they do represent it in one of its most instructive, and we believe valuable, aspects. It is part of Downs' value that he presents a spatial model of party competition. Use of geometric and spatial language and analogies in describing politics is hollowed by practice and endemic. We argue in Chapter 3 that it is not at all accidental.

Downs constructs, for simplicity, a naive one-dimensional model of political conflict. This dimension, or spectrum, he identifies as measuring, from left to right, the degree of control of the economy by governments desired. Any point on it represents such a view, possibly held by a voter. All voters can be placed somewhere on the dimension. In suggesting this as a prime dimension of party conflict in Western democracy, he is on safe ground. No one is likely to challenge it, and we provide evidence for this being true, at least of Britain in this century, in Chapter 3.

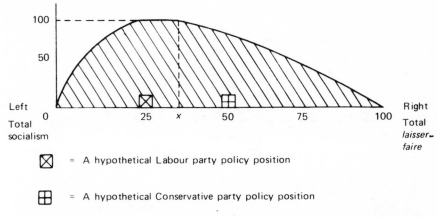

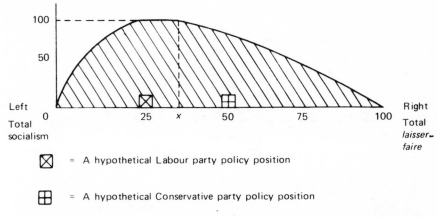 = A hypothetical Labour party policy position

 = A hypothetical Conservative party policy position

Any one point on the left—right dimension, in the example here the point marked *x* represents the number of people who hold that degree of belief in the desirable extent of government control. Here roughly 100 people want a degree of control more or less halfway between the alternatives supplied by the opposing party policies.

Figure 2

Figure 2 demonstrates this. A frequency curve could be constructed, showing, for any point on the dimension, how many voters have that part as their most preferred policy position, and how many lie to either side. 'Either side' here means not only how many would prefer more or less government control of the economy, but how many are more or less 'left' or 'right' wing. If voters can be put on such a diagram, so can party positions, and these are also plotted in the diagram.

Now it follows from the previous four axioms that if both voter preferences and party positions can be reduced to a simple spatial design, we can predict the following. 'Each voter will vote for the party nearest him on the dimension.' For it can only be assumed that the party nearest voter X will be the one which will maximise his likely utility from government. To argue otherwise is to say that a party whose policy is less like one's preferred policy than another's is still more likely to do what you want (what increases your perceived utility). This destroys the link, vital to any democratic theory, between a party's promises and its performance.

From this, and the situation displayed in Figure 3, follows the most vital and interesting conclusion of Down's theory. The distribution of voter opinion on the dimension that represents political conflict determines which party will win an election, and, more important, determines a unique position for each party which will maximise its voting support, given the position of the other party.

28

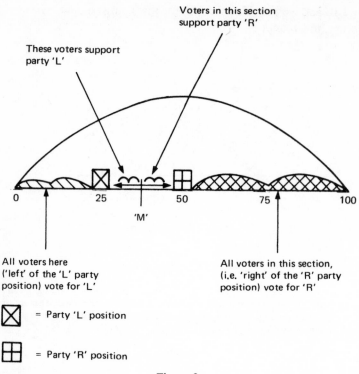

Voters in this section
support party 'R'

These voters support
party 'L'

0   25   50   75   100

'M'

All voters here
('left' of the 'L' party
position) vote for 'L'

All voters in this section,
(i.e. 'right' of the 'R' party
position) vote for 'R'

⊠ = Party 'L' position

⊞ = Party 'R' position

Figure 3

With the situation as displayed in Figure 3, party 'R' is bound to win. If each voter votes for the party nearest his own position, all those who fall between the extreme right wing end of the spectrum and the position of party 'R' will vote for it. All those, a smaller number as shown by the frequency line, who are between the extreme left end and party 'L', will vote 'L'. In addition, those between the parties will vote for the nearer, so that those to the right of the mid point, 'm', will vote 'R', and those to the left will support party 'L'. The result is obvious.

This conclusion follows from the previous axioms, and leads to this conclusion. The further a party moves from its own end of the spectrum towards that of the other party, the higher its vote will be, until it comes to a point where its position is the same as that of its rival. There has been considerable theoretical effort expended on the obvious question of party crossover, of party A moving past the position of party B. We do not consider this question a serious one, and prefer to rule that it cannot happen. Enormous questions of what is meant by the continued existence of a political party are raised by such a situation. There are only a few and rare cases of this at least in one-dimensional terms.

The obvious conclusion from all that has gone before is that, given a distribution of voter preferences, there is a unique vote maximising position in any two party system where both parties are concerned to maximise their own votes. Figure 4 demonstrates this for three possible configurations of voter preferences.

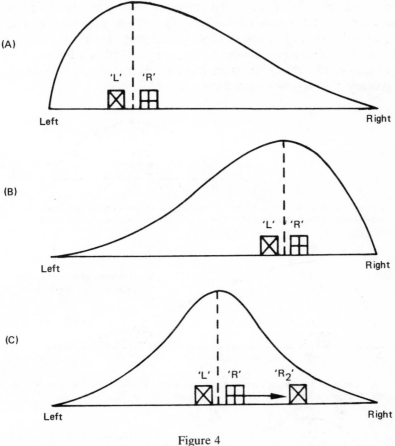

Figure 4

In each of the three diagrams the parties are shown on each side of the mid point of the distribution. How 'left' or 'right' this is depends on the skewdness of the distribution.

In no case could a movement of either party increase its vote, for any move that is not forbidden by the 'no crossover' rule would place the party where there would be less voters nearer to it than to the opposition. This is demonstrated by the second position of party 'R' in Figure 4(c).

Figure 4(a) is Downs' suggestion for the most likely distribution, on the grounds that any 'left–right' distribution that accords with common usage is likely to be class related, and class distributions are, roughly speaking, skewed in a working class or 'left' direction.

The final conclusion for the theory of party competition contained here is this: each political party in a system will be ideologically mobile and will move to the position, over time, which maximises votes. Several other points follow, some of which will be taken up later in our own more complex model. Most of these are related to the choice in distribution of vote support itself; an example is Down's belief that a change in the franchise will change the distribution, and that such a change may produce a new political party. In this case it is possible that one of the existing ones will be squeezed out. This is attractive in that it helps to account for the decline of the English Liberal party over the first half of this century. This is demonstrated in Figure 5.

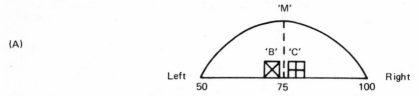

Party 'B' and Party 'C' are both, at time T, close to the vote-maximising position 'M'. But suppose the suffrage is extended, enfranchising a large number of more 'left' wing voters:

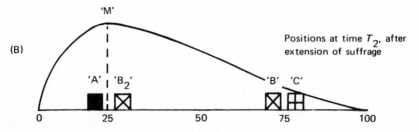

Party 'A' is now on the vote-maximising position. Party 'C' gets the second greatest number of votes. The only chance for 'B' is to move nearer to 'M', say to position 'B$_2$'

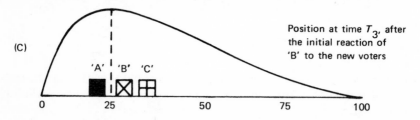

However, even if it does make this move, 'C' can follow suit and cut off nearly all its votes. The result seems to be the inevitable restoration of the two-party system

Figure 5

Finally we must note the most important characteristic of this theory: the actors, both voters and politicians, are seen as rational. This means that they are both factually and intellectually equipped to make decisions between alternatives by calculating which of them is more in their own interests, and that they do so. This is an assumption that has led to an apparent split in the ranks of political scientists between those who are economists and those who are sociologists at heart (Barry, 1970).

This very limited portrayal of aspects of Downsian theory serves in the next section as a starting point for our own brief version of a theory of party competition.

A.3.1. The Missing Elements of Downsian Theory

Those amendments we wish to make in Anthony Downs' model, which cause us to derive a different and more complex prediction about what policy a party will adopt, all concern one point. For Downs there is never any reason why a party might not want, might not be able, might not suffer from failing, or might expect it to be rewarding, not to adopt the vote maximising point on the spectrum. We think strategy is more complex than that. At times we must predict that parties, if rational, will not adopt the position which is, *ceteris paribus*, dominant. This follows from structural elements not taken account of by Downs, and from our 'problem solving' notion of governing.

His model might be said to be over-simple in four ways:

    I. In the number of types of actors he envisages.
    II. In the constitutional structure of the state.
    III. In the motivations of some actors.
    IV. In what constitutes a voter making a rational decision.

We are aware of the arguments for simplicity in models, yet we feel that past a certain point, simplicity and abstraction can be overdone. Points I, II and III above we feel are necessary and unavoidable complications in any model of party competition. Together with point IV (which Downs actually notes himself at times, though without paying it much attention) they suggest to us a radically different theory of party competition.

A.3.2. The Actors in the Model

As far as existing theory on party competition goes, there exist only two types of actors: voters, all of whom are motivated the same way, and political parties. The parties are unified teams who have, as motivation, only the rewards of office if elected, and who, alike, have no personal commitment to any ideology. All members of political parties share the same goals, and if there are any disagreements amongst them, these are purely tactical. Now it is entirely an empirical matter whether this description of the party is adequate, and indeed there is evidence both for and against the suitability of the description. Downs' description is an ideal type, corresponding to some American political parties, or electoral organisations. The 'Presidential party' constructed virtually by one man to ensure his own election, depending on his own or his friends' financial resources, and the bought skills of advertising agencies and similar organisations at the state level, may work very much as Downs predicts [Burns 1963].

The opposite ideal corresponds to the European Communist parties, whose candidates are controlled by the party organisation, are not prepared to make ideological sacrifices for electoral expediency, and may not even gain the rewards of office themselves if elected. Sometimes they are even required to give a large portion of their parliamentary salaries to party funds, Herig and Pinder [1969]. Between these ideal types range a variety of parties, more or less controlled by the parliamentary leadership, more or less prepared to trade ideology for votes, more or less dependent on party membership in their election campaigns.

No party however can be effective without large resources of finance and labour, to buy and transmit propaganda, to canvass and organise voting, to mobilise generally the electorate. Unless these resources can come entirely from the private funds of those who form the alternative government and can expect direct reward from office holding regardless of the policy stance that electoral strategy requires, they must enter into the model. We assume that political parties entirely without financial connections are not frequent enough to matter very much in Western politics.

Although the variety of real world parties with regard to the source and nature of resources is great, and must result in varying party behaviour, one thing is certain and common to all. If someone is to provide resources for a party, whether his own labour or financial contributions, his motivation cannot be independent of the expected action of the party if elected, and hence of its ideology. The motivation may be a direct reward, patronage or the granting of a government contract, or it may be indirect, the adoption of some approved policy. Either way it constrains party policy. A policy has not only to recruit voters, but resources, and there is no automatic correlation between the policy that maximises the one and the other. There is no way in which the relationship can be known *a priori*. Figure 6 shows some possible relations between these.

For convenience we shall adopt for the rest of this chapter one simple model of the party, and believe that the logic, if not the details of the ensuing analysis, are transferable to any other real world party of a competitive nature. We shall assume that political parties are of Duverger's [1959] 'mass' type, consisting of leaders, who are candidates for office, and members who are not, and who are necessary for the party. We therefore omit both professional paid party workers, and external sources of finance.

If a party requires members, their rewards must be derived from the policies the party commits itself to following if elected. The party's strategy, as we shall see shortly, is now constrained by the need to optimise membership and votes; a policy that has the approval of a majority of electors may be useless if it cannot attract enough active supporters to get that potential vote out. Working voluntarily and actively for a party must require a stronger motivation than just voting for it, because it involves a higher cost. Thus while it is rational to vote for party A rather than B if there is any difference between them at all, it may very well not be worth working for it. We shall develop this point in further detail below. At this stage it becomes obvious that there is at least one

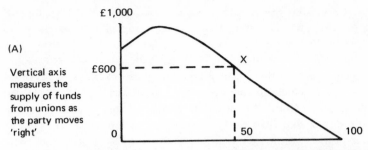

(A)

Vertical axis measures the supply of funds from unions as the party moves 'right'

Horizontal axis measures the percentage of the electorate potentially ready to vote for the party as it moves 'right'. X gives the expected supply of funds when the party reaches the vote-maximising position. The question is whether or not, with only £600, the party can mount a campaign effective enough to mobilise all those potentially attracted by the policy position

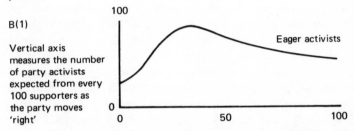

B(1)

Vertical axis measures the number of party activists expected from every 100 supporters as the party moves 'right'

Horizontal axis again measures the percentage of the electorate who will vote for the party position, as it moves 'right', *if* they can be mobilised with the available number of activists. In this situation, it is most likely that the activists will be numerous enough, so that moving 'right' pays off. Below, with more apathetic or more strongly socialist activists, less willing to work for a party as it moves 'right', it looks as if the party can never move far enough 'right without losing too many activists

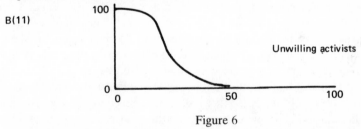

B(11)

Figure 6

significant limitation in Downs' model—it is not true that there can never be a cost involved in taking up the vote maximising position. Parties can be pulled in two directions at once, away from and towards the competitively best position. It remains to be seen under what conditions the strengths of these opposed vectors control the party.

A.3.3. Constitutional Constraints

What we have to say here is straightforward. The Downsian model as it exists suits only one constitutional arrangement, that in which an entire government is elected, en bloc, from one constituency. Such arrangements are not rare. The

Presidency of the United States and of other countries, Governorships of States, where the executive is one man elected by a single constituency of the state or federation, are examples. So are countries, like Israel, in which a legislative assembly is elected on the basis of one national constituency.

Even with such examples the political party in question has to fight, often simultaneously, many elections on many constituencies. When American political scientists refer to the 'Presidential' and the 'Congressional' parties, deriving a four rather than two party system for the United States [Burns 1963], the force of their argument comes precisely from the fact that there are, officially, only two parties, which are supposed to unite the executive and legislative branches. In most countries it is still the case that there are no nationwide constituencies.

Hence we need to introduce a further structural modification to the party. Not only are there leaders and followers, with different motivations and requirements for policy, but the leadership itself is not a single block. Again for convenience we shall consider one example, the Westminster parliamentary system. Under this candidates for election are of two sorts. There is the leadership proper, the senior members of the parliamentary party, who can expect to be members of the government if their party is successful. There is no reason for these men, especially as they will probably hold safe seats, to be concerned with much else but their party winning the election as a whole. However this is not true for the rest, a majority of the candidates, who cannot expect to be in a government, and for whom the rewards of politics lie in their being elected from their own constituencies to parliament.

Only the most severely restrictive assumptions can allow us to ignore the possibility of conflicting motives within this group. The principal assumption is of total homogeneity of constituencies. This implies that the vote maximising position for the country as a whole is also that for each constituency. This is nowhere empirically valid. The empirical conditions for its validity are clear, As voters have different interests, which lead them to vote for different parties, one can only assume that real socio-economic differences, in class, religion, wealth, ethnicity or whatever underlie these differing interests. Any electoral situation where, although the legislature is elected from constituencies (unlike, for example Israel which has one national constituency), each constituency has equal proportions of all major social groups would involve the most complex gerrymandering. In such a case each constituency is a microcosm of the nation, and the vote maximising position in any one constituency is the vote maximising position in all. We have therefore the following possibility: the policy stance that will get the party elected may result in the avoidable defeat of some candidates. The avoidability lies in it being possible for them, by making a different stand in their own constituencies, of achieving a local maximising position. There is more implied here than another internal conflict over what policy to adopt, for the possibility of many different policy messages, and a differentially distributed audience calls into question the possibility of the party having any one policy. The normative aspects of this problem, the possible conflict between representation and government selection, have already been touched on. The predictive theory needs to analyse this area carefully, as we do below.

It is worth noting that even Presidential type electoral arrangements do not escape the problem entirely. If the 'Presidential party' is to have any success in governing, and thus be a plausible candidate in the future, its policy must not be one, however electorally attractive, that it cannot find support for in the legislature, hence a problem about the compatibility of different electorally expedient platforms.

A.3.4. The Voter and his Decision

I. Anthony Downs is careful in his book to point to the place of other determinants of a rational voting choice than the policy of the party. He mentions also the need for a party to be 'responsible' and 'reliable', that is, to act so that their behaviour in the past is some guide to their future behaviour, and their promises are kept. This kind of consideration is the more important in our theory because of our stress on government as solving problems, and the consequent need of the voter to think twice before supporting a party which promises to do what he wishes, but has frequently failed to cope with social problems.

Unfortunately Downs does not go on to explicate the confusing situation that follows from this. In our terms it is more confusing still. How does one calculate the relative attractiveness of parties when their record for efficiency, the problems they now identify, and the solutions they offer may all be at odds with each other? Does one vote for the Labour party, though disliking nationalisation, because it is at least aware of, say, a slow growth rate; or, while believing in nationalisation, and being concerned at the rate of economic growth, might one vote Conservative, despite their being unaware of the problem because, perhaps, they have been much more successful in the past at getting funds from the IMF with which to restore a strong economy? There is no obvious way to resolve such a situation, and it does not seem fruitful to try, *a priori*, to work out the likely voting strategy. But we can see that the parties' records are likely to be taken account of, and we know from empirical research that economic conditions are laid at the government's door and affect public opinion. There is, indeed, the old saw, that oppositions do not win elections, governments lose them.

This suggests, for our purposes, that it is mistaken to assume that a particular position on an ideological spectrum is of the same consequence for all parties. Briefly it may be the case that at times records of rival parties are such that one of them cannot hope to win the election, whatever position it takes up. In such a case there is no short term advantage to be gained, and it may be positively dangerous, for a party to be competitive in the sense of assuming that position which would, were decisions to be made on ideological grounds alone, be a vote maximising point. That has its corollary, that there may be occasions when one party is much freer to take up ideological positions that its members like, because it is enormously likely to win on record alone. Such might plausibly be argued for the Conservative party in 1931, with a completely collapsed and discredited Labour opposition. We do produce evidence in Chapter 4 that on that election, between a party that could not hope to win and one that could not lose, the policy stances from both parties were relatively extreme, this being incompatible with either party trying to get onto an ideological vote maximising point. Why this might be so, why the logic of party competition in our model would predict just that, is spelled out later.

II. One familiar phenomenon that is not compatible with a purely Downsian model is the 'safe' seat. How can it be, with rational voters and ideologically mobile parties, that some constituencies always return enormous majorities for one party? Is this related to the equally familiar finding of survey research that most voters are far too ignorant of party policy, and too unreflectively attached to one party to fit our assumption of a rational and calculating voter? Can both these phenomena be explained, not disingenuously, in the terms of our theory, and if they can, with what implication for party competition?

There are two possible explanations for safe seats, both of which we shall use, and one of which is based on a second phenomenon, the 'safe voter'. Obviously, a safe seat may be one that is full of safe voters, those who do not appear to be sufficiently calculating or informed to fit the rational voter stereotype. That safe voters should be concentrated in some seats is unlikely and inexplicable if they are to be seen as entirely irrational creatures. There is one well established fact about safe seats, which yields the usual explanation for the difference between safe and marginal seats. Safe seats are those where the distribution of social classes or other social phenomena associated with voting patterns is uneven, marginal seats are those with a more matched distribution. This gives us an explanation in our own terms of safe seats, which is that a safe seat is one where the policy stance that fits the nation as a whole, when searching for a vote maximising point, is inappropriate because of a skewed distribution of ideological opinion. As long as one does not grant much local autonomy in the setting of candidates' policy stances, it becomes impossible for one party to compete effectively in such a constituency. As party ideology is largely concerned with economic issues that affect social classes differentially, and as we know that constituencies exist with class distributions sharply out of line with the national distribution, and as these are the safe seats, such constituencies must be admitted in a rational voting model. The assumption necessary, that there is limited autonomy, is argued for later. Figure 7 demonstrates the point graphically.

What this suggests though is also an answer to the rational status of the 'safe voter'. Under what conditions, one should ask, is a knowledge of party ideology or policy necessary for a rational voter? Alternatively, under what conditions will an unthinking loyalty vote for a party one has been taught to identify with through one's class position be any less sensible than a carefully calculated vote?

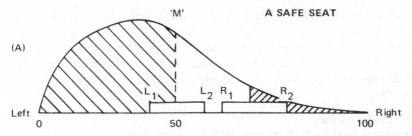

'M' A SAFE SEAT

(A)

Left 0 50 100 Right

The area L_1 to L_2 is the limit of permissible policy variation by a candidate from party 'L'. The actual candidate position here is L_1. Similarly, R_1 to R_2 limits the possible policy modulation by a candidate of party 'R'.

In this example no one from party 'R' can win because a majority of the electorate are distributed to the left of the most left extreme of policy modulation available to any candidate of party 'R'

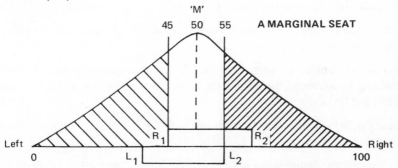

'M'

45 50 55 A MARGINAL SEAT

Left 0 L_1 L_2 100 Right

In this case the loyal votes are evenly split around the halfway position between left and right policy extremes. The ranges of policy variation for the two candidates, L_1 to L_2 and R_1 to R_2, overlap. The most 'left' position available to R, at 45, is further left than the most right position, 55, available to L. They can therefore compete, as their range of permitted variation in policy in both cases lies across the vote-maximising position 'M'

Voters in this area are loyal to party 'L'

Voters in this area are loyal to party 'R'

Figure 7

The answer is that one needs to be ostensibly rational, to take note of ideologies, only when it is probable that parties' ideologies can fluctuate enough to make a previously learned or calculated rational vote no longer appropriate. If we make the assumption that political parties will not shift by any great degree, that fluctuations in policy stance will take place only in a limited area of the ideological spectrum, then voters whose preferred positions lie at all far from this area, will not need to recalculate. For them being 'safe' voters is rational. The result of this is to suggest that party propaganda, and to a large extent records in office, is limited in its effect to a small percentage of the electorate who can expect that the strategic shifts in policy stance may make their rational choice different from election to election. This again we analyse later, more fully.

At this stage the importance is that, just as a party generally may not be able to win, or lose, an election by its policy position, there may be many constituencies in which individual candidates are in this position.

A.3.5. Push and Pull

We have sought so far to derive the following points:

I. There may exist constraints leading a party not to take up an ideologically expedient position, because to do so is to lose vital resources in voluntary workers or finance, to the point that the potential vote cannot be realised.

II. There may be situations in which a party cannot credibly take up an ideologically vote maximising position.

III. There may be situations where a party can win an election without taking up such a position.

IV. Individual candidates may find that they cannot hope to win in their constituency by adopting the official party position, or by modifying it within the permitted limit.

V. Other candidates may benefit from this by being in a constituency that their opponent cannot win.

The rest of this chapter consists of further development of the arguments above, elaborating on the rational model we suggest so as to make the assumptions used above credible. In particular the position of the individual candidate vis-à-vis his constituency and his party is analysed, and the interaction between vote maximising and membership retention is spelled out more fully. The predictions of the model follow in a straightforward way from the assumptions above, and anyone who is either prepared to accept them, or who is uninterested in their veracity, is invited to skip the rest of this chapter and proceed straight to Chapters 3 to 5 where data analysis tests the theory.

There are two basic predictions, one for the party as a national unit, and one for constituency level competition. They are almost the same, and rest on the same major point. This is that competitive behaviour, used here to mean 'taking a position as near as possible to the vote maximising position on the ideological spectrum', will not be the necessary and automatic act of a competitor. Instead we argue that it will happen only where 'necessary'. 'Necessary' here has a particular meaning: it is 'necessary' to be competitive when a competitor can hope to gain by so doing, and will suffer by not so doing.

As far as the central party goes, our reasoning is that a political party, because of its mass membership, has an ideological preference, that this is not the vote maximising position, and that it will be pulled towards this position when (i) it cannot win by being competitive; or (ii) it can win without being competitive.

The prediction for the constituency level activity is nearly the same, that there exists such a 'not maximising' party preference, and that the candidate will be pulled towards it when he cannot lose by so doing. However it is further argued that there is a gain from being competitive even where one cannot hope to win the constituency (for example, candidates who do not have safe seats need to demonstrate their vote winning talents) and that this will lead them to take up competitive positions.

The definition of necessity cannot be filled out, for the central party, *a priori*. It covers, though, those situations in which the outcome of the election seems very likely to be determined by past records, or other considerations, thus making policy irrelevant. That there are other restrictions that may produce this situation, by somehow limiting a party's choice of policy stances is admitted, and dealt with to some extent later.

Necessity at the constituency level involves the safeness or marginality of the seat.

B. Ideological Mobility and Party Activities

We shall continue and expand the previous discussion of the role of the party activist. It will be assumed here that an activist is motivated by a desire to change the world by implementing a certain set of policies. This is simply to facilitate analysis, for as we admit in Appendix 2, other motivations are capable of being fitted in. It will save space, however, to leave them out of consideration. In any case while we accept the possibility of other motivations, we do not expect such people to amount to a large fraction of party members. If one does have a fairly firm conviction of how the world is to be changed, working for a political party is one of very few avenues, short of revolution, which is open. It is not part of our definition of the activist here that there be any great likelihood of success—an activist is not irrational for working for a hopeless cause. Apart from a belief in the chances of educating the voters, one may be perfectly rational in working against enormous odds for the satisfaction of doing one's all. We do not assume rationality in what is perhaps the normal 'teleological' sense. We assume merely that the activist has a political opinion, and sees working for a party of the same opinion as a way to do whatever he can towards realising a desired state of affairs, or even just as a way of expressing his desires.

There is a great difficulty in defining the continued existence of a political party in which both policy and membership change over time. Only continued organisational identity seems to help, and for this reason we must, regrettably, use a cumbersome set of time and policy variables to identify it. Thus we talk about party 'A' at time 'T_1' and position 'P_1'.

We start with party A at T_1 and P_1, relying on members for whom the match of party A and policy position P_1 is a 'salient fact'.

40

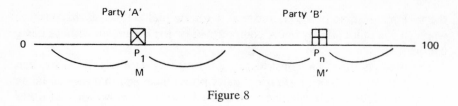

Figure 8

No party activist will lack some tolerance about the exact position; there will be a considerable margin of space within which the exact position does not matter. We can say that the membership will be drawn from the range 'M' in Figure 8.

For any particular member there will be an equivalent range, within which he will work for the party. If, however, party A moves, at T_2, to a new position, P_2, which is outside this range, it will be less consistent for a member attracted at T_1 to continue working for the party—the intrinsic value of working towards policy P_2 for a man committed to P_1 is less. As a party moves away from P_1 it can expect to lose members. They will probably continue to vote for it; if one is to vote at all, it is inconsistent to vote for the party further away from one's own position. But to work actively for P_2, as opposed just to choosing P_2 over a worse P_n in a forced choice situation, is unlikely to seem worthwhile.

The loss of members cannot be ignored by the party leaders unless they can easily be replaced with new members. Such new members cannot be easily and quickly picked up. Parties have to work hard to attract members. In the long run it may be that membership can be made up, but electoral expediency for the leaders is short term—the next election is to be won before anything else can be considered. We can therefore expect a breaking effect—ideological mobility is no longer cost free.

There is a cost effectiveness question here: an ideological move will only be made where it will increase voter support, and membership loss must be discounted against this. More potential vote support is useless if one lacks the troops to get the vote out, but equally a strong and loyal membership is of no avail if the party cannot hope to be elected. If membership is not replaceable the relationship between voting support and membership is easily analysed. Assuming a steady drop in members as the party moves, and a distribution of voter ideology that is roughly normal, one can imagine a graph as in Figure 9.

At a certain point which, without real data we cannot know, it would be senseless to move any further towards the vote maximising point as new membership losses would discount any potential vote gain.

It is likely, furthermore, that even if member replacement is possible, it will not make sense to continue towards a vote maximising position indefinitely. For we would argue that the intrinsic worth of working for party A depends not only on the gap between the members' position and that of A, but on the distance party A and party B. One of the considerations against which the cost of working for A must be judged is the cost of party A being defeated. If the two parties are very far apart, the tolerance a member has for ideological deviation

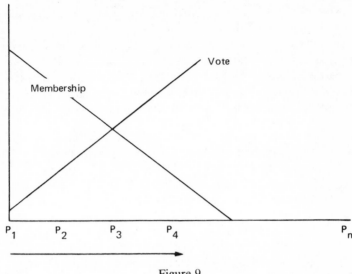

Figure 9

by his own party will be high. However little reward there may be in getting A elected on a platform one does not really approve, the horror of helping, by a sin of omission, the election of a party even further away will make it appear more worthwhile to support A. The overall distribution of parties must clearly help determine the active support for each. But as A moves away from P_1 towards the vote maximising position, it also decreases the distance A–B, making it increasingly less likely that the original members will continue to support it. The only exception would be where party B simultaneously moves in the same direction, towards a more extreme position.

At the same time we can expect that new members will be harder and harder to come by. For if the decision to continue membership depends on the degree of difference between A and B, so, obviously, must the decision to become a member. So the overall effect of the predicted tendency for A and B to converge on the median voter is for both parties to lose membership. This may result in reduced turnout, and increase the chance for 'flash' parties to appear.

We cannot know, until some empirical research is carried out, whether or not this tendency will be serious enough to severely limit mobility, and to make it unlikely that parties will converge. One thing that we can know is this: there is good reason for party leaders not to act competitively if it is safe so to do. That is, if a party cannot change its electoral situation by a move towards the median voter, it will not do so. For there is no point in losing members to no avail.

Under what conditions will it not become necessary to act competitively? There are two. In the one case, a party's position may guarantee election, while the other party's position may be so uncompetitive that it would still be possible for the former to increase its vote. This is the problem of whether a party will seek to maximise voters, or only to maximise the chance of winning the

42

election. Our prediction is that vote maximisation, over and above that necessary to win, will not take place.

In the second case it may be impossible to win an election whatever move, amongst those possible, is taken. One possible reason was adduced for such a situation earlier. Here we consider another, that its opposition has such a dominating position that it cannot be beaten unless the party, violating the 'no crossover' rule, moves past it. Figure 10 demonstrates these two situations.

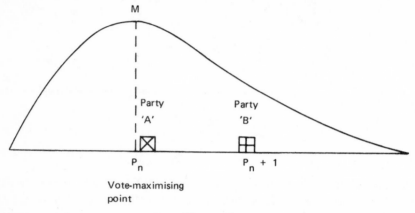

Figure 10

Here party A could increase its vote by moving from P_n towards $P_n + 1$, the 'B' party position. It does not need to, as it is already on the vote maximising position, and we predict that it will not risk losing membership unnecessarily by so doing. In the same diagram, party B could increase its vote, to moving towards P_n, but not to the point of winning. To do so it would have to overtake A and move further towards A's end of the spectrum. We predict that a move which cannot win the election and will lose membership will not be taken.

In general we expect that a party will take advantage of a situation where it does not need to act competitively to take up a more extreme position. Later, when we discuss the voters and the nature of their decision to vote for A or B, we will formulate a more detailed hypothesis of party strategy along these lines, to be tested in a later chapter.

The introduction of an element into the definition of a party which is concerned with the ideology of the party rather than with winning *per se* suggests further areas of research and hypothesis formation which we can only briefly examine here.

One interesting question is of power balances in a party, and the effects of these on policy formation. Although there are innumerable studies of this question, many excellent, they are mostly quite untheoretical, and have not been done with any eye towards generalisation. We have written in this section as though members have no formal power, but have only the recourse of resignation if a policy is unpleasant. The leaders here formulate policy with the limits of feasibility set by the risk of losing too many members. It may be, though, that policy is formulated democratically inside the party by voting amongst the membership. If this is so, it is easy to show that the policy of the party will always be less moderate than the exact vote maximising position given by the median voter in the voter opinion distribution.

The members of the party are a subset of the general distribution. The policy that would emerge from their deliberations should be that of the median party member. He is bound to be a certain distance away from the overall median, as Figure 11 demonstrates. The ideological position of the most moderate

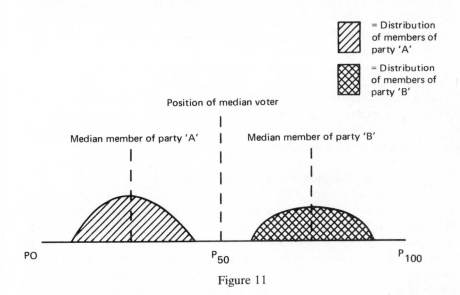

Figure 11

members of each party cannot overlap, or the men in question would change party allegiance. The policy of the party cannot be that of the most moderate member, because in terms of the distribution of opinion inside the party this is an 'extreme' position, and thus party policy cannot actually be that of the median voter. There must remain a gap, into which one or other party could, increasing its vote, were it only less democratic.

A prediction from this that is highly plausible, *ceteris paribus*, is that the less power the members of a party have, and the stronger the leadership, the better its electoral chances. This also invites a direct test of the theory, in that all the argument of this section entails the hypothesis that party members will, on the whole, be more extreme than the leaders. The evidence we could bring to test this is scarce, diverse, and confusing.

Some American studies have suggested it is true, and the same result has been developed, by Dahl and Key amongst others, as a necessary condition for democratic stability (Budge, 1970). But there is some conflicting evidence (Rose, 1967).

For several reasons therefore it is probable that we must oppose Downs and say that political parties will have ideological preferences, though these will be tempered by the need to win elections. The need of a new party to build up a loyal 'safe' vote, may well require that for some years after it first achieves a sizable following it will have to forego electoral victory, sticking close to the preferred position of those most naturally its 'safe' voters. Only once this 'natural' connection has been assured will it be able to play for centrist votes by approaching the vote maximising position.

Of course, as we discuss in Appendix 1, not only the parties move—the voter distribution, or the ideological dimension itself—can shift. We shall discuss this point further in Chapter 4, with evidence of the steady movement in a centrist direction of the Labour party. Much of our argument here either rests on, or is helped by, the presence of the loyal or 'safe', unreflexive voter. Such people are known to exist, but it is sometimes thought that they are incompatible with a 'rational' voter model.

In the next secion we argue that this is untrue, indeed that the safe voter is predicted by our rational model. Having justified this element in the theory, we turn finally to apply an analysis similar to this one, also resting on 'safe' voters, to constituency level competition.

C. The Voter, his Decision and his Political Knowledge

Although the question of the extent, and nature, of rationality amongst voters is one that we must postpone here, one aspect is worth discussing. This is the claim, to be found in any standard piece of voting research, that voters lack the detailed knowledge of policy that would be necessary for them to vote rationally. Backing this up is the general claim that the electors do not have ideologies, and cannot be seen as having more than an emotive and automatic link with parties, through something called 'party identification'.

No one could deny the raw data, derived with great skill and imagination, in the great survey research works, from Michigan and their followers abroad (Campbell, 1964; butler, 1969; Campbell, 1966). What is less well founded is their interpretative framework. Briefly, it does not seem to us that the data leads to a non-Downsian position, but is quite compatible with a flexible rational theory.

To a considerable extent the opinion of survey researchers that voters cannot fit the Downsian description is a result of their having a rather narrow conception of rationality. They seem to expect that an ordinary voter, quizzed by an interviewer, will produce an explanation of his vote in terms of a detailed and specific account of how his own interests will be served by the current policies of the party. An explanation of the sort 'I vote X because my father did', or 'I vote Y because I'm a Y supporter', instead of being further probed and considered, is taken *ipso facto* to imply an almost random and certainly non-calculative approach to politics. Not only in such examples, but in many of their judgments, the survey researchers demonstrate a very rigid interpretative scheme, which at times calls their own use of concepts into doubt more than it does anything at all about their respondents. As an example the findings of Campbell *et al.*, on voter ideology serve well (Campbell, 1964). They define having an ideology as requiring a complex and structured set of attitudes. Yet in their study of the American voter, they discovered that only $2\frac{1}{2}$% of their sample were capable of using even a crude 'Liberal–Conservative' ideological dimension to order the parties. Butler and Stokes, carrying out the same study in Britain, produced similar findings of the capacity of British voters to use 'Left–Right'. Using such definitions and examples, with no respect to the great creative works on ideology, they discover only very few people are 'ideological'. At the same time they report the number of people who perceive politics as 'group conflict', or through the idea of group interest. Although they appear not to regard this as having to do with ideology it is, to any political theorist, the very essence of an ideological approach. If one does accept this point, the percentage of the sample who are ideological rises from 2–3% to over 50%, on their own data.

Returning to their dismissal of attitudes as expressed in the examples above, one might well argue that these actually express a very rational approach to voting. Given the low incidence of social mobility in most Western countries the fact that one's father was content with party X is probably one of the strongest pieces of evidence one could have for the proposition that X is one's own best bet. The idea of an identification with a party being some obscure emotional tie that has no basis in reason is something that electoral sociologists find easy to swallow. But why on earth should there be such an identification, and for what reason should it be seen as irrational? However people develop such an identification, they are usually perfectly sensible, in the sense that most people have an identification with the party which, on balance, can be expected to look after them best.

Rare creatures like the British working class Conservative, always a minority of the working class and declining, cannot even be cited as irrational voters—one would need to have far more evidence of their other beliefs than has usually been collected by surveys to make this judgment. Recently more critical studies have been carried out showing, for instance, that children of voters who were 'deviant' have a greater tendency to change their views, towards social conformity in their voting, than children of conformist parents have of changing to a 'deviant' position (Goldberg, 1969). A further discussion of the clash between survey research and rational choice approaches is to be found in Chapter 6.

Even Butler and Stokes were forced to make a major theme of their research report the fact that Labour in Britain was 'coming into its own', increasing year by year the share of the working class vote that it gained. Other studies, notably the investigation of 'affluent workers' in Britain by Goldthorpe and Lockwood (1968) have found signs of 'instrumental voting' on the part of these men. This is particularly revealing, as it is just such 'marginal' voters, people whose social and economic position is ambiguous, who seem, on our theory, most important.

Nonetheless we do not ignore the evidence that for most voters a rather simple and direct causal link between voting for a certain party, and achieving a political aim, exists, amongst great ignorance of precise policy.

Just as it was necessary when thinking about the political party to accept the existence of more than one element within it, we need to realise that not all voters are alike. We have remarked above that even if voters, in the real world, seem to be motivated by a simple emotive link, a party identification, they are able to vote efficiently.

These attachments to parties, formed early in life and continuing throughout adult political experience, are usually ones that lead the voter to support the party most in his interest. Thus in Britain the working class typically have a strong identification with the Labour party, in America blue collar workers, immigrants, blacks, all have a much greater chance of identifying with the Democrats than with the Republicans. It is by no means surprising, in the context of our theory, that many people should have a straightforward and unsophisticated link to the party that is more in their interests.

Consider the one-dimensional model of party competition in this light. It follows from the need of parties to be both responsible and reliable that the extent of ideological change from election to election will not be great. This is particularly so in any electoral system where there has been time for both parties to approach very nearly the median voter, the vote maximising point. Once there little change is likely, and it would be sensible for any voter to predict only marginal changes in the relative position of the parties.

Given that governments have to try to solve social problems and given the inadequacy and rarity of policy initiatives, one can also expect what Lindblom has christened an incrementalist policy mode, in which rival parties will make only small changes in existing policy when they are elected (Lindblom, 1963). This increases the likelihood that the only ideological changes made will be small ones.

Now we must ask this question—is there any reason to assume that all voters will be equally interested in marginal changes of party position, or are some more likely than others to find these significant? Look at the situation depicted in Figure 12.

For any voter whose own preferred position is in the range 0-40 there is virtually no chance that any shift in the positions of either party would lead him to wish to change his vote from party L. Equally no voter in the range 70-120 has any reason to expect a change that would make him wish to vote for any party but R. Both types of voter exist outside the range of possible or probable party movement. Their vote will not change, from election to election, no matter how precise or sophisticated a picture they have of party ideology. If they ever once learn which of L and R are better for them, and thus start to identify with that party, voting from that identification will always be efficient for them.

. As long as the range within which parties can move is limited only a small percentage of the electorate can need to know a party's position in any detail.

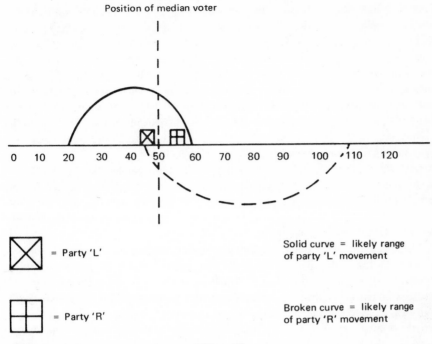

Position of median voter

= Party 'L'

Solid curve = likely range
of party 'L' movement

= Party 'R'

Broken curve = likely range
of party 'R' movement

Figure 12

These are the 'marginal men', voters whose own positional preference lie near to the median. Only they can be expected to have any detailed or sophisticated knowledge of party positions, or to shift their votes between elections.

On rare occasions parties will move more drastically, will take up ideological positions outside the normal range of variability. As these changes will inevitably result in electoral failure, such an action is pathological, and we should expect it to be rare. When it does happen though we further expect that more voters will become aware of the new position than would usually, and will change their voting allegiance. Political history seems to uphold this expectation.

In 1964 the Republican party moved further 'right' than is normal, and the Republican vote dropped considerably. In 1972 the Democrats moved further 'left' than is normal, and their vote dropped. It is hardly possible to maintain that those party identifiers who switched their votes to give Johnson in 1964 and Nixon in 1972 unusually large majorities did so without being aware of the relative positions of the parties. Thus we have some evidence for the following proposition: low levels of voter knowledge or sophistication are a result of there being very little ideological movement by parties so that (i) only those few likely to be affected by small changes will have any great knowledge or sophistication; amd (ii) in times of unusual change larger percentages of the electorate will be aware of party positions.

It is worth noting, though by the way, that these two elections bear out another, earlier prediction. We said earlier that parties would not be 'competitive' unnecessarily, that if for any reason they were presented with a chance to increase votes beyond the winning number by moving further away from their own end of the spectrum, they would not do so. This we deduced from the principle that party supporters would act as a brake on any ideological mobility, and politicians would not wish to upset them if this could be avoided. In the light of this it is instructive to note that neither the Republicans in 1972, nor the Democrats in 1964 took advantage of the chance to move over into their opponent's normal political range.

Mr. Nixon certainly did not present himself as any further 'left' in 1972 than he had in the past, even though Mr. McGovern made this possible for him by taking up what some regarded as a 'radical' stance. Mr. Johnson did not move right, towards Mr. Goldwater, in 1964, and arguably actually moved to the left, with his Great Society platform.

There is some other evidence for our prediction about levels of awareness of voters. As far as British politics goes, the easiest and most obvious way of operationalising a one-dimensional party spectrum is to equate it very roughly with social class distribution. If one does this one can say that, as an example, a working class voter in a traditional and relatively ill paid job, say a miner or textile operative, is extremely unlikely to need much information to decide between the parties. However Labour and Conservative dodge about in the middle of the spectrum, the probability that they will move so far left (towards the interests of the working class) that the Conservative party would be more in their interests than Labour is zero.

Similarly a bank manager, corporation executive, or small scale entrepreneur is most unlikely to need to know the precise positions, ideologies or policies of the Labour party. There does exist a class for whom this is not true. The phenomena of the affluent worker, men who are socially marginal, with the values and consumption patterns of the working class but a middle class income has attracted much notice in the last decade. Part of their marginality lies in their politically ambiguous position. They earn enough to be distinctly interested in the low tax, low welfare policies traditionally attributed to the Conservatives, but they make use of and expect some prerogatives of the working class, in particular public housing and state pensions, to take the place of the private saving habit that they have not inherited from the middle class (Goldthorpe, 1968). Such voters need indeed to be keenly interested in the positions of the parties. Should the Labour party commit itself more seriously than usual to income redistribution, they suffer. Should the Conservative party become sufficiently right wing to wish to charge economic rents for public housing, they suffer again.

The example of the affluent worker is a very good one for demonstrating theoretically the strength of our own model of voter awarenesss and motivation. In addition it provides a neat test. If we are right, constituencies which have a large percentage of affluent workers should exhibit a greater tendency to swing from party to party over several elections than 'traditional' working class constituencies.

Such a prediction has been tested by a political sociologist (Crewe, 1973). He found indeed precisely the pattern that we predict, though his explanation is not quite ours.

No one should be too surprised by this finding: it is additional support for our theory that the parties themselves have shown themselves aware of this situation in the past. As Rose shows in his study of campaigning (1967), the Conservative party in 1964 identified a special creature, the 'target voter', to whom their propaganda should be addressed. He, the target voter, closely resembles our 'affluent worker'. In much the same way the Labour party became most concerned in the late fifties and early sixties about something called the 'embourgeoisement thesis', the idea that the working class was developing middle class tastes in politics as it learned to like cars, televisions, and washing machines.

This thesis later turned out to be false, but with a grain of truth. As the Labour party during the fifties failed to move sufficiently far to the right to be maximally competitive with the Conservatives, more and more working class voters may well have found themselves in the marginal position of being within the likely range of ideological change.

It is our position, then, that voters are of two types, depending on their position on the spectrum. If parties must live in a narrow range of the spectrum, for fear of losing the election by demonstrating an irresponsible and unreliable nature, there may be a group in the population who have a political influence quite out of proportion to their voting strength. These are the people who are to be found within the range of likely ideological change. No other voter is likely to examine very closely the party policies—he has no choice but to vote, as ever, for the one with which he has learned to identify. Quite small shifts of position can lose or win a majority of these 'marginal' voters, and as the parties will be very evenly balanced otherwise with ordinary unsophisticated 'identifiers', this is enough to lose or win the election. The voters who inhabit the region of likely party change will have a decisive effect on party policy, and thus on government output, despite their relatively small numbers. In the following section, on the competitive phenomena at the constituency level, they have an important role.

D. Multi Constituency Constitutions

Perhaps our most serious charge against the basic Downsian theory is that it cannot yield predictions of much interest for us, because the electoral framework it embodies, of a single party and a single constituency, is not the most common system in the real world. Downs was led to use this design presumably for two reasons. One may have been that economics thinks in terms of a single market for any commodity; that producers and retailers are geographically distributed, and that consumer habits vary from place to place apparently does not prevent their theories working. The second reason is that it seems to be implied by thinking of a voter as deciding between alternative governments, that the party as a whole is the significant object, and that any two voters, however geographically dispersed, are presented with the same alternatives when they come to vote.

We feel, however, that as long as strict government selection is not the only motive for voters, a theory of party competition cannot entirely ignore the effects of multi constituency electoral systems. In any case it can be shown that the very possibility of an electorate deciding between alternative government teams, ideologically united, is affected by the existence of such electoral systems.

The typical parliamentary system is one in which a country is divided into a set of geographical constituencies, within each of which candidates from all the major parties stand for election. The selection of government is, *de jure* at least, subsequent, depending on the balance between the parties in the assembly. It is both a fact of political life, and a tautological result of writing a theory of party competition, that the candidates in each constituency should be members of national political parties. What we need to find out is what exactly is implied by their membership.

If the model was purely one of alternative government selection, every candidate would present to his own constituents exactly the same programme as every other candidate of his party. The government would be selected automatically, though indirectly, by the votes in the assembly of these'men who would represent precisely the aggregate support over all the constituencies for the same alternatives. It would be very much like the behaviour of the American electoral college. The policies of the parties would, just as in the single constituency case, be as near as possible to the national median voter's preferred position.

There is a further assumption here. This description of the working of the multi constituency system assume ideological homogeneity of all constituencies. For unless this is assumed, it is not necessarily true that the winning electoral strategy is that of the national median voter's preference.

But to allow that constituencies may not all have the same distribution of ideological opinions is to entail the following: if party A is to fight an election on a constituency maximising platform, some of its candidates are doomed to fight individual seats on platforms that cannot win. If the policy that maximises seats cannot maximise the vote in every constituency, the individual candidate may be at odds with his central party. His own immediate goal is a seat in Parliament for himself, while the goal of the leaders is control of Parliament.

As yet it is not a problem, for it has not been shown that there is a need for the unlucky candidate to accept central party policy, or for the policy to be imposed. Other elements are needed to introduce the conflict. An obvious strategy for the party indeed removes all this conflict—surely it would be better, rather than forcing a central policy on the candidate, to encourage all candidates to adopt whatever may be the *local* vote maximising strategy?

Unfortunately this cannot be, at least as long as we include the idea that voters are deciding between alternative governments. Such a policy would raise serious questions about the definition of a party. Consider a voter in constituency C. He is presented with a choice between candidates A and B. He much prefers A, who has been allowed by his party to take up the *local* vote maximising policy. But looking around he sees that all A's potential colleagues in the future government have done the same, adapting themselves to local conditions. The result is that it is (i) impossible to predict what party A would actually do if elected, so varied are the individual candidates' policies; and (ii) that the median policy of A candidates is actually further from his own desires than is the policy of the local B candidate. Both of these conditions need not arise. Either of them is enough to make the voter discount the A candidates.

It is the requirement of some degree of reliability and responsibility on the part of a political party that makes it impossible to allow the candidates to offer their own strategic policies. Democratic politics requires high internal party discipline if elections are to be mechanisms for public choice.

A party cannot, therefore, allow that much autonomy to its candidates. To allow a man who will otherwise lose to buck the party line may cost it the election of others who could win on a common policy, by creating an impression of incoherence and unreliability.

The same reasoning serves to show why the candidates themselves must belong to, and cannot risk the displeasure of, a party. For the voter needs to know that if he elects candidate A, this has a good chance of producing policy results, and a chance that is predictable. If candidates do not bear meaningful party labels, there is no close connection between voting for a man committed to one's own policy and the action of the future government in carrying out that policy. The local candidate has to show that there is some possibility of his carrying out his promises. Unless he can point to his colleagues in the party, he cannot do this. This at the same time restricts the extent to which a candidate of a party would wish to offer a different line from that of his colleagues. If he fights an election campaign by offering to do X, Y, and Z, which do not please the other members of his party, he must face the next election having failed to carry out those promises, and his reputation for honesty will fail.

The best empirical evidence we have for the difficulties of a candidate who cannot show any good reason why the voters should expect him to be able to carry out his promises comes from France. Analysts have found it impossible to explain repeated Gaullist successes in every election since 1958 other than by showing that a Gaullist candidate can present himself, as no other French candidate has ever been able to, as a member of a team which can form a united, one party, government. This has had its effect by prompting several attempts at unity amongst centre and left parties who have never shown any deep liking for each other, or for the role of disciplined governmental party (Williams, 1970; Charlot, 1971).

There are, of course, other reasons for candidates wishing to be affiliated with, and being prepared to accept the dictates of, a central party. The most important is that financial and propaganda resources are more likely to be available to a member of a team than an individual candidate. There is probably considerable support for the prediction that the greater the reliance on centrally collected resources, the greater the uniformity of individual candidate's policy platforms.

Before we derive any predictions in this section there is a vital aspect of electioneering to note. All that has been deduced about candidate autonomy depends on the assumption that the information available to a voter in a particular constituency is the same as that of any other voter in another constituency. Thus so far the role of parties and of candidates is providing the voter with information has been overlooked. If there is one thing that voting research has shown us, it is that voters have very little, and very inaccurate, information about politics. Therefore any assumption of perfect and identical information made in a theory such as this invites failure. Voters do not know much, and what they know is slanted by their own selective perception and the ideological preferences of their news sources.

With a situation of very imperfect information a candidate's autonomy may well become more feasible. How voters get what political information they have we do not know. It is more than likely that local sources are as important as national ones. The earlier voting studies showed the importance of 'opinion leaders' in the daily lives of voters; these are certainly local men (Berelson, 1948). Political climates, varying from place to place, also affect the voter. Butler and Stokes demonstrated that as the percentage of one class dominance in a constituency rose, so did the percentage of that class who voted normally, and the percentage of the other class which voted deviantly (Butler, 1969). These are all signs that a voter's information sources can well be local rather than national. If this is the case we would expect that accurate information about the stands of party A's candidates in other constituencies would be lacking, and that the A party candidate in a particular constituency would himself be a major source of information and interpretation of the central party line. Not that his speeches and election addresses will necessarily be the direct source of many people's knowledge, but they, filtered through local papers and opinion leaders, are as likely to provide a picture of what party A stands for as are direct messages from some central source.

Again we could hardly claim the candidate will have a very free hand in interpreting central policy; any very great divergence from the line taken by the majority of candidates will be noted by, amongst others, opposing candidates who will make capital out of this sign of dissension. Much more would one expect a candidate to vary the emphasis of policy and promise. By such means it may well be possible for candidate to transmit selectively policy to their best advantage according to the nature of the local electorate.

We still need to know much more than we do about information source and candidates' salience in the voters' mind. We can however suggest the following predictions from our argument in this section:

I. The official party policy will be the one calculated to win in a majority of constituencies, not the one which has majority support in the electorate at large.

II. No great degree of autonomy will be enjoyed by candidates in presenting policy.

IIIa. The less a constitution arranges for accountability for government policy, the more autonomous will candidates be.

IIIb. Even where there is little accountability candidates will need a party affiliation and will try to appear similar in outlook to an appreciable number of other candidates.

IV. Candidate autonomy will increase as the proportion of information sources which are local in nature increases.

V. Variance between candidates of one party will be a matter of emphasis of policy rather than sharp disagreement.

VI. Where there is conflict between them, the goal of a candidate will be his own election to the assembly rather than the victory of his party: the goals of leaders will be the opposite.

VII. VI, as well as most of I–V, depends on this: variance between winning positions in different constituencies decreases with the homogeneity of the electorate.

Why candidates may be prepared to fight in constituencies where they have little or no chance of success is a question of some importance. Seats in Parliament are much desired, and in scarce supply, of course. It seems reasonable that a party would not, if it could avoid it, put weak or unattractive candidates into any seat it has much chance of winning. A candidate may well see even the slight chance of winning in a hostile constituency as a valuable opportunity, if only because it gives him his chance to demonstrate how attractive a candidate he could be. We would therefore suggest another two hypotheses.

I. That a candidate fighting in a difficult seat will be concerned to maximise his vote even when it is improbable that he can hope to win.

II. That most candidates will have to serve an apprenticeship in difficult seats before they get a safe seat.

This latter prediction is a dangerous one, for there are so many reasons why a man might be given a good seat straight away (external party politics being just one) that it can only be offered with so strong a *'ceteris paribus'* clause as to make it very difficult to test.

But how can the small variation allowable be any use to a candidate in a constituency? Following from the arguments in Section C there may exist an element in the electorate, the only group which is likely to be affected by policy at all, for whom it is precisely this sort of marginal change which is important. A candidate who is able to make only a slight change in party policy may nonetheless be able to capture all the votes which can be captured in any given constituency. Also, we can suggest why many candidates will not need to take advantage of the slight competitive change they are entitled to.

Imagine a constituency that is heavily skewed from the national distribution. This does not just imply that it will be likely to vote for one party position over another. It implies that a large percentage of the vote in the constituency can be relied on by one candidate, whatever position he chooses to take up. In such a case the lucky candidate can be sure of winning easily, and will take the opportunity to use his small degree of autonomy to please his party activists by taking up a relatively extreme position. His opponent, at the same time, will be able to use the whole range of variability left open by the strong candidate's taking up an extreme position to capture what few votes are available.

A 'marginal constituency' is defined as one where (i) the numbers of 'identifying' voters are roughly balanced, and (ii) there exists a group of 'marginal voters' big enough to swing the election. If candidates who can expect to win anyway take advantage of this to please their campaign workers, and losing opponents in turn take advantage of their actions to maximise their vote, a regular pattern of candidate positioning should show up. As constituencies deviate from equality in expected vote for each party, all candidates will move towards the end of the spectrum 'owned' by the winning party.

Some evidence tending to confirm our belief in rationality and ideological effect in marginal constituencies is presented in Appendix 3. Chapter 5 shows that candidates do compete as we suggest here.

E. Conclusions

The theory of party competition is a rich and fascinating area for speculation, which we have no more than touched on here. The predictions we draw, stated at the end of Section A.3.5, are not all that could be derived, though they are all that can be tested as yet. In the concluding chapter to the book we shall suggest some further refinements, and at various places throughout we mention additional areas for thought. All we can try to do however is to test this theory, and these predictions, in the rest of the work. At the same time we produce evidence and information that is suggestive of further hypothesising.

What remains to be done theoretically is principally to fill out the statement that competition will not always be 'necessary' (as the word is used in Section A.3.5). Yet this covers a great deal of ground. In particular it revolves round the actual nature of policy dimensions, and the availability of postions. on such dimensions This we pass on to in the next chapter. However the really difficult problem (involved in studying ideological dimensions but of wider import) is that of relevance of a party's record. As we said earlier, this is difficult not only because of weakness of measurement and absence of data about how people do in fact weigh records, against policy, but because, even at the logical and normative level, it is so unclear how they ought to be weighed. On this we can go very little further.

Chapter 3 is a bridge between the theoretical and empirical section of the book. In it we start by discussing theoretically the nature of ideological or policy dimensions, and go on to describe what we take as evidence for their actual nature in Britain in the last fifty years.

Spatial Representation of Party Competition

A. Spatial Representation in General

When we think of politics in dimensional terms, which is to think of it with the vocabulary and tools of geometry, we are using a natural and efficient way of dealing with a complex phenomena. One could reference the French Estates General of 1789, or daily journalistic discussion of the left and right wings of European parliaments. The advertisment for the Italian Christian Democrats in 1972 which showed a stretch of autostrada with 'their' car driving fast down the middle lane is a fine example. There is no doubt that a spatial representation of political attitudes helps make it all comprehensible.

No less a figure, nor a more politically ambiguous one than Winston Churchill regarded as quite serious the question of seating arrangements in the House of Commons. He was determined to avoid the French semi-circular array where parties might compete for the 'left' segment.

All that Anthony Downs and his imitators have done since 1957 on spatial modelling of party competition is to take seriously a metaphor that is quite basic to our conceptualisation of political competition. Take it seriously we should. Sociologists, far more than political scientists, make serious use of geometric and spatial analysis—social distance measures, sociograms, social hierarchy and social mobility studies, with their complex graph theories, have developed from non-technical but very common spatial thinking. To point out a 'distance' between attitudes, ideas, systems, is inevitable, and 'distance' is meaningless without 'direction' of change, movement, reaction. Direction and distance between them, as soon as they are used, raise the question of dimensionality. For if X is to be a certain distance from both Y and Z, it may only be possible to display this in a two-dimensional space. Each extra parameter fitted, an extra person or another distance requirement between two other actors, defines further and increases the complexity of the dimensionality of the space required.

Using geometrical techniques to display, categorise, and describe social phenomena is useful, though there are alternative methods. One could, though only in a cumbersome way, give it up and use descriptive language which has nothing to do with the concept of distance. Similarity, likeness, compatibility, are alternatives. There is a good reason, though, why even these tend to invite us back to geometry. To make judgements of similarity is to rank order. For greater accuracy, and more precise theorising, it is often necessary to attach some numbering, or at least a well-defined logic of ranking categories, to any set of similarity judgements. In a three party system one would have to be enormously unimaginative not to ask which of two parties was more like the third.

Ranking leads us, wherever possible, to measurement, and to the formulation and testing of hypotheses, laws, and theories. These are most conveniently handled by descriptive and sometimes deductive statistics. Yet statistics is, by its very nature, best thought of as dealing with the relationships between points in space—back again to geometry, the only adequate intuitive understanding of statistical relations, and in the first place the easiest way to deal with all but the very simplest distance or similarity judgements.

Despite this, spatial models of political activity are often criticised. One school to make this criticism of Downs is that of the Michigan Survey research institute, in an article by Donald Stokes (1966). Many other attacks on the basic use of left–right have been made by journalists and social scientists, one of the earliest by the latter group being Eysack's, *The Psychology of Politics* (1951). His model of political attitudes is used in a more recent, non-academic and politically dedicated work, Samuel Brittan's *Left or Right, the Bogus Dilemma* (1968). At any time one can see on television interviews politicians denouncing a simple left–right split as being unrealistic, at the same time as they rely heavily on other spatial terms, denouncing one policy as too 'extreme' or advocating the 'middle of the road'. Not a few pamphlets from the British Conservative party have contained the word 'Right' in their title, and metaphors of movement (keep going, etc.) are very common.

What critics (and users of such dimensional accounts of party politics) so often miss are two points that are vital if we are to benefit by taking our geometrical metaphors seriously.

One is that, of course, a too simple or restricted spatial model will be inadequate to mirror political life, just as too small a vocabulary, the socio-linguist's 'restricted code', will distort any social comprehension. The other, in many ways a rider to the first, is that our geometrical tools are exactly that, tools we choose to satisfy our needs.

Left–right, or a much more complex N-dimensional analysis, are all constructs we, as social scientists, create and use to fulfil our own analytic needs. Not only are they not sacrosanct, not 'given' by social reality, but they can only be judged against the purposes we conceive.

Thus to two attacks on such usage: Brittan's claim that left–right is inadequate, or the empirical claim in Butler and Stokes' *Political Change in Britain* (1969) that only 2% of the population does not see politics in left–right terms, we must give the same answer.

First, that if Mr. Brittan finds 'left–right' inadequate, he must show us that we ought to take note of that which left–right misses, for we may not care if it is adequate for what we are interested in. The other criticism is equally misplaced. To use any spatial analogy (or any verbal description for that matter) of society is not to claim it is how social actors think, but that we have found it theoretically useful. Only the social scientist in question can decide how adequate any particular spatial model is for his purpose.

Now it is not our position that the Downsian model, which is, in any case, only offered as illustrative, with its one-dimensional ideological spectrum, is adequate for explaining party competition, though our objections are less directed at the uni-dimensionality than the nature of the spectrum.

However appropriate it may be to see politics in spatial terms, there is room for considerable speculation about the nature of this space, not only in considering its structure, or dimensionality, but its substantive character. As is shown in the journal literature, and most thoroughly by Budge and Farlie (forthcoming), one may have to think in terms of several different spatial frameworks, with some mapping between them.

This is obscurred in the straight Downsian model, and perhaps in much political science, by an incorrect identification between what voters desire, and what political parties offer. We have continually stressed that party propaganda has to concentrate on the policies the party wishes to offer as solutions to problems. Yet except in an indirect way, voters can hardly be seen as desiring policy as such. There has to be a translation at some stage from policy to impact. While in purely redistributive politics, the translation is automatic, between, say, a policy of increasing old age pensions and the actual money income of the old, this is not usually so. Few voters can plausibly be said to have a desire for a prices and incomes policy, though they may have a strong desire for price stability in weekly shopping.

Political parties have to conjure with policy, with methods and proposed solutions, and it is necessary to see this activity as taking place in a 'policy-method' space. Voters are not distributed in this space, however, certainly not the majority of them. They, interested in the results of government activity, must be seen as distributed in a second, 'policy-aim' space in which their desires can be represented. These two spaces, though different, have to have points of congruence; a certain policy will bring about an impact on society which will be more or less desired by the electorate. Thus any policy-method point in one space can be mapped onto the other. As it is the distribution of voters' preferences that determine electoral outcomes, the vote maximising position, in the policy-method space represents, or is a mapping of the actual majority preference for some outcome in the policy-aim space. This restatement may seem unduly complex, but is necessary, because there are features of the two spaces that cannot be ignored, and differ, in a way that is crucial for the understanding of party competition.

Before we take that up, we shall introduce one further refinement of the spatial display of party politics. Whichever space one takes so far only party policy and voter preference have appeared on the map. If one constructs a spatial display, defined by one or more dimensions, whether these be policy-method dimensions measuring perhaps control by government of the economy,

58

or policy-aim dimensions measuring social values or troublesome phenomena, say egalitarianism or the rate of inflation, there will be a point in that space that represents present social reality, the *status quo*. This is demonstrated in Figure 13.

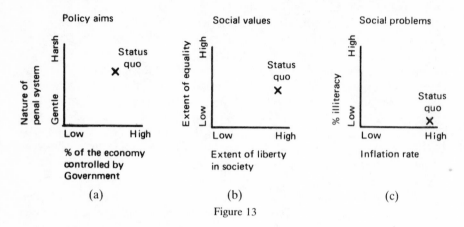

Figure 13

For the analysis and understanding of policy-method, as set out and manipulated by parties, and voter preferences constraining this, the *status quo* has central importance. It helps to give us an interpretation of a phenomenon well-known in voting research, the 'partisan self image', or party identification that predicts voting so well. In addition it leads to the creation of uni-dimensional models that cannot be regarded as so naive as the crude 'left–right' distinction.

As Lindblom has argued (1963) the ability to make policy by comprehensive optimisation of values is not something any policy maker can have, and it is even less likely that an ordinary voter has it. Lindblom's point is that one does not know, in abstract, whether one prefers X% unemployment to Y% inflation, except in specific contexts. We would extend this argument here to say that a voter is unlikely to have an abstract set of desires for party policy, but will have particular attachment to, or dislike of, the *status quo*. He will be worried about some aspect of current reality, to the extent that he is prepared to allow more or less change in his life to remove this worry. He will also have a general direction in which he would be prepared to see society change, if change it must. The degree of his attachment to the *status quo*, and to the preferred direction of change may vary. It is highly probable that the strength of his attachment is inversely proportional to strength of attachment to any direction of change. A man who is very happy as he is is likely to care much less about what direction society moves in than that it should move as little as possible; while one who actively dislikes his present state probably will have a clear and strong idea of how it should be changed. No one however can judge policy, or form desires, without reference to some benchmark, and the present organisation and situation of society seems the obvious one.

It is our suggestion here that strength of partisan identification reflects strength of attraction to some overall direction of social change. The basic image of the party is defined in terms of the values that define also a voter's preferred direction of change, and social reality, the *status quo* is, in its turn, defined by some mix of these values. The less one is enamoured of reality, and therefore the more one is prepared to accept change, the less one needs to know of actual policy; a knowledge of the likely direction of social change to be pursued by one's party, and the likely degree of it, is enough.

For someone who is fairly pleased with the *status quo*, and for whom any very great change in any direction is likely to be unfortunate, a knowledge of proposed change is more important, and partisan identification riskier. It would be interesting to find out, from survey data, whether in fact weak party identification is more common amongst those in such an economic position. There is little evidence, unfortunately, that bears on this.

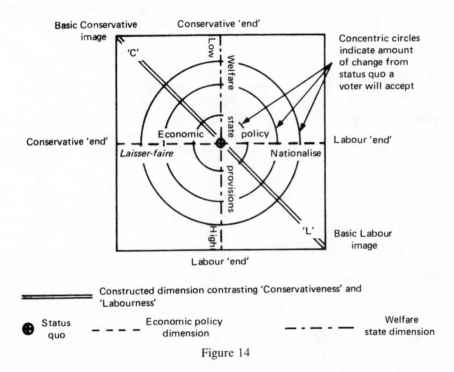

Figure 14

What all this does is to suggest a way in which uni-dimensional models may be very sensible. The dimension in question is one of 'partyness'. In Figure 14 such a dimension is shown. It runs from one traditional party image, through the *status quo*, to the other image. The concentric circles round the *status quo* reflect the distribution of voters according to their tolerance for change.

Such a dimension is not naive, because it asserts neither that only one important dimension of policy or ideology exists, nor that all important issues can be subsumed in one direction. It is just a line drawn in a space that can be as complex as necessary fully to capture ideological conflict, but which itself represents only the distance from the *status quo* to any party stereotype that the voter is prepared to go. We make use of such a 'stereoline' in analysing constituency competition in Chapter 5. Budge and Farlie (1976) make use of a similar construct in their analysis of survey data. Our suggestion here is, of course, only a graphic representation of the discussion in Chapter 2 of the 'safe' and 'marginal' voter.

The *status quo*, as we have said, is equally important in the policy-method space in which parties actually manoeuvre. What the *status quo* represents here is the policies being pursued by the government of the moment. These form the background against which any new initiatives must be seen; indeed policy making at any one time is a matter of changing on-going policy in particular ways. We know already that much that governments do is fixed for quite lengthy periods into the future by programmes which cannot be scrapped overnight. Commitments made by one government frequently are not capable of being terminated by their successors. A very high proportion of government expenditure is fixed and cannot be altered, at least in the short run. All of this goes to make the *status quo* a central position around which party policy must fluctuate. If in addition one accepts the incrementalist thesis on policy making, that the only way to design programmes is to vary slightly the existing arrangements and wait for feedback, it has an even stronger determining or constraining influence.

In particular the *policy-method status quo* is important when one takes into account the popularity of the consequential *policy-aim status quo*. Given the constraints on, and difficulty of, designing policy, a popular *status quo*, one where existing policies are working well, is a very dominating position. One would expect that this position will be one that parties move towards, or back away from, depending on how well it is working, how well the economy, for instance, is progressing. Evidence to this effect is given in Chapter 4.

Returning to an earlier argument, it can probably now be seen why a distinction between policy-method space and policy-aim space is useful, as one considers the different but equally important aspects of the *status quo*. As far as policy-method space goes, this highlights a further question. It is always assumed in the technical Downsian literature that the dimension along which parties compete is continuous, that voters are distributed along the whole length of it, and that whatever position, given voter distribution, is the vote maximising one, will be adopted by the parties.

This is not realistic, though the difficulties in the idea are hidden by the conflation into one space of the two aspects. It may well be that voter preferences are nearly infinitely divisible, and spread over all points in a space. If, in a one-dimensional example, one thinks of a dimension along which people's desires for income redistribution were placed, it is at least possible that every point from total equality to massive income differentials would have at least one advocate. Money is a perfect metric, and one can imagine a society where every gradation from zero pounds per year to a million was earned by someone, and that everyone wanted a redistribution policy as long as it only taxed those richer than himself. The distribution of wealth might be such that a policy advocating a super tax starting at £3250 p.a. would maximise votes. This policy-aim space has to be mapped onto a policy-method space in which the parties actually compete.

In the policy-method space there is no guarantee that there exists a congruent point. While voter preferences may be continuous, methods of achieving them are almost certainly not. Imagine, as an unlikely but heuristically useful example, that the Internal Revenue are only capable of working in fixed £500 intervals; there is then no vote maximising policy. There really exist two similar constraints on policy making. One, as above, is that policy alternatives are not that flexible, and parties may have to adopt policies too egalitarian or too elitist, or whatever, but can never get onto the real vote maximising position. Alternatively, it is true that policy alternatives may just not exist, that there may not be ways of solving certain social problems without imposing unpopular costs. Policies do not exist independently of men; they have to be imagined, devised, and are determined by the categories in which the policy makers think, their experience, wisdom, and imagination. So we must see policy-method space as consisting of discontinuous areas, requiring quantum jumps by any party trying to manoeuvre competitively. Figure 15 depicts such a space, and the problems of competition that might arise.

There remains some question about the plausibility of seeing policy, meaning here 'suggested methods for solving social problems' in dimensional terms at all. What use are dimensions if voters are not arrayed on them?

One may well wish, at times, to ignore the voter and his perceptions, in which case it is indeed sensible to use a complex model in which policy stands are placed in a spatial framework according to their intrinsic nature. One mistake that has often been made, notably by Stokes (1966), is to equate a 'dimension' with an 'issue'. If one does this it is very common to end up with a rather peculiar dimension on which only one position can be adopted. Stokes' example is corruption in government, which he says was a major issue in the American election of 1948. Of course there is only one acceptable position, to be against corruption, on that issue, but this is not to argue against a dimensional model, for any issue is likely to fit amongst a set of similar ones into a complex dimension on which there certainly are many conceivable positions. Even if one does take a single issue case, like corruption, Stokes' argument that there is only one conceivable position does not hold. For it is, to voters as much as to political scientists, obvious that no one can actively support corruption, but it is altogether another matter how one proposes to deal with it, and how one accounts for its existence. In 1948 positions could have varied all the way from a proposal for Constitutional change predicated on a theory that corruption was endemic to a log-rolling federal legislature, to the idea that the President had been misled and there was no cause for worry over something that was 'objectively trivial'.

62

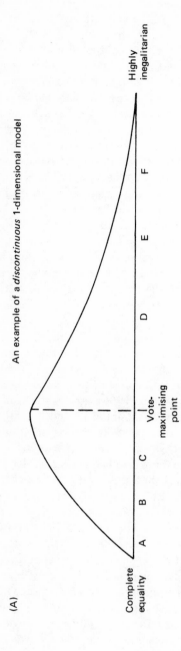

(A)   An example of a *discontinuous* 1-dimensional model

Complete   Highly
equality   A   B   C   D   E   F   inegalitarian
                              Vote-
                              maximising
                              point

Assume the lettered points stand for the following policy sets:

A = Negative income tax, wealth tax, and abolition of private property.
B = As above, but very limited private property allowed.
C = Negative income tax plus ordinary death duties.
D = Current British PAYE system, with some death duties.
E = Roughly proportionate income tax only.
F = Direct taxation only.

In this example, there does not exist a vote-maximising policy. Equal numbers prefer C to D and vice versa. Any party able to invent a policy halfway between C and D would beat either.

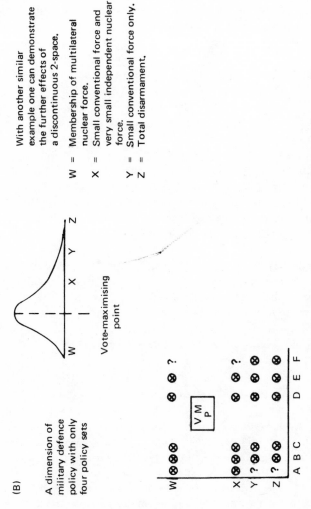

(B)

A dimension of military defence policy with only four policy sets

Vote-maximising point

With another similar example one can demonstrate the further effects of a discontinuous 2-space.

W = Membership of multilateral nuclear force.

X = Small conventional force and very small independent nuclear force.

Y = Small conventional force only.

Z = Total disarmament.

Figure 15

In the discontinuous 2-space that results, there exist, *at most*, 24 possible policy sets, none of them anywhere near the vote-maximising point. If there is, as is possible, a relationship between policies on the two dimensions, there may be fewer possible sets than the apparent maximum.

For example, (?) in the diagram replaces the conjunctions: F/W,F/X, A/Z,A/Y, which are ruled out if military defence and equality policies are related thus. With economic policy 'F' the country cannot raise enough revenue to afford *any* nuclear weapons, and with taxation policy A, nearby Capitalist nations will be tempted to invade, making it unsafe to have a smaller defence capacity than X.

One very good reason for retaining a complex dimensional model which acts to simplify the plethora of issues in an election is that they, or policy decisions about them, are not independent.

One is not free, as a politician, to take up any permutation of stands on a set of issues. Policies are articulated into composite and unavoidable sets. This may be because it is logically impossible, once one has chosen to go for policy A, also to go for policy B. It is, for instance, somewhat illogical to support both a defence policy of a technological nuclear based deterrent, and to retain a compulsory national service. There may be psychological incompatibilities—it is hard, though not illogical, to come up with a policy of denationalising some industries and enforcing mandatory rather than indicative industrial planning. There may be pragmatic incompatibilities—if one is dedicated to a tax reduction policy, one forecloses not only the possibility of great expansion in the social services, but also any very flexible Keynesian demand manipulation economic policy.

There may be theoretical or ideological reasons why policies fit together and others are incompatible. If one has a general world view, an ideology that includes both evaluative, predictive, and explanatory elements, freedom of choice amongst policy alternatives cannot exist to any great extent.

Whatever organising principle a party has, it must have one or more, and policies are likely to be articulated in the light of this. Indeed one would expect, if not a uni-dimensional model, certainly one with only a few major independent dimensions. For dimensions to be independent, unconnected, uncorrelated, or orthogonal, it is essential that any position in one dimension is compatible with any position on another. We shall shortly provide evidence of such a statistically orthogonal model of some major dimensions in British politics since 1924.

Reflect for a moment on the classic long term economic policy debate in Britain. It is clear that there is not a majority of the population in favour of a massive nationalisation of the 'commanding heights of the economy'. But just how many points are there in between? It is not a dichotomy, obviously. But nor is it a perfect metric; there are, in many people's eyes, quantum jumps. One can nationalise certain very basic, ailing service industries without much stir. To add a core industry like steel is going a little far, but still fits into the same framework. Nationalise a successful monopoly, sugar, or a vastly lucrative oligopoly like the pharmaceutical industry, and one has done more than add three or four industries to a list; one has jumped a long way towards socialism. On the other side, to denationalise a little is a moderate step from the *status quo*, to abolish investment grants goes not much further, but to deliberately refrain from using the budget as a demand manipulator, and accept an unemployment rate of more than 5% is a massive leap.

An infinite variety of policy-method positions does not exist, for two reasons. The first is that the electorate are used to thinking in a relatively short list of pretty basic terms; only a few major dichotomies are liable to be noticed, and great odium can come on a party for advocating a policy that it thinks is clearly different from, but the electorate sees as identical to, its opponent's late-lamented failure. How many people, after all, grasped the subtle distinctions between Mr. Heath's 'Prices Commission' and Mr. Wilson's 'Prices and Incomes Board', or between Mr. McGovern's plan to give a thousand dollars to every tax payer and Mr. Nixon's support for a negative income tax?

The second reason is subtler—the electorate are not the only people whose categories of thought are fixed and can be irritating. Ultimately an ideology is a set of categories, a set of collective nouns even, which fixes our thought so that the range of strategic choices we see is limited. Policies do not come from anywhere, they are the product of ideological minds which are prone to carve up reality into tight, non-continuous segments. No greater mistake could be made than in thinking that a competitive politician, one who by Downs' definition cares nothing for what ideology he offers, is free of such an ideology. To the extent that the politician is a socialised (or just educated) human, he has an ideology. An ideology is a complex mental instrument. It contains a value element, which judges what is right or wrong with reality and an imaginative element which conjures up a utopian future. Both of these we can, with risk, ignore in the competitive politician. It also has, however, an explanatory, or sociological element, which defines what is possible, tells the hearer how society works, what human nature is like, how one can coerce, force, bribe or invite desired human action. This part at least cannot be denied to any politician, and makes inevitable the non-continuous nature of the policy dimension.

Whatever difficulties and constraints, ideological and pragmatic, interfere with the smooth making of policy produce further interferences with party competition, because human desires and preferences for policy results do not conform to these.

Such 'category of thought' constraints are not the only ones. A party's ability to find a policy-method which can come close to a policy-aim maximising point can be restricted by other policies. This is particularly likely to be true in the case of dimensions of secondary salience. Even where dimensions are highly independent as far as psychological, ideological, or even technical matters arise, there is always a binding restraint of finance. So a party which has to commit itself to, say, a welfare and education programme which is costly may be quite unable to present the defence policy that would meet with greatest approval. This is hardly a subtle point, though, common a complaint in politics as it is, it illustrates a broader problem of resource restrictions on vote maximisation.

Of greater interest may be general constitutional and social values, not necessarily of the whole population as of a fragment of it attached to the party in question, which may rule out large segments of the policy-aim dimension by making unthinkable some particular policy-method. The long standing loathing of the 'means test' as a social instrument that has so continuously aggravated the problems of policy making in the British Labour party is a good example, as is the opposite, often financially trivial hatred of Conservatives for any policy that did not make such a discrimination and thus paid the poor and the rich alike. What we have in these examples is a strong view on policy-method, held probably by only a small but vital section of a party. Such a minority taste probably could be overruled in the interests of vote maximisation by a party hierarchy sufficiently determined, but probably will not be as they are likely to colour the whole policy thinking of a party research effort. This again points to the way in which some vote maximising policies are available unequally to different parties.

Orthodox categories of thought, failures of imagination, economic restraints, and party and general taboos can all coincide to make a policy-aim dimension which is infinitely divisible badly correlated with a policy-method dimension which may be anything but smooth.

The implications of all this for party competition are clear. Suppose that a certain policy set, 'A', won the election at time T. It has become the *status quo* on the policy-method map. That policy is precisely described in the two-space model and is shown on the one-space degree-and-direction-of-change model. It is a vote maximising policy. There is no majority, amongst the ordinary voters, for a policy that would bring greater social change. Nor is there a majority amongst the sophisticated for any other two-space position, but the policy fails. Do we have any idea at all what a competitive party will do now? As far as existing theory goes we do not. We may assume that a future winning position will have to imply only a little social change but be different from the current policy while remaining plausible.

The plausibility requirement is what interests us here. Downsianism implies that any party can take up any position that does not involve by-passing the other party, and that both will seek to take up very similar positions, as there is a unique vote maximising point. However this is not true, as long as plausibility is taken account of. For it may be equally plausible for Labour to offer a slightly higher degree of central planning and a tax increase as for the Conservatives to offer less research and development aid and to cut taxation. The voter has no way (nor, unfortunately, do the parties) of really knowing what will work, but he does know what is historically the direction in which the various parties deviate from the *status quo*. What is likely to be much less plausible is a policy, offered by the Conservatives, which deviates from the *status quo* in the *same* direction as the Labour party, towards an area of the policy space it has never inhabited (or vice versa). There is good sense in the idea that, if one is to have a capitalist economy, one may as well have it run by capitalists.

What makes a policy plausible is not susceptible to detailed analysis, but it does seem clear that one policy is not equally plausible, necessarily, for all parties, as we argued in Chapter 2.

We must not forget that this policy space, and the party positions, do not come into being, fully-fledged, overnight. On the contrary, it is a slowly emerging and developing social paradigm, and high consensus between parties is a result of convergence over time (see Appendix 1). It is not, logically, ridiculous for a party to leap over the *status quo* and adopt a policy on its opposition's side of it. However, if the voter is to be seen as aware of problems that he wishes to be cured, with a restricted degree of concomitant social change, and with a basic direction partially defined by a party identification, he is most likely to expect policy to be in keeping with the traditional orientation of the party.

We would generally expect, although we cannot show this to be true, that the different parties will come to dominate some dimensions. For, as long as we keep in mind that this party competition goes on in an historically developing situation, policy positions are not party-neutral. The party that first comes up with a policy, say of creating a national health service, which is widely accepted, is likely always to maintain greater credibility in this area than the opposing party which had, over time, denied the necessity of this. It is just not very credible, if there is a crisis in health service provisions, for the long term exponent of private medicine to promise to increase national health funding. This is not to say that it must lose the election on this issue; the electorate may well prefer a policy, in keeping with its traditions, of making easier private health insurance.

As we have said, it is not possible to predict rigorously the determinants of plausibility, but we have shown that, under some circumstances, there may be more than one position on a dimension which is, potentially, vote maximising. Which is chosen could only be decided in terms of the general confidence the electorate has in the parties, or the relative degrees of disruption of the *status quo* implied by the policies.

An obvious analogy is between party competition and military strategy. The general has to deal with a geographically defined battle terrain, the politician with a voter-defined policy space. A battlefield is a continuous surface, filled with targets of varying strategic value and accessibility. Mountains and hills, bridges and forests represent for the military strategist salient points, possibly of different value to different armies. Politically we have the existing or conceivable policies, scattered points around which political campaigning centres. Armies do not fight for spots on a battlefield which fit general war aims for so much territory, or such and such a damage to the enemy, regardless of terrain, but have to fight for landmarks and salient objects. In the same way a party cannot necessarily take up a position, in a policy-method space, correlating precisely with a vote maximising position in the corresponding policy-aim space.

In both cases the terrain is given, consisting, politically, of the conceivable policies or policy mixes. These differ in strategic value, according to their proximity to the vote maximising position, and to their utility for foreclosing the enemies moves. To capture a geographical object, say a river bank, may allow a general to force the enemy to give battle at a place of his choosing, while to adopt, early enough, a popular political position may enable a party to dictate policy on that dimension. This we have already illustrated in the case of social welfare—the party that first adopts a policy of national health provision may well remain invulnerable to any challenge in that direction.

Then there is accessibility, which we have also touched on. Militarily a strong point may be more easily captured by one force, because it has the right weaponry, or because it has strong emotional importance to those soldiers, than by another. Politically not all policy positions are equally available to both parties. This we showed in arguing that, given bad economic conditions, both parties might have to drop previously consensual economic policies, and that this might involve both of them moving away from that position back towards their own end of the spectrum. This is because, if a party has been steadily advancing towards a moderate policy position, a sudden jump over this consensual, *status quo* policy to one on the opposition's side is likely to be much less credible than a retreat into its own area, to a policy more clearly in keeping with and generated by its own basic political attitudes.

Strategy in electioneering can be said, summarily, to be a function of five major factors. The aim is to maximise votes, at least to the point of a guaranteed majority, and this vote maximising point is determined by the intersection of the distribution of voter preferences for policy aims (or problem solutions) and policy-methods. Given a terrain set thus, the availability of issue stands is determined. Choice amongst them is the result of two further factors, the 'plausibility' and the 'effectiveness' of these as policy-methods.

'Plausibility' affects strategy by making some policy positions unattainable at various times because for one reason or another the party lacks credibility. The policy may not be in keeping with the party's tradition, its general articulating principles (or ideology), or the party's past record in the policy area may make it unlikely that much confidence will be felt by the electorate.

'Effectiveness', the extent to which either the party or the electorate expects a policy to be successful must also enter. Where there is a generally successful policy, one that has been tried with apparently good results, this will have a major and dominating influence on political strategy. It is clear though that the electorate's perceptions of policy success are vital, and may be quite inaccurate as judged by apolitical experts. Widespread nationalisation as a policy in Britain is probably foreclosed forever by the public belief, by no means necessarily shared by economists, that public enterprises are always inefficient. Political parties are hardly neutral in this business, and the electorate's view of what is an efficient policy will have much to do with what they are taught. We need to distinguish between opposition by the electorate to a policy because it is thought to be inefficient, and objection on the grounds that it involves too great a change from the *status quo*. The latter is usually likely to be the case, partly because it requires less information, and because we do not expect the electorate as a whole to be very interested in policy-as-method. The electorate is much more likely to be able, or inclined, to judge the effectiveness of a policy that has been tried, that is a fairly familiar social mechanism, than one that is new or untried, and these latter are much more likely to be judged in terms of their general effect on the *status quo* than their specific efficiency as problem solutions. The technical efficiency of a policy does count, because no party is liable to risk advocating a policy which is popular but inefficient for fear of thus damaging its record.

These questions of efficiency and plausibility combine with the general shortage of ideas on how to solve social problems to suggest that policy dimensions may be split into those concerning long and short range social problems. There is usually more agreement, and more objective judgment, in short term areas, and problems of the short term, which may nonetheless be vital, allow parties the least strategic leeway. The best example is in economic affairs. However much political disagreement there has been in Britain or America in the last thirty years on the long range shape of the economy, there has been an amazing consensus on how to deal with immediate problems of inflation, unemployment, and current crises. There is very little room for competitive policy setting in such a case, and we shall shortly demonstrate that, in Britain at least, a dimension of short term economic policy has existed, and that on it the parties have behaved in substantially similar ways as economic conditions have fluctuated.

Before we launch into the empirical part of this book, and argue for a particular set of dimensions as characterising British politics in this century, we have to note a consequence of the fact that any dimensionality is, as we argued earlier, only a construct employed by a social scientist for his convenience in summarising and representing change in party policy.

There are only two ways one can study party competition, and neither can be ignored. Either one can study the change over time of the policy of the party as a single unit, or the variance over candidates at one time of their interpretation of central party policy. That is, one can look, diachronically or synchronically, at variance in policy. This is the choice represented, for instance, by studying party competition between single party blocks, as does Downs, or at the constituency level, as we do in parts of earlier chapters and empirically in Chapter 5.

There is an inevitable problem, however, when one does both, in deciding what the relationship is between the dimensions on which candidates from a party take their stands at any one time, and the diachronic dimensions, through time, on which one plots changes of party policy in general. They are not the same dimensions, for we know that some problems and ideas exist for a while then die away. They cannot be entirely unrelated, else it is impossible to talk of party policy changing over time. It is from not noticing this distinction, and this problem, that we feel some of the difficulties that are seen by Stokes and others arise.

Our solution, as set out below, is to regard the dimensions along which change over time by the central party is plotted as somehow or other basic, a deep structure, which is instantiated from time to time in different ways at elections by policy dimensions that are derived from them, but set in terms of contemporary problems.

We are more than aware of the difficulties and implications of such a theory, but cannot here discuss them properly. It does not seem that there is any other plausible way out.

B.1. Dimensions in British Politics

Just what sort of dimensionality has there been in British politics, and how does one investigate this? We have already argued against the identification of an ideological dimension with an 'issue'. This does not mean that issues will never be separate dimensions of importance, but that in general a dimensional framework is a simplification of the mass of 'issues' or 'topics' of political debate. The simplification, if such is possible, arises from the correlations and interdependency of issues. One can easily formalise the logical relationships that produce a dimensionality out of a mass of 'issues'. Suppose we have six issues, A, B, C, D, E, F, on each of which it is possible to adopt policy 1 or 2. At least one dimension exists if something like the following is true: $A1 \leftrightarrow B2$. Two orthogonal dimensions would exist given, for instance, $(A_1 \leftrightarrow B_2) + [(C_1 \vee C_2) + (D_1 \vee D_2)] + (C_1 \leftrightarrow D_1)$, and we would have a three dimensional, orthogonal, model if we added the following restrictions:

$$[(A_1 \leftrightarrow B_2) \rightarrow [C_1 \vee C_2 + D_1 \vee D_2] + (C_1 \leftrightarrow D_1)$$

$$\rightarrow [(E_1 \vee E_2 + F_1 \vee F_2) + (E_1 \leftrightarrow F_1)]$$

The logical implication signs here stand for either a logical, a psychological, or an empirical/pragmatic entailment. $(A_1 \leftrightarrow B_2)$ means that one can adopt policy A1 if and only if one adopts policy B2. We do not stipulate here why this should be so. Why it does is the subject of the sociology or history of knowledge and ideas.

Nor need the entailment hold for everyone—it may rest on another kind of consensus. Parties that have broken this consensus of entailment, advocating policies otherwise seen as incompatible have had the occasional success; the most catastrophic being the French Poujadiste policy, answering a cornucopian desire in many voters for high welfare and low taxes.

The interpretation of what each dimension 'means' may be difficult—it has to rest on what there is in common and what inherent oppositions there are amongst the different issues. In the end this might boil down to an inexplicable psychological propensity to think the same way on one set of issues and a different way on a different set. We must be careful to avoid pushing explanation or interpretation too far. One interesting example of a psychological political two-space now very well known is Eysenck's (1951) model of orthogonal dimensions, the one contrasting 'tough' and 'tender' minded people, the other 'Conservative' and 'Radical' minds. He used a long set of policy style questions to derive this mapping. It is apparently the case that to believe in corporal punishment is also, very probably indeed, to believe in compulsory religious education. Were these, and the other test questions in his research, to arise as policy issues in an election, we might well end up with very definite but quite inexplicable dimensions.

Nor do we need to be able to explain or even interpret dimensions, as long as we can be sure they exist. Just as we need not ask why any distribution of policy-desires subsists in society, we do not need to know why beliefs in high welfare, controlled economics, and support for the third world go together, and are opposed by beliefs in imperialism, *laissez-faire*, and the 'grace of poverty'.

To take this line though we must be certain that there is an existence to our dimensionality independent of our own interpretation of society. Broadly there are two ways of going about producing a spatial model of politics. One can impose a dimensionality of one's own, making judgements about which issues go together, and deciding for oneself how the actors rank on them. Alternatively, one can seek some way of allowing any latent dimensionality in the world to display itself. If one takes the second line one has to find a way of uncovering, in the mass of data about issues and actors' reactions to them, any patterning that their minds, or their perception of connections, forces on political action and political rhetoric. With the former methodology one has to present good theoretical grounds to justify a patterning of issues one perceives oneself, and also to show why one's own patterning should be held to be useful in explaining and describing other people's behaviour.

As an example one might look at roll call analysis in the study of legislatures and courts. There are many studies which attempt to find a one-dimensional 'Liberal–Conservative' ordering of issues in voting in the American Congress. Many of them proceed from the assumption that this 'Liberal–Conservative' ordering makes *a priori* sense, and struggle to fit actual roll call votes into such a schema. In the same way there are attempts to scale voting in the US Supreme Court on some *a priori* spectrum like this (Schubert, 1959; 1965). Guttman scaling, perhaps the best known of survey research tools, rests on our ability to rank actions, votes, or beliefs, on some underlying scale. To do this successfully one has to be able to show that, for instance, to support Federal Housing and Education policies is a comprehensive 'Liberal position' obviously opposed to supporting military expenditure and states' rights in voter registration. This one may be able to do, but the validity of the exercise always rests, in the end, on the force of one's own arguments that such a dimensional ordering ought to make sense.

Contrast this with a brief unpublished study on seven free votes in the British House of Commons between 1966 and 1970. These were the first and second readings of the social reform bills on Divorce, Abortion, and Homosexual behaviour, and the resolution to continue the abolition of capital punishment. What was done was to collect the voting records of a sample of MPs on these, and look for what statistical dimensionality might be present. Of course we expected to find a dimension of pure 'social liberalism'; to support easy divorce and abortion, to be against capital punishment and the illegality of homosexual behaviour. The two-dimensional model that the principal components analysis yielded did provide a first and major dimension that coincided very well with just such an interpretation. We would never have guessed, and therefore never have built into our analysis, had we not let the data speak for itself, the second dimension. For this was one that contrasted opposition to capital punishment and abortion with acceptance of either, with the other two issues being of negligible importance. The interpretation, *a posteriori*, is easy—a sanctity of life dimension that could interfere with our stereotypes of either social liberalism or conservatism. For most of the MPs there was little variance on this second dimension; to have a score much different from the mean was to be atypical, but nevertheless some were clearly divergent from the mass of it; and as such they were interesting cases. The analysis, by refusing to fit a preconceived dimensionality, told us something about the innate structure of this policy space that would have been otherwise ignored.

This approach, to allow the data to dictate the dimensionality of policy competition, is ours in this study.

B.2. Methodology

We have taken party literature of two sorts, the official party manifestos of the Labour and Conservative parties in the general elections of 1924 to 1966, and the individual parliamentary candidates' election addresses, for samples of candidates in the elections of 1924 and 1955. Why we chose, and how we analysed the latter two data sets is explained in Chapter 5, though we shall make references to the results in this chapter. The central party manifestos were chosen for the analysis of Chapter 4 because they are the only direct and clear statements of party policy available to the electorate and directly attributable to the party as such. Though it is perhaps unlikely that many voters read them themselves, they are the source and official backing for any impression that the electorate may get of what the parties stand for. One has to take them seriously because they are the background for any mass media discussion of party policy, they are discussed and represented by the speeches of party leaders, and they are, as we argue in Chapter 5, the basic source for the campaigns of the constituency candidates. In addition it is very clear that the party leaders themselves take manifestos seriously. This is demonstrated, for instance, by the excitement they cause at party conferences. See, for example, Crossman's account of the 1964/6 Cabinet's concern to carry out manifesto promises (Crossman 1975).

We treat the party manifestos more as the best available indicators, of what voters ought to believe about the parties, rather than what they actually believe. We should stress, at this point, the inutility of a possible criticism. It is not part of our effort here to analyse what voters actually know, or how this affects democracy—that has been exhaustively researched elsewhere. We are investigating the activities of the parties themselves, to see, basically, how they would meet the requirements of competitive democracy given the best of voters. For while it may be that competitive democracy stands or falls by the electorate's capacity and sagacity, it is certain that the activities of the parties are primary. Public knowledge of policy is one question, party manipulation of policy is another. From our point of view party manifestos are policy, whether read or not. As it is we have suggested above that they hold a vital position in determining what the electorate knows. The electorate may be right or wrong, well- or ill-informed. This has to be judged against some standard of truth, and party policy as adumbrated in manifestos is that standard of truth.

As far as these manifestos go we are searching for a dimensional model that is timeless, in that it represents the basic structure of policy competition throughout a time period, neither synchronic nor diachronic but, relatively, permanent.

'Issues' as such cannot qualify for this, for they are too specific. Tariff reform was an issue in the pre-war, and comprehensive education in the post-war, periods, and both were unknown outside their periods. Obviously we cannot search, in replacement of 'issues', for full-blooded ideological statements. To do so would be both to read a structure into the data collection stage, and to force documents which are essentially pragmatic into too theoretical a mould.

Instead we have examined these documents for references to 'topics' or 'symbols': these range from an insistence on aspects of socialist economic policy, say nationalisation, or its opposed *laissez-faire* symbol of de-restriction, to foreign affairs symbols like 'faith in the empire', or 'collective security as the mainspring of peace and safety'. In doing the research we read, over and again the manifestos, making a long list of the basic symbols mentioned, progressively narrowing this list and redefining the symbols until it was impossible to make a list that was shorter and still exhaustive. Having done this we coded each manifesto, counting the number of occurrences of each symbol. The unit of account we took was the sentence: it is the natural unit of expression in our language, unlike the word, more usually counted in similar content analysis (Berelson, 1971; North, 1972). A final score sheet for a manifesto, once the entries have been expressed as a percentage of the total number of relevant symbols (to standardise for length and verbosity) thus gives one a measure of the relative frequency of symbols which we believe account for the basics of policy debate over a forty-two year period. Our raw data is then a set of measures of relative stress on a list of symbols in twenty-two documents, one for each of the two main parties in eleven elections.

The 'symbols' we searched for, and ostensive definitions of them, are given in Table 1. Once we had the data we needed a statistical or numerical operation which would display the frequency of mention of these twenty-one symbols.

Table 1. List of Ideological Symbols (a few examples of the scope are shown)

No.	Name	Scope
1.	Empire	Favourable mentions of the Empire and Commonwealth; the need for cooperation and aid to the Commonwealth; the importance to the economy and defence programme of the Commonwealth and Empire.
2.	Regionalism	Favourable mentions of need for decentralisation of government; need for respecting regional autonomy; need to listen to man on the job; importance of special economic and political consideration for certain areas.
3.	Freedom	Favourable mentions of importance of personal freedom, civil rights, freedom of choice in education, freedom from bureaucratic control, freedom of speech, freedom from coercion in industrial and political sphere.

Table 1—continued

No.	Name	Scope
4.	Enterprise	Favourable mention of personal enterprise and initiative, need for the economy of unhampered individual enterprise, favourable mention of free enterprise capitalist economic system, superiority of individual enterprise over state buying or management.
5.	Democracy	Favourable mention of democracy and democratic procedures in political and industrial contexts, need to make government more democratic or more open to popular control.
6.	Socialist economy	Favourable mention of nationalisation, direct government control over prices, wages, rents, need for economy to be directed by government, application of general principle of nationalisation to any industry or to whole economy.
7.	Economic planning	Favourable mention of central planning of consultative or indicative nature, need for this in the economy, need for government department to plan and create national plan, need for planning of imports and exports.
8.	Special groups	Favourable mention of special care for special groups in society, need for legislation to protect various groups, debt owed by society to certain groups. Groups are of varying sizes and types, e.g., 'manual workers', young workers, shop assistants, miners, servicemen, deprived or crippled children, the blind, ex-servicemen after wars. But does not cover very basic categories, e.g., need of children for health service, provision of old-age pensions, which are covered in other categories.
9.	Culture	Favourable mention of leisure activities, need to spend money on museums, art galleries, need to encourage the development of worthwhile leisure activities, need to provide cultural and athletic facilities in the provinces.
10.	Commonwealth	Favourable mention of decolonisation, need for leaving our colonies, need to convert colonies to dominions, need to train natives for dominion status, respect for independence movements, need to give special aid to make up for colonial past.
11.	Economic stability	Importance of economic stability, balance of payments, need for full employment, stable economy, fear of inflation.
12.	Productivity	Need to encourage or facilitate greater production, need to take measures to aid this, appeal for greater production, importance of greater productivity to economy.

No.	Name	Scope
13.	National effort	Appeal for national effort and solidarity, need for nation to see itself as undivided, appeal for public spiritedness, decrying anti-social attitudes in time of crisis.
14.	Social justice	Need for fair treatment of all men, need for special protection for the exploited, fair taxation systems, need for equality of opportunity and suffering, need for redistribution of wealth and removal of class barriers.
15.	Technology	Importance of modernisation of governmental machine and of industrial administration; importance of science and technological developments in industry, need for training and government sponsored research, need for overhaul of capital equipment and methods of communication and transport.
16.	Military	Need for strong military presence overseas; need for re-armament, need for self-defence for Britain, need for conscription, importance of independent deterrent, need to keep up military treaty obligations.
17.	Economic orthodoxy and efficiency	Need for traditional economic orthodoxy, e.g., balanced budget, strong pound, retrenchment in crises, but also need for government efficiency, economy in government, cutting down civil service, not squandering national resources, low taxation, need to encourage thrift and national savings, support for traditional economy organisations like Stock Market, independent Bank of England.
18.	Incentives	Need for financial and other incentives, need for opportunity to expand for industry, need for opportunity for the young, encouragement to small businesses and one man shops, need for wage and tax policies designed to induce enterprise.
19.	Peace	Declaration of belief in peace and peaceful means of solving crises, need for disarmament and negotiations with hostile countries.
20.	Social services	Favourable mention for any social service or welfare scheme, support for free basic services, e.g., education or public health.
21.	Internationalism	Support for the UN, need for international cooperation, need for aid to underdeveloped countries, need for world planning of resources, need for international court and policing system, support for any international aim, or for a world state.

For a long time now social and psychological scientists have been making use of a technique, Factor Analysis, to display just such latent dimensionality. A simple explanation of what is in fact a rather complex statistical technique would be out of place here; readers would do well to consult either Keith Hope's *Multivariate Analysis* (1968), or A. Child's *The Essentials of Factor Analysis* (1970)—they have the advantage that both seek to explain in arithmetic and geometric terms, which are more easily comprehended by the layman than the statistician's preferred algebraic approach. For that one can do no better than consult H. Harman's classic *Methods of Factor Analysis* (1964). We will attempt only a brief explanation ourselves. One rather famous American social survey researcher has been heard to describe factor analysis as a method in which one grabs one's data by the throat and screams 'Tell me something'. This quite well summarises both what is wrong or doubtful about the technique, and how easily misunderstood its application can be, even by experts. Obviously given a data set like ours, which measures the frequency of mentions of certain symbols amongst a set of documents, one has the makings of a correlation matrix. If symbol 3 only has a high score where symbol 15 has a low one, symbol 15 is low or high when symbol 19 is low or high and symbol 7 low or high at the same time as symbol 9, one has evidence of J. -S. Mill's 'concomitant variations', the statistical correlation. Equally, this is evidence for the existence of the logical model we suggested earlier as a formal definition of dimensionality. $[(A_1 \leftrightarrow B_2) \rightarrow (C_1 \vee C_2) + (C \leftrightarrow D_1)]$ is one definition of an orthogonal two-dimensional model.

Factor analysis lays bare any such latent model by analysis of the correlation coefficients. The implied argument is that if any set of variables are highly correlated, they can be treated each as imperfect measures of the same phenomena, and if several sets of highly correlated variables are mutually independent, one can see the total data set as consisting of a series of imperfect measures of a much smaller number of uncorrelated, 'latent', 'real', or 'underlying', variables. In survey research this has often been deliberately made use of; concerned to measure the respondent's feelings of powerlessness vis-à-vis the government, one asks a series of questions about the topic. The results are highly correlated, and factor analysis is used to extract the common attitude measured imperfectly by the whole set of questions.

Factor analysis can be expressed in terms of an equation. Take the total variance of scores on a test, or (as in our case) symbol frequency, by all respondents. This can be broken into the amount of variance due to a position on the latent dimension that this test, amongst others, measures, the variance due to position on something that this test uniquely measures, and a random, or error, 'noise', which measures either nothing, or nothing we can recognise. Factor analysis proceeds by taking the correlation matrix for all the variables, and finding such a latent dimension as accounts for as much as possible of all the variance. This is then produced as the first dimension, and the remaining variance is subjected to the same procedure to find the second most important latent variable, and so on. A factor analysis result is a table showing how strongly the variables are related to this specially constructed latent dimension.

The identification of these dimensions is not hard, fast and scientific, though the dimensions themselves are definite and objective. They are there, in the sense that they are unique solutions to mathematical problems: given an analysis, a specific dimension, identified by a set of weightings with the original variables, is the only construct that will explain the most variance, and a set of such dimensions does represent a simplification of a data set, or the basic structure of a social phenomena one is investigating. The several dimensions of a factor analysis are, as in our earlier logical example, uncorrelated, and can be geometrically represented as right-angular dimensions. In real political terms this means that any position on one dimension is compatible with any on another.

The application of factor analysis may be demonstrated by the following brief and entirely imaginary description of the analysis of data from intelligence testing.

Suppose we give four tests to a sample of children: one involves the solving of logical puzzles, one arithmetic, one word games, and the fourth ability to invent stories of some complexity around pictures. The resulting scores yield a correlation matrix with the following values:

1. Logic	\			
2. Arithmetic	·90	\		
3. Words	·30	·25	\	
4. Stories	·10	·15	·89	\

A factor analysis would probably reveal the presence of two dimensions, as shown by the strength of the relationship between the variables and the resulting factor.

Test	Factor One	Factor One
1	+·93	·05
2	+·87	−·09
3	·10	·86
4	−·25	·93

Thus one would argue that one's data showed a two-dimensional model of intelligence, one measuring logico-mathematical talent, one descriptive-imaginary talent. More probably the first and most important variable would show all the variables weighted heavily, displaying some general intellectual talent, and subsequent dimensions would make the precise distinctions displayed above.

These, then, are the data sets and techniques we have applied in a search for the underlying structure of party competition in Britain. We have coded manifestos according to frequency of mention of a set of symbols, calculated the resulting correlation matrix, and found the latent factors that account for the variance in these scores.

The symbols we used are described in Table 1.

The concepts given in the scope column are intended to give a more vivid idea of exactly what sort of references are coded under each symbol. Several things need to be said about this table. For one thing it may appear that some of the elements in the scope column appear to have nothing in common with the others in the same category. We hope that this will not often be the case as we have attempted to make each category as homogeneous and exclusive as possible. However there are some categories, notably 17 and 18, which are composites of others. In these cases any oddness about the scope does not represent prejudice but the fact that when the preliminary list of 25 variables was put through the initial analysis several of the categories were ranked extremely closely on all dimensions, even under rotation. As it was technically desirable to reduce the list of variables, and these seemed to represent some redundancy (as they must have been tapping the same underlying political attitude), some categories were 'collapsed' into each other. Thus category 17 was originally two categories, one for Economic orthodoxy and one for Government efficiency; they have been combined, which, in fact, turned out to make the coding reliability higher, suggesting that the original two categories had been badly defined and were indeed the same thing.

Similarly variable 18 represents several less important variables dealing with the provision not only of incentives but also government aid to industry. Because some of the categories are combined it is not possible to compute reliability measures for each of the final list. However the reliability of the code–recode test on all the variables ranged between 82% and 93%, with a mean reliability of 86%. These figures seem adequate, especially considering the clarity of the ostensive definitions given in the scope column in Table 1.

Finally, whether or not this table accords with individual beliefs about the content of ideology in British politics, it has been drawn up as far as possible without any preconceptions, solely on the criteria of what appeared in the manifestos. Indeed several of the variables which we expected to need turned out to be completely useless. The scores used in the factor analysis then are the symbol frequencies in the manifestos, standardised to eradicate any effect that differing lengths of the manifestos or verbosity might have. All scores are positive; originally we had planned to count both favourable and unfavourable references in the manifestos, but this proved too difficult if a desired reliability was to be maintained. Unfavourable mentions were rarely clearly relevant to any one concept. It is unlikely that any useful information has been lost through this: the parties usually refrain from attacking specific points of policy or ideology in their manifestos. There is criticism and comment on their rivals but this tends to take the form of impugning the others' motives or decrying their governmental failure rather than directly attacking the rival's values.

Our analysis presented seven dimensions that seem worth reporting, although the amount of variance they account for declines rapidly. The first three factors account for a large percentage of the common variance. When we remember how much error (random scores due to counting errors, the inaccuracy of the whole procedure in measuring what politicians really meant by any symbol) must exist these figures are even more impressive.

We repeat that, however intuitive our interpretation of these factors is, their existence, and their efficiency as simple describers of the whole data set, is not in question. Where, as in Chapters 4 and 5, we use such factor analysis results to plot party or candidate positions, they are valuable and accurate as data for testing hypotheses about competitive manoeuvering independently of their interest as summaries of political rhetoric. To see this, imagine an American spacecraft en route for the moon. To navigate and manoeuvre the astronauts need a three-dimensional framework, and such a one is quite adequately provided by arbitrary lines drawn between stars. The framework suffices, as do our factors, to fix accurately positions and measure changes between them. The astronauts may, for good or bad reasons, choose to label these lines as up–down, left–right, in–out. One could argue forever about the suitability of the labelling without questioning the utility of the framework. We hope our interpretation of the factors resulting from our analysis is not equally infinitely arguable, but without doubt the value of the results in Chapters 4 and 5 are not dependent on our interpretative powers.

B.3. The Seven Main Dimensions

Of the seven main dimensions or factors we extracted by the analysis of the symbol frequencies in these documents, the first three are of greatest importance. Together they account for nearly 60% of the common variance, and in addition are not only easy to interpret, but are predictable. It may seem strange to hail as a good point the obviousness of our results, but factor analysis suffers from the highly intuitive nature of the interpretations of the factors, and results that conform well with one's *ad hoc* expectations may be preferable to ones that challenge otherwise sensible orthodoxy. Not that there is nothing surprising or new in the structure that presents itself; the surprises are more about what does not appear than what does. These dimensions are necessarily general—as they have to be to produce order from a distribution of political symbols over a long time period during which political problems have changed enormously. There again generality is not only predictable but desirable, for it fits with the idea that, in a policy–method space, rough and broad impressions of the style of policy and the effect it will have on the *status quo* are all that are likely to be perceived by the electorate.

The First Dimension

The first of the seven dimensions, which alone accounts for 26·81% of all the variance, is given in Table 2. The figure in each row is the loading of the variable given in that row. Only the variables of significance for identifying the dimensions are given. As in this case the primary factor loadings produce a sufficiently clear interpretation for the dimensions, rotated loadings are not given, though for later dimensions they are.

Table 2

Variable No.	Name	Loading	
17	Economic orthodoxy	·864	
1	Empire	·735	
18	Incentives	·587	These are the variables
12	Productivity	·555	with the positive loading
13	National Effort	·519	
4	Enterprise	·486	
11	Economic stability	·209	
6	Socialist economics	−·669	
7	Economic planning	−·626	
8	Special groups	−·581	These are the variables
14	Social justice	−·524	with the highest negative
21	Internationalism	−·495	loading
20	Social services	−·435	
19	Peace	−·380	

The picture which emerges from these loadings is beautifully clear, and confirms what most people would probably expect. The major dimension of political conflict has been an economic one. The dimension is essentially polar, expressing conflict over the method society should adopt for handling its economic problems. The high place of variable No. 1, Empire, on the positive side of the dimension should not mislead, one must remember that appeals for unity of the Empire and Commonwealth have very often been argued on an economic basis, as for instance during periods of tariff reform ardour, one of which, the election of 1931, falls into our period, and as an alternative to the policy of getting Britain into the EEC, which must affect our scores for the manifestos in the late 1950s and 1960s. The dimension is not, however, just a crude one of economic policy; the high placing on the negative side of variables 8 and 14, Special groups and Social justice, show that it includes concern over target priorities in relation to economic policy. Similarly, the two highest non-economic variables on the positive side, not shown in the table above because their loadings are relatively low, are Freedom and Regionalism, giving a hint at the non-economic values associated with the policy of economic orthodoxy-efficiency, incentives, productivity, effort, and initiative.

We would thus suggest that this major dimension be thought of as one of conflict over economic policy and goals.

The Second Dimension

This accounts for 19·44% of the common variance. Its interpretation is easier than at first appears, particularly if one looks at rotated factor scores as well as at primary weightings on principal components.

Table 3. Principal Component Loadings of Significant
Variables

Variable No.	Name	Loading
3	Freedom	·711
4	Enterprise	·670
18	Incentives	·658
20	Social services	·443
13	National effort	−·502
11	Economic stability	−·688
12	Productivity	−·709

This, like the first dimension, is a polar factor, contrasting opposed variable clusters, and it is economic in nature. Yet it is clearly non-partisan—the opposed clusters of variables mix symbols from different economic philosophies. On what policy dimension can support for Social services, a left wing symbol, and for Freedom and Incentives, economically Conservative values, be seen united in common opposition to demands for Productivity, National effort, and the search for economic stability? These latter symbols, negatively weighted, are themselves politically neutral in a way, and this is the key. The dimension taps that most constant politico-economic dichotomy, between policies of restraint and financial discipline in crises and expansive use of the economy to provide whatever is seen as good, in times of ease. Whatever our parties have wished most to do, and this has of course been different and at times in conflict, they have both been forced, sometimes, by short term demands for economic restraint, to govern in nearly identical ways.

Whether one sees this dimension as contrasting long term or basic social values with pragmatic restraining responses to crises, or as contrasting policies directed to benefiting from, rather than protecting, the economy, it is a familiar creature. Stop–go, boom and slump, call it whatever, British politics has been marked by close policy agreement on how to deal with short term problems of crisis, alternating with bursts of less consensual activity in pursuit of the parties' separate basic values in the rare periods when the economy has done fairly well. There are at least two, probably equally applicable, explanations. For one thing economic crises tend to overshadow all else, so that government and opposition policy both stress this, and the agreement about how to respond to short term economic problems has always been high. This is true not only in the post war Keynesian consensus, but earlier, when orthodox policies of economic stringency were shared by all parties. Perhaps it is because in the short run academic economists are agreed, and win the day. Secondly, although the preferred economic philosophies of the two parties, at least as shown in this analysis, are different and opposed, the one desiring a free and uncontrolled market economy, the other a service or welfare economy, they are both incompatible with the restraint and effort policies needed for coping with crises. To spend a great deal on welfare is not compatible either with the Keynesian solution to inflation, our post war theory and problem, or the orthodox salary and expenditure cutting solution to unemployment, the theory and problem of the pre war era. Nor is *laissez-faire*—Keynesianism demands high taxation and possibly a price control policy, its predecessor restrictions on the free settling of salary levels and, as the Conservatives thought anyway, the abandonment of free trade.

The idea that this second dimension is one of consensual restraint versus striving towards one's ideological preferences is strengthened by looking at rotated weightings. Rotation is a technique used with factor analysis to make clearer the nature of the factors extracted. Briefly, a straight factor analysis produces a set of dimensions known as 'Principal Components', defined so as to maximise the amount of variance explained in the first few factors extracted. The usual result is to produce factors that are significantly weighted by several variables. Sometimes it is desirable to impose a particular structure on the factors. The most usual structure is known as 'simple' structure—in which the first factor is a general one, significantly weighted by as many variables as possible, and subsequent ones are selective, being characterised by one, or a very few, variables. Thus in intelligence testing work it is frequently desired to extract a first, 'general' factor of undefined 'intelligence', the ability to do well on all forms of tests, and to split up the remaining common variance into a few highly specialised 'talent' factors. Though rotation does produce more clearly interpretable factors, there is no justification for using it unless one can provide good theoretical reasons for expecting, or needing, 'simple' or any other specific, structure. We do choose here to apply such a simple structure, for a political 'space' characterised by a very general 'left–right' dimension followed by more specific value dimensions seems to us useful. As Table 4 shows, a rotation leaves us with four variables, in two opposed pairs.

Table 4. Second Dimension Varimax Rotated Weights

Variable No.	Name	Rotated Weighting
20	Social services	·880
8	Special groups	·786
13	National effort	−·765
12	Productivity	−·776

'Special groups' here, variable 8, is in some ways a Conservative version of the welfare variable, with the Conservative preference for seeing welfare as directed to particular deserving sectors, rather than a blanket social 'right' of the citizen. Again we have a clear contrast between a position in which the citizens in general, or those especially deserving, are looked after, that is one in which the economy is seen as a provider, and a position where sacrifice to defend the economy is stressed.

Just as with our interpretation of the more complex unrotated case, we have an easily recognisable dichotomy which is without doubt part of the deep structure of twentieth century politics in Britain. That this dimension should be so important in explaining the variance among the symbols, and be a non-partisan one at the same time, fits perfectly with all we have argued about the consensual, problem solving nature of competitive politics. As we shall show in Chapter 4, the parties have indeed behaved on this dimension in a way compatible with this interpretation.

Given two economic dimensions, a highly partisan, long term economic philosophy dimension, and a short term pragmatic consensual one as the two main factors, it is to be expected that the next will be primarily non-economic. This is so, but we would wish to stress how dominant the economic factors are—together they account for nearly 50% of all the variance, and even the second, accounting for nearly 20% of the variance, is roughly twice as important as this third factor. Truly economic problem solving has been primary in politics, and the stuff of which party competition has been made.

Table 5. Third Dimension Factor Weightings

Variable No.	Name	Weight
5	Democracy	·597
7	Economic planning	·521
6	Socialist economics	·392
4	Enterprise	·347

The principal component scores are not easily interpretable, though the dominance of Democracy as a symbol gives the main character to the component. Rotating for simple structure heightens this impression considerably, for the major symbols then become much more similar, and variables 7 and 6 drop out completely. So again from the rotated values we make our interpretation.

Table 6. Simple Structure Rotation of Factor Three

Variable No.	Name	Rotated Weighting
5	Democracy	·525
4	Enterprise	·775
2	Regionalism	·496
18	Incentives	·432
1	Empire	−·417
2	Economic stability	−·359

Here we have a dimension in which support for open government and democratic procedures (in and out of public political institutions), preference for personal initiative and enterprise, dislike of centralised bureaucratic control, and faith in the efficacy of incentives gives a very clear picture of the Conservative faith in traditional liberal freedom. The opposition of the negatively loaded Empire, the ultimate symbol of unfreedom, and the economic 'stability' symbol, associated as the second dimension shows with economic constraint, underscores this interpretation.

It is worth noting that from the principal component scores of this dimension, its nature would not be much different. Democracy is still the vital symbol, and the high score for Economic planning combined with this supports an interpretation of a more 'positive' liberty—the need for the government to intervene to improve a situation so that ordinary citizens are free from economic pressures and free to control their own lives. Democracy as a symbol includes references to the need for industrial democracy. Even the third ranking Socialist economics, with its heavy element of nationalisation, invites the notion of freedom as control of institutions and forces, rather than freedom as absence of control by institutions. Still it is obvious that the negative concept of liberty is more common and easily understood, and has, of course, been a major theme of Conservative debate in British politics since the emergence of the Labour party.

The fourth dimension presents no difficulty in interpretation, and rotation does not materially affect its nature. It is an interesting one; after two economic and one 'political' dimensions we have a general social morality factor.

Table 7. The Fourth Dimension (accounts for 9% of common variance)

Variable No.	Name	Principal Component Weight	Rotated Weight
14	Social justice	·472	·826
19	Peace	·398	·462
1	Empire	−·473	−·529
17	Economic orthodoxy and efficiency	−·043	−·481

Social justice and Peace, opposed by belief in the Empire and concern for Economic efficiency and orthodoxy, (which usually meant cutting government expenditure on promoting Social justice) is delightfully clear. Had the phrase not been taken, of recent, to describe less fundamental questions, one would be tempted to call this dimension 'The quality of Life'. As it is we could see it well as being Humanitarian—uninterested in technical economic efficiency, opposed to Imperialism, but concerned for peaceful solution to international problems, for disarmament, and above all desirous of social justice with its implication of egalitarianism. If dimension three is one of freedom in a negative, Conservative sense that has been in many ways the 'spiritual value' of the British Conservative party since the First World War, this is the Labour equivalent, the driving concern for this form of general humanitarian goal. Neither factors three or four are practical policy dimensions, as is the second; nor are they well articulated theoretical or ideological dimensions, as is the first, but deep and even slightly inchoate primary social values.

These four dimensions are the heart of the analysis; they are not strange, and not unpredictable, and not difficult to interpret. They have structured the political rhetoric of party manifestos, have delineated the space within which parties have changed and modified their ideologies over the years. They are well balanced, covering economic ideology, economic pragmatism, and the core social values of the two parties. They are balanced in another way: the first is a polar dimension with clearly marked partisan ends on which neither party is dominant, the second is a non-partisan dimension on which both parties would prefer to take the same position and yet are likely to be forced to agree in being at the end they both dislike. The final two are clearly party dominant dimensions—the whole dimension is 'owned' by one or other party. The Labour party is not against freedom, any more than the Conservative party is opposed to social justice, yet the two values have tended, perhaps still do, not to be held simultaneously with equal force. They represent the one party dominance of a dimension we discussed earlier. For the Labour party to compete with the Conservatives in the defence of individual freedom, or the Conservatives to seem more concerned with social justice than Labour is never likely to be credible. These four factors together account for 67% of the common variance in the data set, and such a result compares very favourably with psychological studies, where 60% is a high target.

In fact the full model, with seven dimensions, all of them relatively clear, accounts for 86%, but the final three factors are so small, and substantively uninteresting, that we will spend little time on them. They are summarised below.

The Fifth Dimension

This accounts for 7·44% of the variance and is summarised in Table 8.

Table 8

Variable No.	Name	Primary Loadings	Varimax
9	Culture	·657	·828
16	Military	·597	·492
21	Internationalism	·287	·200
10	Decolonisation	·121	·412
8	Special groups	−·469	−·342
17	Efficiency	−·249	−·273

Once one gets to the point where factors are tapping only a few percent of the variance of the whole set of variables it is reasonable to expect that the dimension will be overshadowed by one variable and thus interpretation takes the form of finding the major variable in the list of loadings. Here we see such a case, for where the primary loadings show just two variables of any importance, numbers 9 and 16, the rotated loadings both show an overwhelming dominance of one variable, 9, Culture. This is the sort of dimension we might well expect to be evident but of only minor importance in political life. Both parties do at each election announce plans, usually very similar ones, for enriching the cultural and leisure life of the population, and of course they do not dwell for long on the subject, thus producing consistent but low scores on the variable with little variance between parties, though some over time.

We think we can thus safely call this dimension that of Cultural provision, the constant placing of Military as the second variable perhaps underlying this in that it is only a safe and stable country that ever spares time to think of such things as leisure life. Perhaps also the negative loadings, principally for the variables Special groups and Efficiency, underline this by serving as the reminder of economic and social obligations that make the spending of public money on cultural activities unlikely.

The Sixth Dimension

This dimension accounts for 6·05% of the variance.

Table 9

Variable No.	Name	Primary Loadings	Varimax
15	Technology	−·594	−·550
14	Social justice	−·426	−·208
7	Economic planning	−·121	−·534

This variance is of some interest despite its low share of the common variance (probably mainly due to the fact that the dimension is one that has only been significant in politics in Britain since the Second World War). When one looks at the rotated figures in Table 9 the confusing presence of Social justice drops out, leaving the combination of Technology and Economic planning, denoting a clear dimension of modernisation in economic, governmental and social spheres. This is an ideological stand, part of the ideology of pragmatism, that has come to sound very familiar to us. The negative loadings have not been given in the table because they are far from clear; the two rotations and the primary loadings produce differing orderings. However Military, Economic stability, and Empire, are fairly consistently placed highly, traditional variables, standing opposed to the voice of modernisation. Furthermore they are all of greatest relevance to the earlier part of the period and thus are opposed much more by their distribution over time than by negative correlations. We consider this a clear variable of modernisation, and one that would probably become more important should this research be repeated on a sample of manifestos drawn from the near future and recent past.

The Seventh Dimension

This dimension, which accounts for 5·37% of the variance, is not easy to interpret. There is one overwhelmingly dominant negative variable, 3, Freedom, on all loadings, but given that the third dimension is one of political and economic freedom this is not a convincing interpretation for the dimension. However, considering the positive loadings in this dimension one can see a pattern by which freedom (and its economic echo, enterprise), is opposed to a combination of Productivity, Efficiency, Economic stability and Internationalism. This suggests a dimension contrasting the need for effort and international obligation with the desire for a free life; there is also the relatively high negative loading of Military and Democracy, turning the freedom into something more akin to peaceful, protected, politically safe, life, versus the economic and political demands made by governments on the conscience of their citizens. We think that this dimension can best be seen then as one of civil duty versus apathy.

The seventh dimension, however, is not one of great importance and is discussed more for the sake of completion than because of its innate interest. In addition, we can still produce factor scores that place the parties on the dimension even if we do not find it very clear; as the dimension exists in the sense that it is statistically present in the space delineated by the variance of the symbol scores it is useful to do this if we desire as accurate as possible a picture of party movements in the ideology space.

As a technical note we must mention here that Kaiser's criterion of the number of roots greater than unity has been used in this research to extract the factors, and this seventh factor has a root slightly less than unity.

B.4. Some Comments on the Dimensions

But before we go on it is worthwhile considering how the dimensions produced by this factor analysis relate to the traditional left–right spectrum with which these ideas originated.

A very simple ordinal left–right scale has been created with which to measure this. Like any such simple scale it incorporates all the disadvantages of an historical or philosophical dimension, but it may still be of heuristic interest. It was constructed from an intuitive conception of left–right, based on reading the manifestos. A second scale was derived actually using the symbol scores. For this we used the 'simpliste' definition that left wing was concerned with Socialist economics, Social justice, Internationalism, and Decolonisation, and that to be right wing was to be concerned with Economic orthodoxy, Incentives, Initiative, the Empire, and Military strength. We have not considered more abstract concepts like a 'Christian nation' or 'Respect for tradition' that properly belong in wider definitions of right wing Conservative ideology because we used the manifestos, which do not talk much about such things, in order to produce a scale that was relevant to the factors above. These two preliminary scales had a high rank order correlation of $+\cdot92$. The final result is a scale derived from both these previous ones, choosing what seemed most reasonable where the two scales differed in rank order of the parties. Nothing can make this a scientific process, nor is it offered as such.

We give our original left–right ordering of the British Conservative and Labour parties during this period below: the extremes are at either end, so that the top position represents the extreme right wing position, the bottom represents the extreme left wing. Being purely ordinal no assumptions are made about the size of the differences between any positions.

Table 10

	Years		
	1931		
	1929		
	1950		
	1924		
Right Wing	1955		
Conservative	1951		
Party	1945		
	1959		D1 D2 D3 D4 D5 D6 D7
	1935	L–R	
	1964		$+\cdot89$ $+\cdot39$ $+\cdot24$ $-\cdot12$ $+\cdot01$ $+\cdot04$ $+\cdot05$
	1966		

Above are given the correlations between the basic left–right rank order and the rank order produced by each of the seven dimensions

	Years
	1929
	1966
	1964
	1924
Left Wing	1959
Labour Party	1950
	1951
	1955
	1945
	1931
	1935

As can be seen from Table 10 six out of the seven dimensions produced by the factor analysis have no correlation with the left–right spectrum. This would be expected, if the criticisms levelled at it are accurate. It is very interesting however to see the very high correlation of $+\cdot89$ between the first (most important) of the dimensions and the left–right spectrum. The first dimension is the one referring to economic policy and goals, and this high correlation suggests two important points. The first is that while 'left–right' is by no means an exhaustive dimension of politics, it is an important one because of its high correlation with the most important of the factors from this analysis.

It is necessary here to report briefly the result of a second factor analysis that was carried out with a very much reduced list of very much broader variables.

This was done because the smaller list of variables made it possible to get a simpler model with only three dimensions. Happily the three resulting dimensions give us more confidence in our original model, for they correspond to dimensions in that model. The first dimension in the simpler models is exactly the same as the first one in the more complex model, being concerned with economic policy and goals in the same way. It accounts for 39·62% of the variance.

The second dimension, which accounts for 28·02% of the variance, is very similar to the second dimension in the complex model, being concerned with the contrast between variables like National effort, Productivity, and Empire, that make demands of a basically economic nature on the citizen, and the compensatory economic and social aid implied by variables like Social services, protection for groups and, in this case, Peace. The third dimension does not correspond to any particular dimension in the full model, but is a dimension contrasting Economic stability, Peace, and Social services with variables calling for an adventurous spirit in economic life. To a great extent it is a combination of the third and fourth dimensions of the full model, contrasting the humanitarian preference for Justice and Peace with the love of freedom, especially in economic life.

Taken together the three dimensions account for roughly the same percentage of their common variance, 82·68%, as the seven dimensions do in the larger model. The similarity between the models extends to the correlations between the left–right spectrum and the three dimensions, for while the second and third are respectively only −·14 and +·27, the correlation of left–right with the first dimension is again very high, +·90.

B.5. Synchronic Dimensions

These models both present a set of very general and very broad dimensions, and this, as we have argued, is inevitable where we are dealing with the movements over time of the central parties. When we wonder about the nature of ideological space we must be careful to stipulate the vantage point. Nothing less broad or general could be used for the investigation of party change between elections, and these questions must be asked. One might well wish to argue that social problems are very different at different time points, as of course they are, and that no such dimensionality as this exists. But to do so is simply to refuse to ask questions about change and continuity in party policy. It might well be to deny the continued identity of a political party. For if policy can only be investigated in terms of here-and-now specifics, if no a-temporal framework exists, there is nothing but institutional continuity to define the Labour party at two different elections as the same party. Yet the whole mechanism of party competition, perhaps of responsible and representative government itself, requires more than this organisational identity. In any case the dimensions suggested by our analysis are not of so broad, nor so transient a nature as to be bad candidates for defining such continued identity. Precise policies not only change, but are very frequently nearly identical; actual visions of the good life must change, if only because it is hard to have such a vision which is not partially defined by expectations of possibilty. How could the policy-aim desires of a Labour voter in 1931 and 1966 be similar, when the latter lives in an age of affluence thoroughly inconceivable to his ancestor?

There are three things that are less likely to change with time, and thus can serve to define parties, and to provide a framework into which succeeding generations of voters can be socialised. One is a rigorous long term theory—an ideology, such as the one of the first dimension. Another is a fundamental question of the economic and productive capacity of a nation—that, surely, is not only a diachronic but a synchroninc constant, and is represented by the second dimension. The third 'thing' that can be relatively invariant over time is a very basic value premise, or set of them. This is particularly the case where the values in the set are not likely to spring from the same social environment. Many political theorists have suggested that a desire for freedom is not likely to be primary amongst those who have more immediate and less esoteric problems of survival (Berlin, 1969). Positive and negative freedom concepts lie at the heart, not only of low key practical political rhetoric in this century, but the prime philosophical debates between Liberal and Marxist–Hegelian thinkers; this is just such a set of values as are represented by the third and fourth dimensions above.

We suspect it is because of a lack of clarity on the question of what exactly a dimensional model is supposed to be defining and contrasting that there is so much confusion and occasional hostility to dimensional models. Take the argument in Stoke's article, that 'issues' cannot be seen as simple dimensions, and the furtherance of that idea by Converse in two articles, one on French and the other on Norwegian voting, that *ad hoc* dimensions of a 'one-off' nature are needed to explain or describe voting preferences in particular elections (Converse, 1961). Naturally they are both correct, because their view point is strictly synchronic, concerned with identifying and distinguishing parties at one time period. Yet the Downsian style of model is both—it has a synchronic element because it deals with who gets elected at a certain time, but because it relates this to change over time, to the progressive manoeuvering of parties from election to election, it is diachronic as well. Admittedly we cannot have two entirely separate dimensionalities. If the 'issue stands' or ideological positions that discriminate between party A and party B at time 1 have nothing whatsoever to do with the policy space in which one can map parties A and B at times 1 and 2, then something is very odd indeed. Such a situation would be one in which either there were no long term values, ideologies, and constraints, or where these existed but had no effect at all on the values and ideologies that were dominant during any particular election. Either of these ideas are nonsense.

During any election campaign debate will focus narrowly on particular problems, and the dimensionality of the policy space at that time will probably mirror this greater precision. To examine competition at a fixed time will indeed require the presence of ephemeral dimensions. To examine competition at a particular time is not to inquire into the positions of political parties as such, but of particular candidates from the parties fighting in particular constituencies. For elections are only indirectly the election to office of parties. However, the dimensional space within which policy-methods are advocated for policy-aims is predefined by the basic ideological structure of party competition in that nation. Policies will only be offered if they are feasible, desirable, or legitimate in terms of where in this deeper structure the parties and the *status quo* are, and they will be restricted by the competitive feasibility of positions in the diachronic general policy space.

When one investigates voter preferences (as does Converse) or candidates' positioning (as we do in Chapter 5) at some election, there is no immediate need to know what is this more basic, or to borrow a Lévy–Straussian term, 'deeper structure'. But either of these topics is inextricably tied in with the position taken by the central party. Why this is so we have partially suggested in Chapter 2, and deal with in detail in Chapter 5. So we must come to the conclusion, in no way unusual or original in the sociology of values, that the policy space at any particular time is derivative of the deeper structure of party rhetoric. One cannot hope fully to understand competition inside the derivative space fixed by the momentary positions of the parties without understanding how these came about, and to understand this requires the investigation, as here, of the deeper structure.

As an example, consider the dimensionality of the party space we report in Chapter 5. Here we are investigating competition at the constituency level in the elections of 1924 and 1955. The election of 1955 seems to have been carried on in a policy space of perhaps four important dimensions.

The first is a general dimension contrasting Labour and Conservative positions on economic policy and foreign and military affairs, like the first dimension in the model discussed earlier, but including a stronger foreign policy element. This was particularly important in 1955 but not generally of importance in our period. The second is again similar to our second dimension here, being concerned principally with a contrast between immediate pragmatic concerns with short term economic affluence and Butler's recent low tax budget, and long run criticisms or support of the free enterprise economy. In the new found affluence of 1955 there could hardly be a credible demand for economic restraint, but that dimension nonetheless seems to determine economic debate, which focused on confidence in the permanence of the economic prosperity. The third and fourth dimensions are specific and, as Converse would expect, more or less unique to the moment. The third, relating to home affairs, is again an economic one, consisting almost entirely of long run economic policy and conflict over nationalisation versus free enterprise. The fourth is, to fit with the tenor of Stokes' article, a single issue dimension, of attitude to the independent nuclear deterrent.

A candidate's position on these temporary dimensions, say about the bomb or the recent budget, would be constrained by the 1955 positions of the parties on the permanent, 'deep structure' ideological dimensions.

Furthermore, only one of these dimensions is really unique to, or specially coloured by, the conditions of 1955, the one dealing with the nuclear deterrent. This dimension must remain derivative on the third and fourth deep structure dimensions, those of negative freedom and social justice.

Then again the analysis of 1924 displays two vital dimensions. The first is, as usual, a general, primarily economic philosophy dimension of a long term nature. The second is again like the second deep structure dimension, about short term economic policy, the correct reaction to financial crisis, and contrasts above all a free trade policy, dominated by the Liberal party, with various restrictive and protective policies advocated by the other two parties.

In both these examples the more precisely policy relevant dimensions of the elections, used to contrast candidates, are fairly clearly derivative of and constrained by the general value dimensions of the deep structure models. The right language might be to describe synchronic policy spaces as instantiations of the diachronic space.

In this chapter we have tried to do three things. The first is to be clear about the different ways one can conceive of an ideology-space; as policy-aim or policy-method space. Then, given that, to suggest how much more complex will be party competition in a policy-method space, and how strategy there will be more like military than economic strategy. In so doing we have introduced a way in which a one-dimensional model of such a space may be far from simplistic and can be a perfectly sensible and realistic way of dealing with party competition for less informed voters.

Finally we have described a multi-dimensional model for party competition in Britain over the period 1924 to 1966. This is further investigated in the next chapter where we study party competition in this space. The contrast between the momentary dimensionality of any particular election, used for synchronic investigation of candidate competition, and the deeper structure of the diachronic dimensionality is brought out further, along with the utility of a uni-dimensional model, in Chapter 5.

CHAPTER 4

The Correlates of Ideological Change

PART I: DATA ANALYSIS

1.A. Introduction. Measures of Change in Party Positions

In Chapter 3 we introduced a dimensional framework to describe party competition in Britain between 1924 and 1966. This has two different uses. In the previous chapter we used it to describe and characterise the terms and shape of policy debate. Here we shall be concerned not with the substance of this debate, but with the dynamics of it. We shall be focusing not on what precisely was the position of party X on dimension 1 at time T, but on the changes between elections, the social and electoral phenomena that are associated with such changes, and the dispersion, scatter, and patterning of party positions in the N-space of the dimensions.

Another military analogy might help to show why this is interesting. If a military historian is studying a previous battle, he may need to know exactly what hill or bridge was threatened or held by which regiment at some moment in the battle. For the general study of strategy, however, one could as well work entirely from map references and heights above sea-level (a three-space), because it is the relationship between positions, and the causes of movement from one to another that is important for strategic theory. Strategic theory, this time of party electoral competition, is what we are searching for here.

In Part I of this chapter however we are engaged not in theoretical but pre-theoretical work, presenting the salient facts that emerge from the data analysis of party positions and concommittant socio-economic changes over time. In Part II a sketch of an explanatory theory is given.

We do not bother to use all seven ideological dimensions here. To do so would be unnecessarily complicated, given the low importance (in terms of variance explained in the factor analysis model) of some of them. Instead we examine three ideological measures for each of the two parties. The two major dimensions, the first of economic ideology in the long term, the other of economic policy in the short run, are used, and in addition we use specially constructed summary measures for each of the parties.

Essentially these summary measures are operationalisations of the concept of 'moderation'. If one assumes that in an N-dimensional space the origin, or 'centre' of the dimensional array represents the point of greatest moderation, one gets a general measure of moderation by taking the euclidian distance in N-space between the position of one party and the origin. Each party position at a given time is, of course, perfectly defined by seven coordinates, as is the origin. The greater the distance from the origin *in any direction*, the more extreme the party at that time.

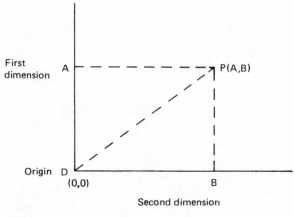

Figure 16

This is shown for a two-dimensional model in Figure 16. The party is at a totally defined position (A,B), the origin is (0,0), and the distance (A,B)–(0,0) is simply the hypothenuse of the right triangle (D), (P), (B). Thus the moderation score is calculated easily as $\sqrt{A^2 + B^2}$. This is trivially generalisable for any number of dimensions.

The use of these measures, which we will call LMOD (Labour moderation score) and CMOD (Conservative moderation score) is that they convey nearly all the information of seven separate dimension positions, providing for an analysis as simple as the naive one-dimensional Left–Right model. The drawback, requiring us to look also at at least the first two dimensions separately, is that they are direction–unspecific. Thus to know, say, that the Labour party and the Conservative party have both become more moderate over a period of time says nothing about how near they are to each other. A joint move to moderation may have been accompanied by a great disconcensus. One way this could come about is demonstrated below in Figure 17.

If L_1 and T_1 show the respective positions in a two-space array at time one, and L_2 and T_2 the positions at time two, we can see that at the latter date the parties are both nearer the origin, but are actually further apart than they had been. That a growing moderation in both party policy stands is compatible with a breakdown of consensus may seem odd. It reflects, though, only how imprecise our usual thinking about both these concepts is, and the need to be very much more careful.

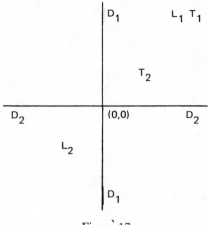

Figure 17

There is a simple way to check on whether or not increasing moderation has been compatible with growing consensus. The final measure of policy change to be used in this chapter does this by directly measuring the consensus between party positions over time. The measure, which we shall call 'C' (for Consensus) is again a euclidian distance in the seven-space of the whole factor model. It measures in this case the distance in the seven-space between the Conservative and Labour positions at each election. Correlating CMOD, LMOD and 'C' together shows that the fuzzy thinking behind our usual notion of moderation and consensus remarked on above is not, as it happens, at all misleading. There is a strong positive relationship such that the distance of either party from the origin (our operationalisation of 'moderation') decreases as the distance between the party positions themselves decreases

Table 11. Correlations between
CMOD, LMOD, and 'C'

	'C'		
LMOD	.710		
CMOD	.884	.415	
	'C'	LMOD	CMOD

1.B. Notes of Explanation and Caution

(i) A Note on Significance Levels

Throughout this chapter and the next we report the significance levels of correlations, and certain other statistics derived. Usually the results we wish to comment on are safe from the charge that they could have arisen by accident, because they pass the standard significance tests at the 5% level or, at worst, the 10% level. However, we feel it necessary to make the following observations about the relevance of significance tests in this kind of research.

(a) The orthodox interpretation of a significance test is that if a result, as for instance the correlation between 'C' and LMOD above, is significant at the 5% level, there is only a 1 in 20 chance that we are mistaken in asserting that there does exist a relationship between the variables. It is very far from clear what this means. In addition, it must be said that if that interpretation is taken seriously, our statistics are more reliable than we believe our theory is because, in the current state of the art of political theory, the thought that there was only a 20% chance of our being wrong about *any* social phenomena is incredible. What level of significance *is* relevant? There is no obvious answer. Clearly we do not wish to base a theory on observations that have a fifty-fifty chance of being nothing but random fluctuations, but whether a social scientist has any business to be demanding odds as good as 10 to 1, let alone 20 to 1, is less obvious. The whole significance test controversy is now old hat, and well covered in a book of that name (Henkel, 1970) though not resolved.

(b) These doubts about the utility of significance tests are multiplied by the second point; normally the justification for using them is that the statistics to which they are applied are derived from a data set based on a sample of a much larger universe. One is asking, in effect, 'What are the chances that I will make a fool of myself if I expect the rest of the world to conform to my sample of it?' In our case it would be odd to argue that the elections between 1924 and 1966 are a sample of anything. We are not generalising from a sample to a universe, but commenting on relationships that seem to hold in a universe.

(c) Despite all these quibbles, the use of significance tests does provide a crude rule of thumb for showing which statistics can probably be ignored, and which ones, if they clash with assumptions or arguments, cannot lightly be dismissed, so we use them to some extent, and quote them most of the time. It can do no harm to do so, and may make some people happier. Rather than using the normal 5% level, however, we use in this chapter the 10% level. What we do is to mark out those statistics that are not significant at this level. Unmarked ones are significant at this or a higher level. In fact most are at 5%, some at 1%. The underlined correlation in Table 11, between LMOD and CMOD is thus marked as not significant at this level.

At no point however would we argue that some finding had to be accepted as truth *because* it was significant, any more than small and insignificant statistics will be ignored if they provide any interesting or useful indication of the phenomena they are supposed to be measuring.

(ii) A Note on the Signs in Correlation Tables

A careful comparison with the tables in this chapter might make them seem inconsistent. This is because in reporting them we sometimes reverse the signs to make exposition clearer. The trouble is that our measures can be very confusing, intuitively. Take, as an example, 'C'. As the 'C' score goes up, the parties are getting further away from each other. It is used to measure the consensus, and thus the statement 'Consensus increases as the economy improves' would show the confusing correlation coefficient of, say, $-\cdot655$ as evidence. For, of course, an improved economy is negatively correlated with the 'C' *measure*, if there is a positive relationship between increased consensus (*decreased* distance between the parties) and economic growth. If this last paragraph has been confusing to the reader, my explanation is made. It *is* terribly confusing to keep in mind always the way the variables are scored. So we hope that each section will be made self-explanatory, without the need to repeat passages like the above all the time, by some judicious reflection of the relevant signs. Any apparent inconsistency between one table and another results from this.

1.C. Maps of Ideological Change

At this stage it will help most if we provide in a pictorial from basic data about just what the party positions have been at different times during the period 1924–1966. For this we use the first two dimensions of the factor analysis of Chapter 3. Figures 18A and B, 19 and 20 give this information.

Figure 18A presents the twenty-two positions (one for each of the two parties at each of the eleven elections) in a two-space array of the first and second dimensions.

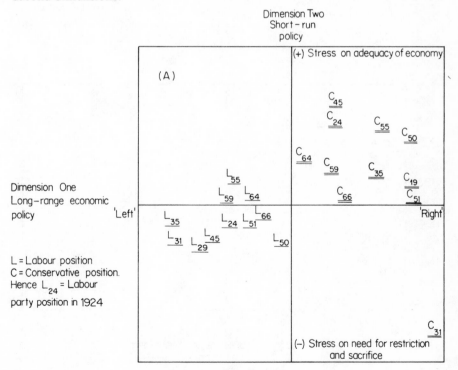

Figure 18(A)

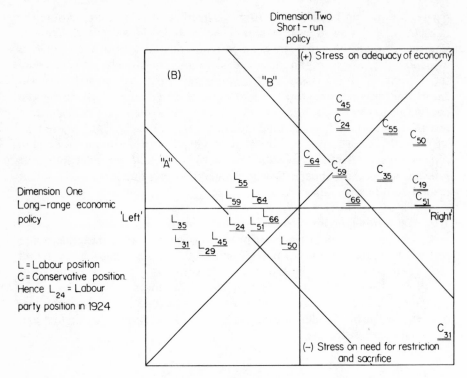

Figure 18(B)

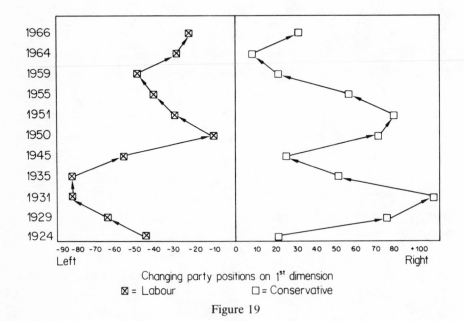

Changing party positions on 1st dimension

⊠ = Labour   □ = Conservative

Figure 19

To make the election-by-election changes of the two parties clear, Figure 19 and 20 show the positions on each of the two dimensions separately.

Dimension one requires no reinterpretation. It is the basic economic policy dimension; a position on the left, or negative, side of the origin is one favouring socialist economics, one on the right (positive) side a position of support for a free enterprise economy. The second dimension is less easily interpreted. Later we shall present evidence of the way party positions on this dimension are correlated with economic changes which supports and clarifies the interpretation given in Chapter 3.

There we argued that this dimension could best be seen as one contrasting views on the state of the economy. High scores indicate confidence. They imply a belief that the economy can afford welfare measures or anything else, like absence of controls, which may be seen as coming with a boom. Conversely low scores indicate a need for control, for cutting government expenditure, for the immemorial 'spirit of Dunkirk'. All in all the dimension contrasts a boom, 'You've never had it so good' policy stance where economic rewards are stressed, with that cry for productivity, effort, and consumer restraint that has been so familiar a demand in Western politics this century.

If one takes Figure 18A, an intuitive interpretation of the party positions, (which we shall shortly attempt to 'fit' statistically to other social phenomena) can be made which will lend substance to the data analysis.

The two very similar Labour party positions of 1931 and 1935, for example, represent the most extreme commitment to economic socialism that our party system has seen, with a pessimism about the economy's health. They are policy positions dominated by stress on the required effort and control of economic initiative. Similarly the neighbouring Conservative positions of 1950 and 1955 are deeply committed to free enterprise and *laissez-faire* economics, coupled with policies that see the economy as capable of producing social rewards. The policy of free enterprise is not coupled, as it was in 1931, with an abandonment of welfare and public expenditure, because of basic confidence in economic capacity.

What is important to us here is not the actual position of a party at any one time—these are, after all, highly relative constructs—but the changes over time and with other social phenomena, such as electoral success, economic indicators, and time itself. Change itself, the amount of change, in party platforms *per se*, is crucial. For, though we may not yet know what would count as evidence for party competitiveness, it is easy to see what is definitely *not* compatible with the *alternative thesis* on party behaviour. This latter is a model of a 'sincere' party, one which sticks resolutely to a policy line its members believe in, and changes this only when objective social conditions change. Here one can fairly argue that there ought not to be any very great change in policy positions over the short run.

Now a casual glance at Figure 18A indicates an interesting difference between the parties—the spread of Labour party positions is much smaller than that of the Conservative party, in both dimensions. Even ignoring the extreme

Conservative party position in 1931 (on the grounds that it was a most peculiar election in which the Conservatives sought to hide themselves behind a national coalition front) there is surface plausibility for the idea that the two parties have not been equally consistent over time. This is borne out by the following table, which records average change between elections.

Table 12. Average Change of Party Position

	Lab $\bar{x}$	Lab $\bar{x}$ Pre-war	Lab $\bar{x}$ Post-war	Con $\bar{x}$	Con $\bar{x}$ Pre-war	Con $\bar{x}$ Post-war
D1	1·25	1·22	1·28	3·47	5·82	1·92
D2	·67	·43	·83	4·72	7·47	2·90
D3	2·25	1·88	2·51	2·28	4·11	1·06
All D	34·65	40·08	37·03	69·39	142·43	20·70

This table shows that the mean distance between elections for Conservative party positions, on any of the first three, or across all, dimensions, is higher than the equivalent Labour figure. The Conservatives have, overall, been prone to change their positions more often, and more violently. However this is largely a product of the pre-war days. The total mean Labour change before and after the War is not very different (40·08 compared with 37·03), but the pre-war Conservative figure of 142·43 is nearly seven times greater than the post-war figure. Indeed the Conservative party has changed, on average, less than the Labour party since the war. As we shall show later, this fact of less consistency on the part of the Conservatives has another, and perhaps more interesting side—the Conservative positions are also less predictable. Whereas we have had some success finding predictive regression equations which 'explain' quite a high percentage of the variance in Labour positions, we have met with less success in finding economic and social phenomena with which to 'predict' Conservative positions.

We cannot know why this is so, and it is possible that it is purely an artefact of the data analysis. Alternatively, it is quite in keeping with the theory we sketch in the second half of this chapter. The idea there, in brief, is that the competitive status, and thus performance, of the two parties has been different over the time covered. The explanations most readily to hand for the Labour party are in terms of its need to build up a loyal vote following, and to demonstrate its reliability and fitness to govern. The same problem has not been faced by the Conservatives, and the broad socio-political variables we use do not, for that reason, explain or predict variance in Conservative positions as well as they serve the Labour party.

This is not to say that there are not explanatory variables which might be used on the Conservative party, but that they will be more complicated and perhaps subtler. Equally it is necessary, for any theory of party strategy to be possible, that decision making in the party be shared, or influenced strongly, by many members. The Conservative party with its greater reliance on the individual views of the leader is less amenable altogether to prediction. The collective action of a group is the stuff of the social sciences, the private actions of the individual are not.

1.D. Policy Positions and Time

Something else fairly visible by inspection of maps in Figures 18–20 is change over time. It is not only a Downsian prediction, but a commonplace of both academic and journalistic commentary on British politics, that the parties have come closer together, have 'converged' on the middle of the road, over time (Beer, 1965).

Another casual glance at Figure 18A supports this. The way the party positions are scattered in that two-dimensional map suggests a 'typical' Conservative and Labour position. Most of the Labour positions are in the bottom left hand quadrant, on the negative side of the origin in both dimensions, while the typical Conservative position is the upper right hand corner. If we imagine a line drawn from bottom left to top right, through the origin, one would have in effect a dimension that was arranged along a 'Labourness–Conservativeness' continuum. This is a technique we use in Chapter 5 where we investigate the ideological positions of individual candidates in constituencies. Such a line is superimposed over the map of party positions on dimensions one and two in Figure 18B. The line is cut by two others, A and B, on each side of the origin, producing a square box around the

Changes of position on dimension Two

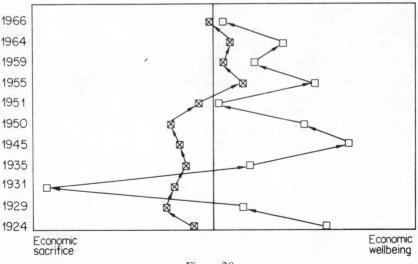

Figure 20

origin which represents, as it were, the 'middle', most moderate position, of this pseudo dimension. It is notable that all the Labour positions that fall into this box are after 1945, and the three Conservative positions inside it are the last three elections in the period, 1959, 1964 and 1966.

We can show this more rigorously and less cumbersomely by correlating the party positions on our several measures against time in years, counting 1924 as 1. The tables below report these correlations and the average distance between the parties at various times.

Table 13. Correlations between Party Positions and Time

Labour first dimension	·652
Labour second dimension	·707
LMOD	·774
Conservative first dimension	·421
Conservative second dimension	·345
CMOD	·636
'C'	·718

The Labour party moves towards the '*laissez-faire*' end of the first dimension, over time, while the Conservative party moves towards the Labour party's end, characterised by a belief in the needs for control and nationalisation. As we know, both parties came over time slowly to accept the need for a 'mixed' economy, and this is reflected in these correlations. At the same time the correlations between time and Lab 2 and Con 2 show that both parties moved towards the optimistic end of the second dimension. This is unsurprising, for the economic capacity of the country has increased greatly.

The direction and extent of movement in this two-space is shown to be typical of all the dimensions by the way CMOD, LMOD and 'C' all demonstrate, for the whole seven-space, a tendency for the parties to move towards each other and towards the origin (which we have said represents moderation) as time passes. They are all quite high, showing that there is little doubt that a process of convergence has taken place over time. It is also clear, as it is indeed by inspecting the diagrams, that the Labour party has been more consistent, and has moved more smoothly over time. The correlations between time and the three Labour measures are higher in all cases than those with the three Conservative measures.

Table 14. Mean of the Distance between Parties

	D1	D2	D3	D4	D5	D6	D7	All Ds
1924–35	11·6	3·6	2·4	2·0	1·6	1·0	0·9	216·6
1955–66	5·2	1·0	1·8	1·8	1·2	1·2	0·7	48·9

This table, as we say, bears out the correlations. Only in the one case of dimension 6, which accounts for a tiny proportion of the variance, has there not clearly been a convergence; here the distance between the parties has never been significant.

One has to be very careful when thinking about time. Where there are high correlations between a measure of time, and the variables one desires to explain, there is a temptation to use 'time' as an explanatory variable in a regression or causal model. Time, however, does not *do* anything. We must talk about change happening 'over time', and only in a poetic sense, of the passage of time 'causing' anything. If we use 'time' in an explanatory model, it can only be as a summary 'error' term. Several of our economic and electoral variables are intercorrelated with time quite heavily, and it is the changes in these which must be looked at for explanation of changes in ideology. Having said this we must make one special exception which is important for considering the Labour party case. There are circumstances where one does expect the passage of time to be fairly directly important. For example there may be some sort of developmental sequence, or process. Once started, this must go on, with unavoidable and uni-directional time lags. Such a case is provided by political demography. It has been convincingly argued by Butler and Stokes that, if the Labour party is in some sense the 'natural' party for the working class, it has necessarily taken time for it to come into its own. The vote-support for the Labour party could only increase slowly through intergenerational change. The Labour policy positions, if influenced by electoral popularity, must show a secular time trend.

1.E. Policy Positions and Electoral Success

The Conservative party, it could be argued, has had its maximum loyal vote (as opposed to percentage share) since the beginning of the period. Naturally its vote fluctuates, and this may cause policy change, but the fluctuation in its total vote does not follow any particular trend, and for this reason its policy change cannot be expected to be influenced so directly by time itself.

It is noteworthy, in the light of these considerations, that if we use two measures of voting support, total votes cast for a party, and percentage of the two party vote going to it, the Labour and Conservative effects are different. Table 15 shows this.

Table 15. Correlations between Ideology Measures and Vote Support

	Actual Vote	% of Vote		Actual Vote	% of Vote
LD1	679	704	CD1	·592	·446
LD2	403	438	CD2	−·720	144
LMOD	−638	−725	CMOD	+·708	+·232

The Labour party positions have been slightly more highly correlated with its share of the vote than the actual total vote, while the opposite has been definitely the case with the Conservatives. This is hardly surprising, because the Conservatives have not varied very much over their proportion of the vote. As the party that has remained from a previous period of party competition, it has retained its basic loyal block of party identifiers through intergenerational inheritance, while the Labour party has had to break through old traditional ties to the Liberal party. Neither time nor electoral success has much affected the Conservatives. Essentially the dominant party, but the one needing to guard itself from the attacks of the newcomer, it has been quite sensitive to any change in its total vote, for this might herald the destruction of its own firm base, but it appears that it has been relatively unconcerned about the loyalty of the rest of the electorate which Labour has taken over from the Liberals. Given that the *total Conservative vote* has a rather slim correlation with time, at $-\cdot314$, while Labour's *percentage share of the vote* is very highly correlated at $\cdot875$, we have further reason to expect the Conservatives to show much less of a temporal trend.

What this rather suggests, which is of considerable theoretical interest, is that the Labour party has, over time, developed into a party able to compete. Its ideological positioning has seemed to follow a dynamic strategy, changing systematically over time. The Conservative party, though varying their policy greatly, from election to election, have not displayed any particular temporal trend because they were *already* a competitive party. Though they may have reacted to particular electoral conditions in a tactical manner it is the Labour party who have had to develop a strategically competitive position.

In support of the suggestion that there is a radical difference between the behaviour of the two parties *vis-à-vis* electoral success are the signs of the correlation coefficients, which indicate the direction of change. Electoral success has affected the two parties in opposite ways. As the percentage of the two party vote going to Labour has increased, it has moved towards the *laissez-faire* end of the first dimension and towards the 'economic optimism' end of the second dimension. As this is backed up by LMOD, the summary measure of Labour's distance from the origin in seven-space, we may say that electoral success tends to move the Labour party away from a radical left wing stance into one that is more moderate. The Labour party, as its percentage of the vote increases, is more prone to accept that the economy can be run in a quasi-capitalist mode and still produce surplus for social welfare.

The Conservative case is strategically different from this. For instead of reciprocating and moving towards the Labour party position, or even the moderate position of the origin, electoral success is accompanied by a move towards Conservative extremism. It has moved towards *laissez-faire* with electoral success, and has tended to take up the pessimistic end of the second dimension, decrying the possibility of social welfare as too much of a strain on an enfeebled economy, again when it has done relatively well electorally. CMOD demonstrates, with its high positive correlation, that the distance between the Conservative party and the origin in seven-space has increased with Conservative electoral popularity, in contrast with the Labour party example.

If one then concentrates only on electoral success, ignoring the other phenomena like the relationship between time and party position, electoral success makes the Conservatives more, and Labour less, extreme.

There is an ambiguity in the use of election results as a measure of popularity for strategic calculation that requires caution. As there is no reliable way of getting an index of the popularity of parties *before* elections for the whole of this period, we have used the results of the election itself. We intend them primarily as an indicator of what it is thought likely would happen, but of course there cannot be, strictly, a casual relation between party position and the vote, unless we wish to argue the former causes the latter. As it is we prefer to fall back on a non-causal argument and talk here only of 'association'. The whole question of political popularity and policy formulation is complex and we will return to it shortly. At this stage we wish only to make the point that the two parties have certainly behaved differently, as witnessed by most of the data we have presented so far, and that this may well reflect a difference between them that is fundamental, a difference not of ideology, but of competitive security.

One of them seems to have been very much a creature in a process of development, becoming steadily more moderate over time as its voting support has built up. The other presents no particular temporal trend, and tends towards moderation only when it loses from its loyal voting block, with little of a patterned sequence. The suggestion is that in the Conservative party we can see a truly mature, stable, competitive party, which description would not be true of Labour, we shall now try to support with further data.

1.F. Policy Positions and Economic Conditions

There is one type of variable that everyone must believe affects party policy, the condition of the economy. We know from other research that economic conditions definitely affect voters' preferences between parties. The studies by Goodhart (1970) and by Kramer (1971) are referred to elsewhere. There is also a finding that voters' ideological preferences are so affected. Macdonald (1973) mentions that the Butler and Stokes survey data on British voting contain such evidence. He shows that while all Conservative voters in the panels were prone to say that there ought to be no more nationalisation in Britain, this tendency was much stronger amongst those Conservatives who had a pessimistic view of the immediate future of the economy.

Whether one adopts a competitive or 'sincere' model of the party, economic conditions are relevant to ideological positioning. The 'sincere' party, advocating whatever it thinks is the best solution to current problems, with no eye to electoral expediency, must nonetheless change its prescriptions as the health of the economy fluctuates. So must a competitive party, for as the economy varies, so must the problems and desires of the voters it wishes to attract. Indeed the target voters themselves, the 'marginal voters' discussed in earlier chapters, may change. The social class from which marginal voters come will probably not be the same in two periods with sharply different levels of affluence.

We need therefore to investigate the relationship between measures of economic success and of policy position. Which party reacts how to what sort of economic condition is a question of very general interest. It is also vital knowledge if we seek insights into competitive stategy.

This is particularly true given the nature of the two major dimensions disclosed by the analysis of Chapter 3. The first dimension is really the most 'ideological' in the sense of pertaining to a relatively rigorous theory of how the economy works, and how it should be run. The second, however, which we have characterised under a series of related labels, may be the more interesting. For the second dimension, covering reaction to the immediate condition of the economy, in terms of its ability to confer rewards or its need of sacrifice and effort, is clearly a spectrum of short run economic policy. It is the dimension along which most of the real governing of the economy, as opposed to the expression of long range ideals, has centred. In a quasi-Keynsian nation where all governments are dedicated to economic tinkering in an incremental mode, it is vital. There should be a closer relationship between objective economic conditions and policy stands on this dimension than on the first. What a party advertises as the long run shape of the desired economy can be relatively autonomous of economic actuality. What one proposes to do immediately if elected cannot.

We have a series of measures of economic change against which have been correlated the measures of party position. They are described below in Table 16.

Table 16. Measures of Economic Change

A. Static Measures
These are simply the figures for each election year on the following variables:
1. Unemployment. The percentage of the Labour force registered as unemployed at the beginning of the election year.
2. Index of industrial production. For the first month of the election year.
3. Balance of payments. The overall balance of payments figure for the first month of the year.

B. Government Averages
These, calculated for each of the above variables, show the average change in the indexes over the period a government has been in office, thus reflecting an improvement or worsening in the relevant index during an incumbency:
4. Average change in percent of Labour force employed.
5. Average change in index of economic production.
6. Average change in balance of payments.

The variables described in Section B of Table 16 are perhaps more theoretically interesting, as they carry with them some aspect of responsibility, reflecting change during a period of office. At the same time, because they are in some way measures of economic trends, they ought to be more important, ought to influence policy more. A party which reflects more concern with one, momentary, economic statistic, *in an election year*, than it does with a trend that has been evident over some time may well be seen as showing some element of competitive behaviour. At least it may be said to fail in its duty to inform the electorate honestly of the economic situation.

The results of the correlations are given, for all six economic variables, and for all seven ideological variables, in Table 17.

Table 17. Ideological and Economic Intercorrelations

| | Economic Variables | | | | | |
	1	2	3	4	5	6
LD1	−802	666	·053	−421	674	732
LD2	−472	760	−·100	−234	465	403
LMOD	731	−773	083	144	−567	−699
CD1	569	−471	·265	377	−587	−307
CD2	−819	328	−197	−645	779	572
CMOD	697	−676	004	365	−776	−506
'C'	·810	−776	·130	420	−768	−631

N.B. Economic variables are numbered as in Table 16:
1. Unemployment
2. Index of production
3. Balance of payments
4. Unemployment change
5. Index of production change
6. Balance of payments change

The table certainly supports the expectation that the economic conditions and the policy positions are connected, often very closely. Furthermore all the significant correlations (and the non-significant ones that are at all non-zero) point in the same direction—improved economic conditions go with moderation and increased consensus. As unemployment drops, the Labour and Conservative positions on the first dimension approach one another, Labour deserting socialism, Conservatives deserting *laissez-faire*. With decreased unemployment goes a stress by both parties on the optimistic end of the second dimension. This means for both parties a relaxation, an attitude of using the economy to provide the good things (whatever they may be) of economic life, a boom as opposed to a slump policy set. The general measures, LMOD, CMOD, and 'C' all agree with the move towards moderation and consensus as unemployment decreases.

All the other economic variables on which the party ideological scores correlate highly show the same pattern. There remain two curious points about the table. Firstly, that variable 3, the immediate strength of the balance of payments, is completely without significance in explaining policy position. It seems very likely that this reflects its inadequacy as a measure, for its counterpart as a trend measure, variable 6, has high correlations, all in the expected direction. There can be several explanations of this failure to capture the phenomena that it is supposed to indicate. The most probable is that the balance of payments of all the measures is the one that can least be taken in isolation. Fluctuations in monthly trade returns, as we know from recent experience in Britain, are peculiarly sensitive to *ad hoc* events, strikes or big purchase orders, and do not well reflect the condition of life for the average voter. This is not true of trends in balance of payments which are more noticeable to the electorate. (Balance of payments measures were the ones that Goodhart found least associated with public opinion poll data.)

The other point refers to the hypothesis that trend measures would be more highly correlated than momentary measures of economic performance with policy positioning. The situation here is not straightforward, for the two parties again behave somewhat differently. For the Conservatives the hypothesis is true except in one sphere. As far as unemployment goes, the parties are alike in reacting much more strongly to the unemployment situation at the time of election than to its trend over the period of government. All the other pairs of correlation coefficients, for year-of-election and trend economic variables against the three ideology measures are, for the Conservatives, such that the trend/ideology correlation is the higher.

For the Labour party, six of the nine pairs demonstrate a greater relationship between momentary measures of the economy and ideology. If one leaves out the balance of payments coefficients, for the reasons suggested above, there is no case where Labour pays much more attention to trend than year-of-election figures. What can we make of this? There is one obvious fact about party competition that we discuss in detail later. That is that in any election campaign one party is the opposition and the other the government. The government must defend its record in office. The Conservatives have far more often been in the latter position than the Labour party over our period, and of the five elections where Labour has been the incumbent, in three of them, 1924, 1931 and 1966, the period of office has been so short that there was no real record that could be defended or attacked. Which suggests that where a party can, it will choose to aim its policy positions at the more favourable way of looking at the economy. Of this we have more suggestive evidence in the next section.

Unemployment is the exception to this, we suggest, because it is or has been electorally the bombshell. It has, according to Goodhart, much the biggest effect on the public opinion polls, it is the first attention of journalists, and unlike the other measures has a very direct and quick effect on people's lives. No one is directly affected by the index of production, though they are after a while affected by its concommittants, like inflation. Men are immediately affected by being made unemployed or seeing their friends and relatives so affected. While it may be rational and proper for a political party to ignore current unemployment figures, because the public interest demands that they consider the general state of the economy, no party even slightly competitive can afford to do this.

Some of the most revealing entries in the table are for dimension two. We have argued that this dimension, being tied more closely to economic reality, should show a different pattern from the others, and should be more highly correlated with economic indicators. This is true for the Conservatives, for whom this is the highest correlation registered. Labour however has an insignificant correlation—its general economic philosophy dimension has been more closely correlated with change in unemployment than has its short term policy. It is true, and interesting, that on this dimension both parties move (as they surely must) in the same direction. While their faith in their own general prescriptions for the economy is strengthened by economic disaster, they are both forced to move to the negative end of this dimension (stressing the need for effort and productivity, and playing down the importance of rewards to the citizens from the economy) when unemployment is high. This serves to show that economic reality constrains policy making at least a little.

The whole table presents a complex picture which can best be summarised thus—the objective conditions of the economy do indeed affect party positions, nearly always tending to make them more moderate as things improve, but the effects of particular aspects of economic health on different party positions on different dimensions vary considerably.

1.G. The Strategy of Economic Interpretation

Whatever ideal type of party behaviour one chooses, objective economic conditions ought to be correlated with ideological change. If unemployment gets worse, or production booms, either a competitive strategy or political sincerity will prompt a policy change. If a party is competitive, is concerned principally to adopt a vote maximising programme, economic objectivity may not be the whole picture. Whenever something goes wrong with the economy the government in power is liable to be held responsible, and may lose votes. An economic disaster has one objective nature to any individual. For *competing* political parties an economic disaster has two *different* strategic natures. For the incumbent, disaster is both objectively and strategically bad, for the opposition it can be strategically beneficial. Inflation in 1969–1970 was economically a bad thing, and for the incumbent Labour party in Britain, was also strategically bad. For the Conservatives, able to hark back to their success in stemming inflation in 1951, when they had taken office away from Labour, it was politically a very good thing indeed.

It is clear that only a competitive party, one concerned to adapt ideology to vote maximising, will show any correlation between strategic–economic variables and ideological positioning. A non-competitive party ought doubtless to react to economic conditions, but without regard to whether it forms the opposition or the government.

Special economic variables are needed to trap any signs of competitive behaviour where the incumbency status of the party affects its policy. We have created six of these 'strategic value' variables, one for each of the previous six 'straight' economic variables. The first step is to define a dichotomous variable which takes the value +1 when the Labour party is in power, and −1 when it is in opposition. This is a multiplier which then transforms the straight economic variables into strategic value measures. The logic is as follows. The index of economic production, variable 2 above, is highly and positively correlated with Labour party positions on the first dimension (+·666). When variable 2 has a high value, the economy is doing well, Objectively. If in such a situation, Labour is the incumbent, the situation is strategically favourable for them also. The better the economy does, the more favourable the strategic situation. So if we have multiplied, previously, the production index by the dichotomous incumbency variable, a high positive score will result in such favourable situations where a Labour government had been presiding over economic success. Had a Conservative government had a similar success, a situation strategically bad for Labour, a very low (negative) score would have arisen, as the high index score would have been multiplied by −1.

Similarly, bad performance by a Labour government results in a low strategic value score, and bad performance by a Conservative government in an intermediate score. High strategic values are reported in both the situations where the Labour party is helped (success in office, disaster out of office) and low scores in the bad situations (own failure, Conservative success). This same procedure is applied to the other five economic measures. (An exception, for convenience, is with unemployment. Here the dichotomous variable is reversed, because as high unemployment in office is strategically bad, to use the same procedure as above would involve remembering that in this case high strategy values were *bad* for Labour.)

We can take these six measures, labelled S1 through S6 to distinguish them from the ordinary 'objective' economic measures, and correlate them against the ideology measures used in the previous section. Bear in mind throughout that a high strategy value is good for the Labour party, bad for the Conservatives.

Clearly there ought to be no correlation at all between the variables S1–S6 and the ideology variables. No political party that is not competitive (in such a way as to tailor its policy stands to electoral expediency rather than the public interest) ought to be influenced in its policy setting by the strategic convenience of the economic situation.

Not very many of these strategic variables are significantly correlated with the ideological measures, yet we must remember that none of them should be. It is impossible to provide any explanation of why a political party should react to similar economic circumstances in different ways, depending on whether or not it has to accept responsibility, other than with some version of the competitiveness thesis. The evidence for this position is in any case stronger than it looks from the figures in Table 18. As we shall shortly see, when one takes account of the effects of other variables, controlling for straight economic or political conditions, in almost every case some strategic variable is important in explaining the positions.

Table 18. Correlations between Stategic Variables and Ideology Measures

	S1	S2	S3	S4	S5	S6
LD1	396	539	406	−094	308	100
LD2	153	−281	−285	157	−438	−044
LMOD	−280	−347	−242	272	−206	−060
CD1	−594	193	226	−398	392	−469
CD2	507	021	−080	337	−232	523
CMOD	−750	−056	−086	635	317	−094
'C'	−668	−213	−162	−272	077	−203

In this case the normal proceedure is reversed—only those variables underlined are significant.

On the surface there is a sharp contrast between the two parties. Only one of the entries for the Labour party is significant—the correlation between Labour's position on the first dimension and S2. S2 measures the strategic convenience of the index of industrial production. A high value on it is good for Labour—coming about either when they have presided over an increase in production, or when the Conservatives can be held responsible for a decline. What is of most interest is the sign of this correlation; the relationship is positive, indicating that the Labour party has tended to be moderate, to move towards the Conservative end of the first dimension when in a strategically favourable situation. This direction of change is true also for most of the other variables on the first dimension, even though they do not reach significance, and in most cases for the overall measure, LMOD. This contrasts sharply with the Conservative entries; not only are more of these significantly high, but in the opposite direction.

On each of the three ideology measures there is at least one significant correlation with a strategic variable. The first dimension position appears to become more extreme as the unemployment level becomes strategically favourable to the Conservatives, and the overall level of moderation, CMOD, is very strongly and significantly correlated with this same strategic variable, again in the same direction.

The Conservative position on the second dimension is also significantly correlated, with both S1 and S6 (the strategic value of the change in balance of payments). Dimension two is one that in a sense is really bipartisan. Neither party has proprietary interest in one or other end, for it reflects short term policy choices between options in such a way that both would prefer the same end, and both be forced to choose the other in times of crisis. All we can say is that the negative correlation between CD2 and S1 implies a tendency to demand restraint and effort where the strategic situation is favourable to the Conservatives. The correlation with S6 echoes this, for a strategically good situation for the Conservatives (one with a low S6 value) is associated again with a low position on the second dimension.

What this means can best be seen by translating the S values into typical economic situations. A bad strategic situation for the Conservatives is one in which they have presided over a rise in unemployment (or Labour has been in office when it has fallen). Either of these will be met, if that correlation is to hold up, with a high score on the second dimension, that is, one in which the economy is seen as not being in crisis. Conversely a crisis policy has to be associated with *either* a rise in unemployment under Labour or a fall under the Conservatives. The importance of correlations with these strategic variables lies in the necessary irrationality of the policy response. To stress economic crisis when the unemployment rate drops, or to deny it when it rises, sufficiently systematically to produce a significant correlation, betrays a massive gap between the setting of policy and economic reality.

Equally one can rationalise a tendency to become a more extreme devotee of *laissez-faire* economics when the economy is doing either well or badly. But one cannot rationalise such a tendency when the economy is doing well *or* when it is doing badly, dependent *only* on whether or not one is in office. The only way around these arguments would be to produce the (false) historical argument that it just so happens that there has been a strong correlation between incumbency and economic success, i.e., that a Labour incumbency at election times always has been associated with a rise in unemployment. Again this argument could maintain that, whenever the Conservatives have played down a crisis, this has coincided with a genuine drop in unemployment under a Labour government. Either way the argument is that transforming economic

Table 19. Correlations between Objective and Strategic Economic Variables

Objective Variables	Strategic Variables					
	S1	S2	S3	S4	S5	S6
J–1	−·458	−·150	−·085	−·189	080	−·371
2	+269	−124	·105	+144	−052	026
3	+126	312	233	+045	·217	−498
4	−058	−290	−256	−340	−046	−·153
5	+500	160	172	+452	−156	287
6	+363	373	369	−067	165	070

indicators by multiplying them by an incumbency variable leaves them, because of historical accident, unchanged. This, the only defence against the charge above, is easily countered. If it were true there would have to be high correlations between objective economic variables and the strategic ones, else one cannot argue that correlations between policy positions and strategic variables are compatible with a responsible reaction to economic reality. As can be seen from Table 19, this has not been the case.

The only two correlations, of those that apply here, of any size at all, are between 1 and S1 and 4 and S4, but neither are anything like big enough to suggest that the transformed variables are, in effect, not very much changed. A correlation of 0.458 not only is not significant, but reflects a situation where the transformed variable, were it used to predict unemployment rates, could account for only 23% of the variance. So there is no way round the conclusion that to some extent the Conservative policy positions on all three measures have been, technically, irrational.

1.H. Relative Strengths of the Various Effects
So far we have presented a series of tables, all giving single correlations between variables of different types and the policy measures. Such tables are rich in material for speculation, though difficult to compare and contrast effectively. They also raise the problem that, interesting though it may be to note that X, Y and Z all affect A, unless one has some idea how X, Y and Z are themselves interrelated, one cannot say anything about relative effects. A host of questions are likely to occur. We know, now, that Labour seems strongly affected by economic fluctuations, and especially the unemployment rate. As unemployment declines, the party becomes moderate. But anyone could have said that with much less effort—the man in the street has always said that Labour has become terribly moderate in the last few years, and of course we know that unemployment now is nothing like as terrible as in the depression. Have we really shown any very strong or precise association? Do small post-war fluctuations in unemployment have any effect? Is there, indeed, any causal connection at all, or is it all a coincidence?

Statistical analysis can never, as we all realise, convincingly demonstrate causality—but perhaps at least we can do something to show that there is some association over and beyond historical coincidence. Generally, to say anything of theoretical pertinence we have to sort through the mass of intercorrelations and try to weed out the spurious ones. Of what is left, we must somehow produce a ranking of importance. Only if we can produce some few simple statistical models of the interrelations between the several ideological measures and the various indexes of electoral and economic phenomena can we hope to go beyond the unsophisticated presentation of incomprehensible 'facts'.

In pursuit of this we use regression techniques to produce a set of two variable 'explanatory' equations for each of the measures. We do this not to predict, but because it is the best way of comparing the strength of different

114

variables. We have to restrict ourselves to models with two independent variables because with so small a sample it is hard to achieve significant results with larger models. This can be very convenient however; in a world (or data set anyway) in which one can plausibly insist that everything causes everything, there is no point in seeking for that regression model which has only the quality of explaining more variance than any other. We are using them mainly as convenient comparative tools and summaries, and the simpler they are, the better.

To begin, let us take up the point raised earlier—how precise is the fit between economic change and dedication to socialist economics? Is it all just a coincidence? One way to answer this is to compare the relative importance of the unemployment rate and the passage of time itself. As we have said earlier, 'time' is no sort of explanation at all. It can be no more than a conveniently labelled error term. This helps, for in comparing the effects of these two variables on policy positions, we are in effect asking "Once one controls for time, are the fluctuations of the economy around what one expects from an economic time trend related to similar fluctuations of ideology from its time trend?" As broad a composite error variable as time ought to 'explain' as large an amount of the variance; unless economic fluctuation really is important, it should have a smaller effect than time. Does it? This is the work for a regression equation of the form:

$$L1 = a_1 + b_1x_1 + b_2x_2, \text{ where } x_1 = \text{time and } x_2 = \text{unemployment rate.}$$

The equation, when run, has an R^2 of ·657; healthily large, significant at the 5% level, as one might expect. Compare the relative strengths of those two variables (using standardised Beta Weights), and one comes up with the model shown in Figure 21.

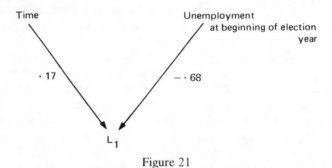

Figure 21

We need have no fear that there is only an historical coincidence; controlling for the passage of time does not reduce the effect of the economy. Of the two 'causal paths', that from unemployment rate is much stronger. It is, in fact, the only path significant if one applies a 't' test to the regressional coefficients.

Having disposed of that problem, what other variables affect this ideology measure? The variables which, for Labour first dimension positions, seem most likely to be important can be spotted from the reports of simple correlations in the previous tables. They are the vote percentage for Labour, the index of economic production, and S2, the strategic convenience of the production index. Together with the unemployment rate, these suggest four two-variable equations:

L1 = Unemployment + Strategic production $\quad R^2 = \cdot806$
L1 = % Vote + Unemployment $\quad R^2 = \cdot691$
L1 = Unemployment + Production index $\quad R^2 = \cdot671$
L1 = % Vote + Strategic production $\quad R^2 = \cdot640$

The R^2 coefficients make the choice obvious. The first equation, L1 = Unemployment + Strategic production, accounts for about 81% of the variance in L1, compared with 69% for the next best, L1 = % Vote + Unemployment. The causal models in Figure 22 show why this should be so—the other sets of variables are all so highly dependent on unemployment that they have little explanatory power by themselves.

In (B) and (D) of Figure 22 we have introduced a third (dotted) arrow to express the influence of one of the independent variables on the other; in these cases the direction of any causal chain is obvious, and it is possible to do so. The usual practice in this type of analysis is to count the total importance of a variable as a sum of its direct influence (the figure next to the arrow linking independent and dependent variable) and its indirect influence. The indirect influence is the product of its influence on the second variable and that variable's direct influence. Table 20 takes account of this in summarising, for (B) and (D), the relative influence strengths.

Table 20.

Variable	Direct Influence	Indirect Influence	Total
% Vote	·110		·110
Unemployment	−710	−090	−800
% Vote	·601		·601
Strategic Production	400	145	545

This explains why unemployment and strategic production index are so much more powerful than any other set of variables. When put into an equation with unemployment no other variable but the strategic one retains as much explanatory power. Combined with the voting variable, the strategic economics variable appears relatively unimportant until one takes account of

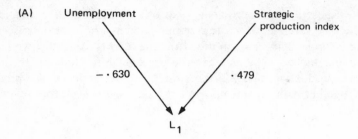

(A)

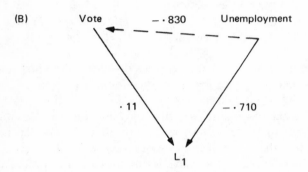

(B)

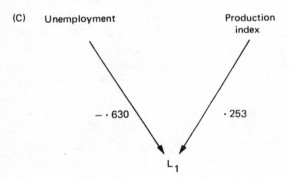

(C)

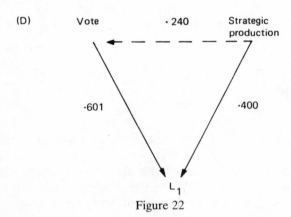

(D)

Figure 22

indirect effect, when it becomes very nearly as important. As the voting variable has so little individual effect when one controls for unemployment, the strategic variable takes on considerable importance. The straight production index is so much less powerful than the unemployment variable that one concludes that, for Labour party positions on the dimension of overall economic policy, the objective state of unemployment, the strategic value of the level of production, and, marginally, the likely political fortunes of the party are the primary influencing variables. It is worth mentioning that the index of economic production is probably the best single monthly indicator of the overall state of the economy and as such is most important where it has explanatory power. A low unemployment situation, a strategically favourable general state of the economy (flourishing when Labour can take credit or bad when the Conservatives are responsible) and a favourable political climate will combine to produce a distinctly moderate policy stand.

We shall skip over the Labour second dimension positions here, because we wish to discuss both parties' positions on this oddly bi-partisan dimension together at the end, and go on to the overall measure of Labour's moderation, LMOD.

There are here only three variables that seem of importance, Labour vote percentage, industrial production, and balance of payments trend. Again the equations are displayed along with the causal models, in Figure 23.

There is no difficulty in interpreting this diagram. LMOD, the measure of overall moderation, is more or less equally influenced by two economic variables, the industrial production index for the year of the election, and the trend in balance of payments over the immediate past. Political popularity has a secondary importance. In terms of direct influence the political popularity measure is rather more important, *vis-à-vis* the other explanatory variables, than with the first and second dimension cases. Even in this case the fact that the economic conditions can be said to have an indirect effect (they influence the political scene), makes them more important overall.

There is only one regression equation which reaches an acceptable level of significance for the Conservative position on the first dimension, although many of the variables are, of course, by themselves highly related to it. The equation that does emerge fits well with the idea of a competitive party.

The best explanatory equation available is entirely in terms of strategic variables, acting so as to move the Conservatives in general away from moderation whenever the economic situation is strategically favourable. Thus where the economy has done well under a Conservative government, or badly under Labour, there is a tendency to the *laissez-faire* position.

Table 21 contains the important equations for the overall Conservative moderation score, CMOD. It is a familiar set of variables, two of them being from the strategic list, the strategic versions of the two unemployment variables, for the election year itself and for the recent trend in unemployment. The straight unemployment variable, the trend variable for the production index, and the Conservative voting variable are also important.

118

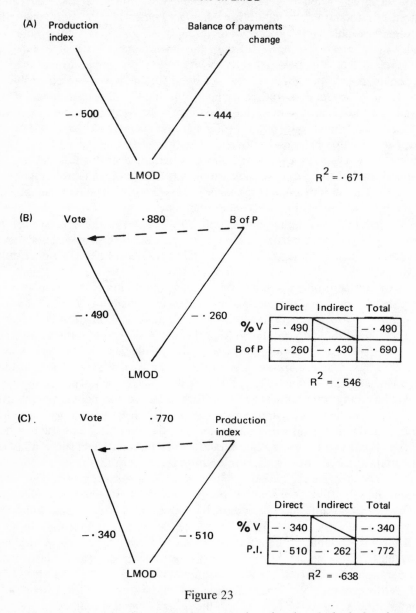

Figure 23

In this case the objective unemployment situation is relatively less important, compared with both Conservative voting and with industrial production change. It is in fact, less important than a strategic unemployment variable (see equation II). The consistently important variables are industrial production change and the two versions of strategic unemployment. As usual for the Conservatives the direction is such as to move them away from moderation

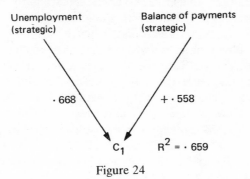

Figure 24

Table 21. Influences on CMOD

	Variable	Direct	Total	R^2
I	Index of production change	−540	−540	·786
	Strategic unemployment	480	480	
II	Unemployment	450	450	·759
	Strategy of unemployment change	540	540	
	Production index change	−62	−62	725
	Change in strategic unemployment	36	36	
	Strategic unemployment	590	590	715
	Strategic unemployment change	460	460	
	Unemployment	400	400	715
	Conservative vote	430	430	

whenever the situation is strategically satisfactory for them, or when the vote support is high, and yet to make them moderate where the objective economic variables indicate an improvement. Again, of course, there is a possible contradiction—a tendency to become moderate because the economy is doing well, balanced against a tendency to be extreme because the Labour party will get the credit for these improvements. It is worth repeating that earlier we have reported a check that there is a close correlation between ideology and the economic situation, and that it is not simply an historical coincidence. We repeat a version of this test.

Running the equation CMOD = Industrial production change + time again produces an insignificant coefficient for time ($-·167$) as against a high one of -660 for the economic variable.

We have reserved discussion of the party positions on the second dimension until the end because it is substantially different in meaning from the others. In itself it is bi-partisan. That is, neither party has a preferred position that is not shared by the other. The negative end of the spectrum represents, as we have said several times, a policy position stressing the need for effort, productivity, and restraint; it is the 'slump' end where the parties fear that it is not possible to do much of what they would wish. What they wish to do does not have to be the same, and probably is not. To stress the pessimistic end for the Conservatives means, for instance, to regret the impossibility of letting affluence and spending power shoot ahead, to feel the need for deflationary tax policies, in contrast to letting the market have its head. For Labour restraint means more that welfare spending cannot surge ahead, and pay rises may not be easily available.

Increasingly over the period, as we know, the actual preferences in a time of affluence (the positive end of the spectrum) and regrets and restraints of the negative end have come to be the same for both parties. Even when this is not so, however, the implication of the ends of the spectrum are the same—both parties would prefer, *ceteris paribus*, the positive end, and feel obliged to advocate the negative end, under the same conditions. Or so they should, anyway. The dimension is non-partisan so there is no suitable concept of the 'extreme' on it.

This does not mean that competitive behaviour cannot show up, however. Precisely because it is a non-partisan, short term, and technical dimension of what ought to be agreed economic policy, competitive behaviour may be clearly displayed. For while there may not be any ideological grounds for holding one rather than another position on the dimension, there is clear electoral expediency attached to what position one takes up. Appeals for effort and sacrifice are never likely to be popular, and if one party offers this, while the other offers an optimistic interpretation of the economy, voters may well be strongly influenced. More than with the other dimensions even, strategic considerations can, and ought not to hold sway.

Going to the Labour positions on the second dimension only the following variables seem to have surface interest: Labour vote percentage, industrial production index, and the strategic version of the production trend variable. The resulting equations are given along with the causal models in Figure 25.

Again the influence of the vote is diminished because its high correlation with the straight economic variable ($+ \cdot 771$) reduces its influence enormously when one controls for the economic fluctuations. The most interesting point here is what happens to the effect of the vote if one does control for industrial production. The change of the sign shows that, controlling for economic conditions, a high vote is associated with a move towards the negative end of the second dimension. Which seems to suggest that the party has tended to stress the need for economic effort and drives for productivity if in a good electoral position to the extent that real economic production has made this possible. A basic pessimism about the economy, from a party whose long-range economic philosophy is to favour considerable change in its structure, is not surprising. That such an emphasis should be related to popular support is less predictable. Too much faith should not be put in this, however, for while the

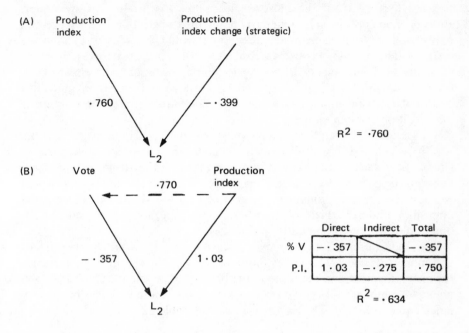

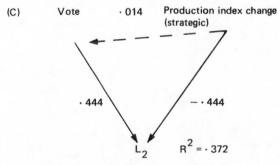

Figure 25

equation as a whole is significant at the 5% level, the individual effect of the vote percentage variable is not very high.

All that one can say with confidence about this dimension is that it is strongly influenced by economic production. That strategic variable which is a transform of trend in production indicator appears to have some theoretically very important explanatory power. As is shown by (A) in Figure 25, the party has tended to be pessimistic about the economy in the short run when production is low.

This is counter-balanced to an extent by the tendency of the party to react to a strategically unfavourable recent trend with optimism, whether well-founded or not. Certainly it would be natural for a competitive party to react to a bad period when it has been in office with misleadingly optimistic forecasts and policies, particularly if the most recent figures for production are better. Equally, if an opposition Labour party has to fight an election after a successful period of Conservative economic direction, it would be foolhardy to advocate restraint. There could of course be conflict between these two forces. Were the economy to have worsened under a Labour government, the effect of the objective conditions would be to pull the party down to the restraint and effort end of the second dimension while its unfavourable strategic position was pushing it into 'boom' policies.

Such a tactical situation is easy to imagine and does help to make clear the way in which those 'causal' models do underline comprehensible political situations. If such a situation was to occur it is safe to say from the difference between the path coefficients that the tendency to short-term restraint would win out, but that it would be toned down by the desire not to help the opposition unduly. Which, when all is said and done, sounds very much what one would expect of competitive politicians.

With the Conservatives the record is substantially the same. Four variables are important: unemployment, Conservative vote, and the strategic variables for unemployment and the trend in the balance of payments. Once again the unemployment variable is the strongest, the other three variables being very much equal in weight. The results are given in Table 22.

Table 22. Influences on C2

Variable	Direct	Indirect	Total	R^2
Unemployment	−610	−210	−820	735
Vote	−290		−290	
Unemployment	−720		−720	
Balance of payments trend (strategic version)	250		250	730
Unemployment (strategic version)	−560		−560	
Balance of payments trend (strategic version)	680		680	·652

The voting variable is considerably more important here than in other examples—the less popular the Conservatives, the more they will be attracted to a 'boom' position, for obvious, if unsatisfactory, reasons. Only when one takes into account the effect of unemployment by itself on the vote do the two strategic variables come up as equally important with the voting variable. They both act the same way, such that a negative relation between strategic favourableness of the Conservatives and their position on the second dimension exists. This means that the more unpopular the economic situation is likely to make the Conservative party, the more they are likely to go to the positive, relaxation of restraint, freeing the economy, end of the spectrum. Overall, a drop in unemployment, or diminished popularity in terms either of the vote as cast, or the convenience of the strategic situation, are all likely to move the Conservatives towards the positive, 'boom' end of the dimension. The comparison with the Labour party is obvious, and the same tensions between objective and strategic effects are possible.

It is of the greatest importance that the direction of the short-term economic policy is undoubtedly affected by the interaction between the incumbency status of a party and economic reality, rather than by economic reality alone.

We have now completed the presentation of the data, and turn in Part II of the Chapter to sketching a theory that can account for and make intelligible, this suggestive mass. Before doing so the most important parts made so far are summarised, with brief (English) explanations.

Best Equations for all Six Ideology Measures

Labour First Dimension

$$L1 = -\cdot630 \text{ (Unemployment)} + \cdot479 \text{ (Strategic production index)}.$$

$$R^2 = \cdot806$$

Explanation: L1 is in part a function of the unemployment rate and the strategic convenience of the health of the economy as measured by the index of production. A rise of one standard deviation in the numbers of unemployed workers moves the Labour position ·63 of a standard deviation to the left in general economic policy. This tendency is countered by a move of ·48 of a standard deviation to the right for every one standard deviation improvement in the strategic economic situation. In brief, the equation says that a rise in unemployment pushes the party left, and this may be mitigated or increased depending on how economic production is going and who is the government.

Labour Second Dimension

$$L2 = \cdot760 \text{ (Production index)} - \cdot399 \text{ (Production trend strategic value)}.$$

$$R^2 = \cdot760$$

In brief: as productivity declines by one standard deviation, the party moves ·76 of a standard deviation towards the 'pessimism' end of the short-term economic policy dimension. This is mediated, however, by a tendency to move ·399 of a standard deviation towards the optimistic end for every one standard deviation worsening in the strategic favourability of the trend in productivity over the last government.

LMOD

$$LMOD = -\cdot500 \text{ (Production index)} - \cdot444 \text{ (Balance of payments trend)}.$$

$$R^2 = \cdot671$$

For every standard deviation improvement in productivity the party moves half a standard deviation nearer moderation, and this is reinforced by ·44 of a standard deviation for every standard deviation that balance of payment trend improves.

Conservative First Dimension

C1 = ·668 (Strategic unemployment)+·558 (Strategic trend in balance of payments).

$R^2 = ·659$

In brief: as the strategic value to the Conservatives of the rate of unemployment improves by one standard unit of deviation, they move ·668 standard deviations towards their own (*laissez-faire*) end of the first dimension, and this is increased by a similar movement of ·558 standard deviation for every one standard deviation improvement in their strategic position from the balance of payments trend.

Conservative Second Dimension

C2 = −·610 (Unemployment) −·290 (Conservative vote).

$R^2 = ·735$

A drop of one standard deviation in unemployment moves the Conservative party ·610 standard deviations towards the optimistic, 'boom', end of the short-term economic policy dimension. This is mediated by a small move in the same direction for every standard deviation worsening in the Conservative's vote support. The second equation, given below, suggests that in addition there is a similarly sized move towards the relaxation end of the spectrum for every one standard deviation worsening in the Conservative's strategic situation re balance of payments trend. Taken together they suggest that a natural tendency to stress economic restraint and effort when the economy is doing badly can be reduced by a tendency to stress 'boom' policies when the electoral situation, either in terms of votes or the implication of the economy for their incumbency position, is bad.

C2 = −·720 (Unemployment) −·250 (Balance of payments trend strategic).

$R^2 = ·730$

CMOD

CMOD = −·540 (Production index trend) +·480 (Strategic unemployment).

$R^2 = ·786$

In brief: for every standard deviation that the trend in production improves, the party becomes roughly half a standard deviation more moderate overall, but where the strategic value of the unemployment rate improves for them, this is countered by a similarly sized move away from moderation.

PART II: THE LOGIC OF PARTY COMPETITION

What we have shown so far of the background to change in party ideology does not constitute a theory. It does not even constitute a set of facts, or a description that can stand on its own, for no such abstract and contrived 'facts' have any meaning outside some special intellectual framework.

We cannot here hope to derive any rigorous or complete theory. All we shall attempt is to point out what aspects of the analysis offered above strike us as most interesting, and suggest one way in which they could be accounted for. At the risk of over-repetition, the statistical analysis seems to make the following points:

1. As economic conditions improve, both parties tend to become more moderate.

2. As voting support increases for Labour and decreases for the Conservatives, they both tend to become more moderate.

3. The effect of economic change is mediated by the incumbency, in such a way that a strategically favourable economic situation is associated with increased moderation of the Labour party, but increased extremism for the Conservatives.

On point 2 we find it also interesting that the parties differ on which of the measures of political success is most strongly correlated with ideological change. The Labour party's position is associated with the percentage of the electorate which supports it, but the Conservatives appear more affected by the total number of votes they get.

Finally there exists an important ideological dimension, the second to emerge from the factor analysis, which is non partisan. It represents a conflict between economic optimism, the absence of restraint and the emphasising of whatever one considers economic values (e.g. the provision of welfare or the exercise of freedom on the one hand) and economic panic, restraint, and caution about the economy's capacity on the other. On this dimension the positions of the parties are affected in the same way by economic conditions. Under bad economic conditions both parties tend towards pessimism, and vice versa. In both cases strategic economic indicators are important in explaining the party position, but less so than direct and immediate conditions as indicated by employment and production indexes for the year of the electron. This should not blind us to their great theoretical importance.

With no particular difficulty one could produce piecemeal 'explanations' for each of these phenomena, but there would be no way of choosing between any sets of these. The real question is this: is there any relatively simple explanation that will fit all of these reactions and help unify them into something like a 'theory of party competition'? Downs' *An Economic Theory of Democracy* certainly does not contain one, though that is not to say that his theory is or will be incompatible with any satisfactory answer—he simply does not have anything like a detailed theory of ideological change.

One reason, as we have already suggested, for Downs' inadequacy is that he lacks any real conception of the development over time of a system of party competition. All he has to say is about a mature system in which both parties are equally able to be competitive, have an equal chance, depending only on strategic competence, to get elected. Admittedly he does discuss the foundation of new parties, and probably has as good an explanation as can be given for the emergence of parties and the concomitant (causing?) change in the structure and distribution of ideological opinion in society. Yet because of his extreme idea of a rational voter as one who is solely and intensely concerned and able to make a utility calculus judgement on the parties, he is led to assume that a newly formed party and the surviving party from the old system are equal competitors. This we know, both from electoral research and historical common sense, is untrue. It is untrue in almost every way. The new Labour party in the early years of this century was not an equal competitor with the Conservatives, who did not lose their position as a 'natural government', or the 'dominant party' until recently, if indeed they have yet lost it. Most voters, even in the working class, had no particular loyalty to, or perceived reason to support, the Labour party immediately it appeared. The members of that party were far from sure that they wished to play the consensus-implying game of competitive politics. Finally Downs makes no mention of one vital precondition for competitive politics—that centres of power and authority outside the new party have to be prepared to allow it to win. That too takes time. Extending the franchise to the whole adult population, which is usually regarded by political scientists as opening the political arena to all, is not the same as accepting as legitimate a government supported almost exclusively by the previously disenfranchised.

Baldwin's self avowed aim in the twenties and thirties of helping to train and make acceptable the Labour party speaks to this (Middlemas, 1972).

There is another aspect, not unrelated to the need for slow development towards competitive equality, that is ignored, or rather made impossible to consider, in the straight Downsian framework, but which is perhaps the key to finding a theory of party competition.

This aspect of the problem is vital to the development of a theory predicated on the quasi-Downsian assumptions that we make. It is also important for a 'sincere' theory of party competition, one in which they are seen as solely concerned with the public interest.

To Downs, and to all those who have worked along his lines, the ideological dimensions on which parties take up position are continuous metrics, infinitely divisible interval scales. A party, once elected, has only to direct utility flows to those it wishes to provide for, and any such division of the public cake is possible. Hence electoral strategy is in no way complicated by the enormous difficulties of government. A party 'takes up' an ideological position, and is more or less free to take up any such. In fact, as we argued extensively in Chapters 1 and 2, this is a simplification of the model which is distinctly counter productive. Rather we ought to recognise that ideological positions are policy proposals, solutions to problems, and they are not there to be 'taken up' but have to be invented. Certainly they can be mapped onto a metric as we have done, and this mapping may even be done by the voters. Still the policies which are to be mapped have to be thought out and designed by the parties.

This is trivially so; imagine a case where politics was really fought out on a naked 'equality-privilege' axis. Theoretically any degree of income distribution may be electorally dictated to the parties, and they may compete eagerly to get on to the maximising point. One cannot, though, stand for election on a promise of ensuring such and such a degree of equality. That may be what matters, it may be a very precise way of maximising votes, but it still requires a policy, a design, a method of implementation. In all honesty it would be difficult to condemn either major British or American party since the war for not desiring to diminish inequality, or for not promising it and even trying to accomplish it. All of them could, though, be condemned for failing to achieve this goal, for lacking effective policies, for being at times intellectually bankrupt and generally having almost no ideas about how to solve this, and other, social problems.

To say that Downs takes insufficient notice of the fact that parties and governments have to come up with plans and ideas, have to try to solve very difficult problems, and that this must very largely constrain and determine competitive strategy, is not to criticise him particularly. Political science and political criticism generally has been characterised for a very long time by an apparent inability to see that politics, if it is to be seen as problem solving, must therefore be seen as deeply involved with the production of ideas. It is so much easier, and perhaps more satisfying, to blame parties for weakness of will or bowing to entrenched interests, that we have almost forgotten that passion, determination and will-power are cheap and in plentiful supply compared with ideas.

When political parties fight elections, in the two party systems of Anglo Saxon democracies, one of them is the government, defending its past performance, one is the opposition. They are both faced with an objective social and economic reality consisting of problems and existing government policies. They have to compete against each other in a situation where no policy makers have any very clear idea of how to solve the problems, how to modify the existing policies, or what new ones are available. Both are tied in complex ways to the government's policies, successes, and failures, for these represent topics to dwell on or avoid for the opposition as much as for the incumbents. Those are the similarities.

In Britain over the period we have covered, there are equally important differences, arising as we argue, from the way our party system since the first world war has been developing towards maturity.

One party has been dominant, antedates the new competitive system, has not changed its percentage share of the vote significantly, has stood only to lose loyal voters rather than having to build up a loyal voting block. It has always been the party of pragmatism, a 'non-idealogical' party because pragmatism means, in essence, reacting conventionally inside a consensus of acceptable policies, and it is the consensus of Conservatism that Labour has had to accept, rather than the reverse.

The Labour party came onto the scene with only few loyal voters, with the need to build itself a loyal vote block which could only come from those who were already attached to one or other of the consensus 'pragmatic' parties. At the same time, it started as, had to start as, an 'ideological' party outside this pragmatism. How else could a new party start?

Only by taking up an ideological position outside that covered by the existing parties, a position on the spectrum only recently come into existence as a result of expansion of the suffrage, can a new party emerge. To do otherwise, to appear, say, right next to the Liberal party, is to provide no reason at all for anyone to support it. Then the new party has to become moderate, has to approach slowly the median voter, winning adherents from the old middle party, in this case the Liberal party, but to do this in such a way as not to lose the hard core of loyal supporters it has been built on. The new party in such an emerging competitive system has to start from a distinctive, necessarily extreme and non consensual position, and converge on the middle ground, but without, if at all possible, losing everything that made it distinctive.

Most of what is said in the last paragraph might come straight from Anthony Downs. We wish though to point out that this process of moving towards moderation is not one in which parties approach a position which is, historically, equally accessible to all parties. The significance of the process is not the same for both parties. The special characteristic of the median position is that it is inside the area of consensual pragmatism in which the surviving old party has always performed. The middle ground 'belongs', has, in the period of our study 'belonged' to, this survivor, the Conservative party. Not that the Conservatives have not had to change, to accept policies and values they would rather not; the welfare state and a Keynsian economy are far from the Conservative plans of 1923, but the change is different, perhaps easier, reflecting a modification, an acceptance of new *ad hoc* solutions, into a pragmatic position, and not entailing the dropping of an ideological outlook in politics.

All of this points to one conclusion. If there are to be regularities and constrains on ideology imposed by a competitive system, we ought not to expect both the dominant and the emerging party to react in the same way, inasmuch as they do occupy these different developmental roles. On the other hand we must expect that, as they occupy the same status as competing alternative governments, other constraints arising from the nature of governing in a consensus society, will present essentially the same challenge to them.

Why do both parties react in the same way to objective economic conditions on the first two dimensions? For they do, contrary to what one might at first think. At first, all one sees is that on the dimension of grand economic policy they go in different directions, in that they each move away, to their own extreme, when things go badly, and come together, towards moderation, when they go well. Oddly enough they go in the same direction on the short range economic dimension, both towards restraint in bad times, both towards relaxation of restraint in good times. The key is that the first dimension is ideologically polarised, with separate and opposed 'natural' ends for the parties. The second is different—the preferred end for the two parties is the same, though possibly with a different meaning for each. Neither of them can advocate its preferred end under economic conditions that prevents its opponent from doing the same. The reaction of each party to economic reality is the same: 'Times are bad; clamp on restrictions in the short run, promise radical solutions in the long' is opposed to: 'You've never had it so good; do what we've always wanted in the short run, don't disturb a working system by threatening any long run changes'.

The same reaction, and one that follows from the problem of government itself, an overwhelming ignorance about how to solve social problems.

Several writers on policy making, most notably Charles Lindblom (1963) have advanced the theory of 'Incrementalism' in planning. This has a mixed purpose, being at the same time normative, recommending a strategy for policy making, and purporting to be a realistic description of how politicians and civil servants do actually try to solve social problems. The basis of it is a somewhat Burkean rejection of the enlightenment faith in reason and the possibility of a utility calculus. They argue that we do not usually know, and could not hope to calculate, the ramifying effects of a policy initiative, and that it is vital that we learn from painful experience, monitoring what we do carefully and reacting as quickly as possible whenever anything goes wrong. It boils down, as its title suggests, to doing very little to alter the *status quo*, but trying very small tentative changes, watching for a reaction, and taking further small steps if anything unpleasant occurs. While we have no intention here of arguing for this theory in its normative aspect, or even supporting it wholeheartedly in its descriptive one, it seems a very plausible description, if not a new one.

Let us accept then that governments behave incrementally, at least in part. The most important implication of incrementalism is that governments will not try to change anything very greatly. A second implication, perhaps following more from the Burkean scepticism than the more refined part of the theory, is that if things are going well, no policy maker will advocate change. Finally there is the great stress implicit in the theory on the short run, and on using any easy tools of policy that we do understand to affect this. The shorter the run, and the simpler the tools, the more probable it is that everyone will agree on them. It would seem to follow from an acceptance of the reality of incrementalism that on a short run policy dimension like our second dimension all parties would be substantially in agreement. There is one important rider to this—they will be in agreement to the extent that they share, or expect the electorate to share, a common definition of the situation.

We see from the analysis earlier just this; common reaction on the second dimension to objective economic phenomena, coupled with a slighter tendency to react to its strategic value. Thus, if things are going well the opposition may react to it as though conditions were bad—there is an observable tendency for labour to stress economic restraint when the *strategic* situation is unfavourable (which may mean that in reality the economy is doing very well, under a Conservative government).

Equally the Conservatives react to the possibility of the electorate not showing its apparent definition of the state of the economy. When the *strategic* economic situation is unfavourable they stress restraint; again an unfavourable situation can be one where the economy is actually improving, but where they cannot claim the credit.

That movements on the second dimension fit neatly with a thesis of incrementalism is not surprising, by its very nature. The thesis serves well to explain the other movements, however. The strongest of all the correlations is between objective economic improvement and the shared tendency to moderation. If the economy is strong the tendency to support incremental policies which seem to be working is bound to be marked, and the hall-mark of incrementalism is that policy consists of small changes from the *status quo*.

Political extremism can best be defined as suggesting a major change from the *status quo*. Where the economy is doing badly the promise of radical change is safe; not only does it avoid contamination by identification with failing policies, but because it is a long run matter it is not likely to be an embarrassing commitment later. There is one problem here raised by the Downsian theory: if we think in terms of there being a vote maximising point on a spectrum, then it is hard to see how competing parties should move in opposite directions; clearly they cannot both be going to a unique maximising point. We have already covered this point in the argument in Chapter 3 about ways of conceiving of ideological distance. What voters are presumed to want is a solution to a problem. The means, unless they represent too great a disruption of the *status quo*, are secondary. What is important when the economy is doing badly is that a solution, which does not look like the existent failing policies, should be offered. It is impossible for both parties to offer the same radical solution, for they need to be distinctive, they need to seem responsible, and they need to attack their opponents. In any case policies have to be invented, and they have to come from somewhere, most naturally a general tradition, something like an ideology, shared by their loyal voting group. The only time when parties not only need not to be different, but cannot afford to be, is where one set of policies appears to be working, that is when the economy is doing well. That it is foolish to advocate the same policies as one's opponent when they fail, and foolish to differ when they succeed is a rule that not only fits our data well, but is entirely consonant with common sense. It also fits very well with incrementalism.

There is a final piece of evidence that we have not yet mentioned and which highlights this point about incrementalism. Any regression equation, even the successful ones we report, leave something unexplained. Statisticians talk about the percentage of variance that is 'accounted for' by an equation, and the 'residuals' from these, equations. This means that the regression procedure is quite, but not completely, successful at predicting one variable from others. It is more efficient, say, then just guessing, or than taking some simple estimate, like the overall mean of the variable that is interesting one. The residuals are the left-over bit. One has, perhaps, succeeded in explaining a lot of the variance in party ideology with a set of socio-economic variables, but the actual value for Labour on a left–right dimension in 1955 is a bit lower or higher than what one predicts with the computer. A positive residual then would mean that, in fact, the party had been more right wing than the economic and electoral factors one has taken account of would lead one to expect. (Assuming that left–right is measured from $0 =$ left to $100 =$ right.) A negative residual would indicate a more left wing position than expected.

Part of this discrepancy between prediction and the actual world will be measurement error, randomly distributed over the cases. With data as 'soft' as ours this error component will probably be very high. Leaving that aside, the residual scores invite the question: 'what did we leave out', what other factors account for party ideology? Doubtless there are many, but there is one type of explanation that is particularly interesting. After one has taken account of as many important exogenous variables in any system of behaviour as possible, one is left with the system itself, with the way the rules of the system and the basic natute of the elements in it impose behaviour of a certain sort. Electoral conditions and economic trends are exogenous to our basic system, as even are party labels. What is basic, simply part of the structure of the game is something we have mentioned before, the mere fact that at any election, two or more parties compete, with the necessary fact that at least one party is the incumbent, and one the opposition. We need to know whether this in itself affects the policy position adopted. Note that we are asking here only about these basic 'system-structure' points. We are not asking whether being the incumbent has a particular effect on the policy of the Labour party, or whether a Conservative opposition party, when the economy is doing well and the electorate dislikes the Conservatives, will act in any particular way.

We are concerned only with the status of a party as incumbent or opposition, because only that is endogenous to the system. For the same reason the dependent variable, that which we seek to explain further, has to apply as generally as possible to all parties. So we look at the residuals in the overall moderation scores, CMOD and LMOD, after the best possible set of explanatory variables has done its work and taken account of party identity, and electoral and economic trends.

Ignoring the data from 1945, because it is hard to rule on which part could be regarded as the incumbent in any serious sense leaves us with twenty party positions. Ten elections, two parties at each, and thus twenty overall moderation scores, or what is left of them after the best possible prediction is subtracted for each party-year. Twenty undifferentiated scores, divided only between incumbent and opposition, there naturally being ten scores in each box. Because the overall moderation scores are actually measures of distance from the centre point, the higher the score, the less moderate. With the residuals this means that positive residuals indicate parties that are even less moderate than we would expect given the exogenous variables that we have controlled for.

Taking the average residual for each category, incumbents and oppositions, we find that incumbents are significantly more moderate than oppositions. The mean incumbent residual at 48·6 is notably lower than the mean opposition residual of 72·4. (This effect is also to be found for some of the other ideology measures, but this is the most useful one to quote, because CMOD and LMOD are more generally interpretable) Incumbents are, apart from anything else, more moderate than oppositions. Why? Where one party is an incumbent government, and one an opposition; the incrementalist thesis forces us to predict that, of the two, an incumbent will be the more moderate. Incremental-ism tells us that change of governments will change policy very little. The assumption that governments are forced to defend their record in office, coupled with this, suggests that the ideological position of the incumbent will be very moderate indeed, tied as it is to the *status quo*. To suggest extreme policies after several years of incrementalist governing is to invite two questions—either 'Why now, why not five years ago?', or 'So what's wrong with what you've given us, then?'

No opposition is going to be as moderate as an incumbent, so closely tied to the *status quo*, again for two reasons. First, it has to advocate something different: if two parties promise precisely the same thing, and one has been doing that effectively for five years, there is little rationality in electing the one who has not been doing it. Secondly, no government is ever that successful. Every government leaves enough room for bitter criticism of its failures, and as the opposition has both the competitive chance, and even the democratic duty to capitalise on this, it will stand some way off from its governing opponent.

These 'system effects' will probably be swamped by the effect of varying social phenomena, but when one has removed these effects, and is left with what cannot be predicted in any other way, they should and do show up.

All in all the acceptance of incrementalism combined with the basic tenet that parties do modify their electoral stands to increase their chance of election serves very well as a unified and comprehensive explanation of the phenomena described above. It helps us considerably towards the goal of theorising rigorously about party competition and its logic.

The developmental aspect of our viewpoint is important for the two other points we noted, that the two parties are not equally affected by the same electoral variables, and that their reactions to strategic variables, though equally definite, is opposed.

The tables showing the correlations between Labour and Conservative positions and the six strategic economic variables above all show the same thing. Two points emerge: (i) the Conservatives are clearly more affected than the Labour party, though neither is innocent; (ii) where the strategic situation favours the Labour party, it tends to be moderate, while the Conservatives react to a favourable strategic situation by becoming extreme. Why should there be this difference? Is it in any way connected with the tendency for the Conservative party to be sensitive to its actual number of votes, while the Labour party is more sensitive to its percentage of the electorate?

Nothing but an insight into the competitive status of the parties can answer this. The mere fact of correlations between votes and strategic conditions and ideological positions is enough to establish competition as part of political reality, but we want to understand it, not just to state that it happens. We have already argued that the two parties occupy very different competitive statuses, one being a dominant survivor from an earlier epoch, the other an emerging challenger. How do these statuses tie in with the phenomena with which we are now concerned?

In Chapter 2 we outlined a theory of party competition predicated on the idea that, where it was possible, parties and candidates would prefer a non-competitive position, one nearer to their own ideological heart. This is because parties consist partly of, and are dependent upon, activities who do have ideological preferences and are not motivated solely by the desire to win at any ideological cost. If such a centripedal force exists, the behaviour of the Conservative party is easily understood. A strategically favourable economic situation is one which relaxes the need for competitive moderation. It can come about because the economy is doing well under a Conservative government, in which case one can accept that the electorate would be predisposed to vote Conservative anyway, making it safer to advocate less moderate policies. Or a favourable strategic situation may mean economic failure for a Labour government. It is well to keep in mind that whenever the economy is going badly there is a tendency for both parties to abandon moderation, for the consensus policies are then partially discredited in anybody's hands. If, into the bargain, they are policies which have been implemented by the Labour party, a move to the right by the Conservatives is less likely to be penalised by voters. For reasons both of satisfying the activists, and disassociating themselves from failed policies, the Conservatives naturally move towards a more distinct and right-wing position.

All of that follows easily from our previous sketch of a theory. But why should it not hold also for the Labour party?

We suggest that is to be explained by the difference in the competitive status of the two parties. Our theory in Chapter 2, just as much as the original Downsian theory, is intended to hold primarily for mature parties. A mature party, in our case the Conservative party, is one which has been, often, a governing party, which 'owns' a large traditional pool of voting support, and which probably expects, and is expected, to win elections. It has nothing to prove to anyone, and is likely to be more normally at home with the pragmatic politics of the moderate consensual area. Given a chance it will indeed repair to a more extreme position, but it is not likely to need to do this to retain its support. In our case the consensual position is not one that is particularly strange or ill fitting with the original faith of the party. Extremism is a luxury to be indulged in whenever possible, but not a primary need.

In contrast an emerging party is one which has its roots in a quite different ideological position, with activists and loyal voters who have deserted one previous party for it. It has to build up painfully what the old party has securely, a large block of voters who will be predisposed to support it automatically. There is a difficult tension here; to catch such a voter it is necessary to be relatively moderate, and to display 'responsibility' and competence to govern, but at the same time it must show itself as distinct, as new, as being something other than the traditional parties. What we suggest is that an emerging party has to justify moderation, can probably only afford to be moderate where there is a very good chance of this being rewarded by electoral success. In contrast to the Conservatives, who need to be assured of success before they will risk extremism, the burden of proof is on the other side—the Labour leaders may have to show that it is worthwhile being moderate. Hence a strategically favourable economic situation, one which predisposes the electorate to vote for Labour, is one to be taken advantage of, to be maximised. One could sum up this as a difference in expectations and costs. The cost of moderation to the Conservatives is low, for in most ways the centre ground is like their preferred position, and the expectation of winning is fairly high. The more one expects, and is accustomed to win, the less the likelihood of risking a defeat, particularly where there is little cost attached to moderation. Such a calculus makes plausible the strategy of taking advantage of specially favourable situations to be immoderate.

On the other side, the cost of moderation for the Labour party is high—it means deserting a rather different ideological home for a consensus politics which is strange. In addition the expectation of success is low, hence only specially favourable situations are likely to make it seem worthwhile to be moderate. One might well also argue that the cost of losing an election is much higher for a Conservative than a Labour activist. If a Conservative government wins, the Labour activist is faced with a situation which may be detestable, but is familiar, is what one has come to expect, and indeed the shape of things to come from the unusual situation of a Labour government is vague and uncertain. When a Labour government is in office a Conservative activist is faced with the possibility of unprecedented and perhaps irreversible social change.

Obviously all this is highly inferential; one cannot prove that such a calculus has ever been, consciously or otherwise, in the minds of politicians. It is an explanation which fits the observed facts, which is relatively economical, and which is drawn from a theory which does more than any other to make comprehensible the activities of the parties. We would stress that the facts do need explanation—nothing in our normative theory of democracy is compatible with the demonstrated correlations between strategic conditions and ideological positions. It is an *ad hoc* explanation, in a way, but this appearance is valuable—it comes from refusing to try to force a simple Downsian model. We insist that it is not sensible to expect an explanation to work which assumes the essential similarity of the two parties, when they are historically not very similar.

What we have suggested as an explanation comes down, in the end, to assuming a difference in power balance inside the two parties, and most intelligent analysis of this question would seem to back up our beliefs.

In time the Labour party will, may already have come to be, a mature competitive party, as used to governing and as at home in the middle ground, as the Conservative party. When that happens, the parameters of competition will change, and a model more like the one we suggest in Chapter 2 will probably fit British politics better.

The other phenomena which we feel can best be explained by noting the maturity-emergence characteristic is the sensitivity of the parties to popular support measured on the one hand by percentage of the vote, and on the other by raw vote totals. This is a fundamentally ambiguous area: the results of an election, in themselves, cannot be a cause of the ideological position taken up before the election, yet we use them as the best (indeed the only) index of what popular feeling for the parties will have been before it. That the Labour party should be sensitive to the percentage of the vote cast is fully in keeping with any crude theory of party competition, for it had slowly to build itself up to a potential winning position, which is defined in percentage terms in a majority vote situation like a general election. The actual total of Labour votes matters little—it could only increase, particularly given the demographic advantage a working class based party has; the Conservative sensitivity to total vote is no more surprising however, as long as we remember its position as the dominant, and surviving, old party.

At no time this century has the Conservative vote deviated far from the 50% share, except marginally in 1974. Having been one of a two-party mature system competing against the Liberals, and thus getting approximately half of the votes, it sat confidently at this position while the share out of the other 50% was fought over between the Liberals and the Labour party. No party needs more than a majority, and the surplus votes that a party is expected to aim for in a vote maximising model are quite unnecessary, and probably costly, luxuries. The Conservative party's majoritarian position has never been challenged in the way the Liberal's was, and has never been a target, as it was for Labour.

The absolute number of votes gained is very important indeed though, for a dimunition of these means a loss from the solid traditional Conservative support which may never be replaced. As we have pointed out, the positions of the two parties are very different in this respect. The surviving party from the old regime stands only to lose, and need not build up, its loyal voting block, while the emerging party must seek to gain such a one, and one which will give it a majoritarian tradition.

The Conservatives have lost votes over the years—if the studies of the working class Conservatives, which show this as a diminishing group are anything to go by—and the Labour party has certainly increased not only its numbers, but its percentage of the vote (McKenzie, 1968). One good reason for treating electoral results as indicators of popular support standing prior to ideological commitments, rather than being the results of them is that it is impossible to produce a coherent account of how the latter has come about.

Impossible because the theory would have to explain why the Conservatives lose votes by becoming moderate, and the Labour party gains them by a similar move. No existing theory of spatial competition, or indeed of rational or irrational voting can do that. Surely we expect and believe that there is a causal phenomena there, and we do provide brief suggestive evidence, at the constituency level, in the appendix to Chapter 2 for this. It is not likely however to show in the crude and simple measures we have, while there is strong evidence for the phenomena and explanation we provide above, which helps further our contention that the party competition of the period 1924–1966 is that of a developing rather than a mature two party system. This thesis, coupled with the idea of governmental incrementalism seems to provide a satisfactory and interesting explanation of the data we provide on ideological change.

The next step, in Chapter 5 is to report similar, but more precise, data about constituency level electioneering.

CHAPTER 5

Ideological Competition at the Constituency Level

1. Theory and Introduction

So far we have discussed the evidence on party competition entirely in terms of central parties, political entities which manoeuvre in a dimensional framework before the electorate as a whole. This, of course, is not the actual experience of voters in many real situations, particularly in two party systems. What actually happens is that voters have only to choose a representative for their own constituency from a narrow list of candidates. The choice of government is indirect, not direct. As we have already suggested, and will develop further, this changes considerably the problems to be dealt with by a theory of party competition.

In this respect the deliberately simplified model of Downs' book may be dangerously simple, for institutional frameworks, though they may seem easily abstracted from, condition almost all aspects of the situation in politics. Not only the details of competitive behaviour, but all the descriptions of ideological space, and even the definition of rational voting may have to change when one transfers from a central-party–one constituency to a multi-candidate–multi-constituency scenario.

There are two good reasons for shifting the focus to the multi-candidate, multi-constituency level.

1. It is more important in Western European politics where we either do not elect national Presidents, or where they are not as strong *vis-à-vis* the legislative as in America. The differences in the systems are not trivial, particularly as the modifications necessary to convert Downs to a constituency level theory are also non-trivial.

2. One of the greatest difficulties many find in accepting a Downsian framework, strange though it may seem, is that his assumptions about politicians' behaviour and motivations, seem, apparently, unduly critical. What we require is some evidence that the men who go to make up a national party leadership are capable of manipulating ideologies for electoral ends. It is hard to show this from an analysis of the central party because such organisations tend to opacity in the gaze of the researcher. But one can look at these same

men in an arena where their responsibility for their political actions cannot be hived off, and where they are open to scrutiny, i.e., to their performances as individual candidates in their own constituencies.

If one can offer good evidence that candidates at the constituency level do 'act competitively', then it would seem no longer too hard to assume that in the role of collective leadership of a party they will also act the same way.

No connotation of political immorality is contained in the phrase 'competitive politics', nor is there any implication about the derivations of these policies. The grounds for decision on what sort of political noises to make in any election are not contained in the concept.

There is however a certain sense, or feeling, that the model of a politician is he who stands up and advocates what he believes to be right and just, regardless of the effect that saying this will have on his electoral fortune. It is this courageous (and foolhardy?) norm that is being referenced when politicians talk about their 'integrity'. It is an amusing thought that one seldom hears a politician talking about his integrity when he is on to a winner. Amusing, but beside the point. It is the opposite of this norm that we cover here with the idea of 'competitive' politics, for we use it to cover the action of deliberately moulding propaganda to suit the audience, of taking up a policy stand because it is more likely to win votes than any other available to that politician.

One can never strictly prove that this is done. The most that can be done is to show that variations in ideological position are such as to be compatible with that assumption. If the variations are also such as to be not obviously compatible with any 'integrity' interpretation, so much the better.

This enterprise will take up Section 2 of the chapter, where we shall discuss briefly some data from the 1955 election in Britain.

As an aim, however, it would be rather slim. The main aim of this chapter is to attempt an investigation of the conditions determining such competitive behaviour. This is where the modifications of Downs come in. Obviously if we grant that politicians behave competitively, then we are granting they perform rational, goal oriented behaviour, in a complex institutional setting. We are, in short, saying that here is a perfect setting for the development of a detailed theory of political action that has close analogies with the archetypal economic theory of the firm.

Such a theory, inevitably, will be based on a simplified model which will abstract from reality. But it need not be, indeed to be any use and to avoid indeterminism of predictions it cannot be, quite as simplified as the original Downsian model. That, after all, for all its heuristic value, does not in fact contain a complex model and 'logic' of competition, mainly because as it is set up there are no costs attached to competitive behaviour. It is only when one sets up a scheme of relative costs and conflicting goals that one requires a complex model. That the political world is one of conflicting goals and relative costs is obvious. Moreover we require complexity to our models because we are not in fact mainly interested in prediction, but in explaining. Prediction has a vital role, but more to evaluate theories which are primarily designed for explanation and understanding.

The theory of party competition at the constituency level, drawn from our earlier comments, which informs this chapter is as follows:

1. Elections take place simultaneously in different constituencies.

2. Constituencies differ in their class distributions, and therefore have differing vote maximising points.

3. The political parties each have a candidate in most of the constituencies.

4. Voters intend to elect governments rather than local delegates.

5. Therefore each candidate has to associate himself with a party.

6. This severely constrains his ideological mobility; there must not be so much variance between the stands of different candidates from one party as to call into doubt the homogeneity of the party.

7. However, it is from the local candidates, amongst other sources, that the local electorate get their information about the stand of the party. Thus the propaganda output of the candidates is important, and can affect the voting.

8. Political parties exist because of the need to let the electorate have a chance, even in a multi-constituency system, of selecting the government. They also exist because of the need for a body of political labourers to organise the vote.

9. A party consists then of at least three discernible groups:
   (a) The leadership, those who hope to be the government;
   (b) The candidates in the separate constituencies who hope to be elected personally to Parliament;
   (c) The mass membership, organised in the constituencies, who are needed by (a) and (b) to gain their own ends.

10. The (c) group cannot be accounted for in the way Downs accounts for the party leaders—they have nothing to gain by the election of a party or candidate *per se*, but only by the election of a party or candidate committed to certain policies.

11. There is therefore conflict between three groups over the position to be taken up by a candidate. Group (a) requires that the several candidates take up positions fairly near to whatever is the position likely to win the greatest number of constituency contests. If any candidate varies too much from this the electorate may not, as a whole, get the desired impression of what the party stands for, and thus diminish the chances of the party forming the next government.

Group (b) requires the right to set their own positions so as to maximise their chance of winning their own constituency election. These positions may not, however, coincide with the needs of group (a), because the image the electorate in any area gets of the party as a whole depends, at least in part, on the propaganda output of the individual candidates.

Group (c) requires that candidates take up positions which reflect a commitment to goals which are in the interests of group (c).

12. All of these influences on the position taken up are elastic, particularly that of group (c). For of course no activist is to be seen as a purist in ideology—they may be but may be quite selfish rational actors. Thus though an activist may have a preferred ideological position, he is not likely to give up

working for a candidate because of any slight deviation from this position. There is clearly a pay-off calculus here. The more the candidate differs from the activist the less will the activist find his work rewarded, and clearly there is a point beyond which he will not go out and canvass. But this calculus is affected by the probability of electoral success. If it is extremely likely that a candidate will not win unless he moves to a position away from the activist, then the activist will be more prone to allow this deviation. On the other hand, if the candidate has a good chance of winning from a position that pleases the activist, he is less likely to accept the need of the compromise.

13. One is thus led to expect that there will be some preferred ideological position on the part of the candidate, rather than the Downsian indifference to the ideological product on the part of parties. It will work according to the predicted ideological fortunes of the candidate. That is, it is precisely a 'preferred' rather than an inevitable, ideological preference. It is a position to be taken up when it can be afforded, not otherwise.

14. By this time it must be obvious that what we have said implies another change to the Downsian model. According to Downs, there ought not to be times when candidates can afford to be non-competitive. Being non-competitive means taking up political positions that are not best calculated to win elections. If one does this, then it is assumed one will lose the election, as one's opponents will have taken up the required position, and voters, taking note of the positions, will vote accordingly.

This flies in the face of one of the oddest phenomena in Western politics, that of safe seats, held election after election, by the same party, while others fluctuate each time. This is only accountable for with a theory that allows while voters change at each election, most of them will not change; the only constituencies likely to change hands in any election are those where the marginal changing voters number something like the majority at the last election. If all voters were equally likely to decide their vote on the ideological positions of the parties, all parties would be marginal in all constituencies. What one needs if the rational choice model is to fit certain facts of the real world is something to account for the fact that the number of voters liable to be influenced by positions (or anything else) is small in any constituency. Hence if most voters are not liable to change their minds from one election to the next, a constituency where one party has won a large majority in the past is one in which competitiveness is unnecessary for that party. Unnecessary here means that the number of votes likely to be lost by taking up a position of greater extremity than the vote maximising position will not be thought worth that ideological sacrifice given the propensity of the activists (and hence indirectly of the candidate) to prefer some positions to others.

It has always been the case that rational-calculating theories of politics do less well in explaining voter behaviour than the behaviour of political elites. The opponents of the school put it down to the theory's ignoring 'sociological' factors. This may be so, although when one tries to explain observed voter behaviour one usually can come up with explanations equally as plausible as sociological ones. The trouble is that both sorts of explanations are inherently untestable—explanatory paradigms become a matter of personal taste.

15. For what it may be worth there seems to be one assumption that accounts for this observed behaviour and which is in keeping with rational decision-making theory. It is to point out that the need to vote on candidates' present positions, promises, performances or whatever is very much dependent on one's own position on the spectrum. With Western politics being 'incremental' (which follows from the spirit of the Downsian model anyway), it is unlikely for most people that a choice of party at time t_0 will become irrational at any future time t_n because it would take a great shift towards them by their favourite party, or the appearance of a new party further towards their end of the spectrum for their rational vote to be different. More concretely, the Conservative party would have to change very much more drastically than is at all likely for it to become less good a bet for a retired colonel or less bad a bet for a retired coal miner. If they have decided at any previous time that they should vote for either the Conservative or Labour parties, most people are in fact safe in voting that way for the rest of their lives.

Now this is not to say that it matters to no-one what the parties are doing, and accordingly it is not to say that the whole theory of party ideological competition is useless. Rather it helps us to point out precisely who is likely to be influenced by their positions. The answers in detail can be left out here. Marginal voters, people on the edge of class or other groups, do need to take notice of detailed positions. There is no evidence at all in the cannons of political sociology that contradicts this prediction, and there may indeed be, in the work on affluent voters, evidence that supports this. We have touched on this earlier.

This points to the previous assumption that it may often be the case that competitive behaviour is unnecessary, and that candidates will then be free to (forced to?) take up more extreme positions to please their party workers.

The prediction of this model is that candidates' positions will be related to the previous or to the predicted voting strength in their constituencies. The safer they are, the more extreme they will be.

The model needs also to deal with the effects on one candidate of the other's position. It becomes important in this model in a way that it does not in the straightforward Downsian model because there one does not expect either party to make mistakes. Yet there is no other reason to expect a party to fail to take up the vote maximising position. As this model is constructed the vote of both candidates in a two-cornered contest depends on the relative voting strengths. In a safe Labour seat the Labour candidate should take up a relatively left wing position while the Conservative also moves leftwards into what is, for him, a moderate position. There is additionally the effect of the Labour position on the Conservative. Because the Labour candidate is predicted to be taking up a position more left than the vote maximising position he would take were he in danger of losing the seat, the Conservative has two choices. On the one hand he could avail himself of the lack of competition on the part of his opponent to be himself non-competitive, to retreat to a more extreme conservative position which is preferred by his activists. This, however, is unlikely, for by definition this chance will only happen in a constituency with a predicted large Labour majority, i.e., a constituency where non-competitiveness by a Conservative can only be a counsel of despair. Rather it seems likely that he would take the chance to gain extra votes by taking up a position to the left of that which would be possible for him were the Labour candidate to act competitively.

This remains to some extent a situation of theoretical ambiguity which can only be cleared up empirically, for it can be argued that competitiveness is two-edged, that activists will not be prepared to allow ideological impurity in a hopeless cause any more than in an inevitable one. What is predicted definitely by the theory is that under certain conditions there should be an effect on candidate position over and above that of the voting strength. The actual direction of the effect is non-determinate.

16. One final point that needs to be covered in this section is the problem of uncertainty inherent in this model. In the basic Downsian model uncertainty, though at times mentioned in connection with elite activities, is usually discussed in relation to the voters. Nonetheless the problem is important for analysis of candidate competition. Given that the positions they take up are directly related to the voting strengths of the parties in the constituencies, and indirectly to predictions about how the positions will be perceived by the voters, uncertainty is clearly important.

There are two sorts of predictable effects, only one of which is at all easy to check on. The one that we cannot deal with is uncertainty on the part of the candidates about what the best position is. One can predict that the more uncertain a candidate is about the right position the more vague or broad his own position will be, or, alternatively, the less he will try to commit himself to any position at all. This is not at all easy to test, mainly because we can never know how uncertain a candidate may be. The other sort of uncertainty is in the realm of vote prediction; here one is saying that parties may vary greatly over time about how sure they are of getting their own voters out, uncertain in other words about the size of the marginal electorate that may swing and lose or win the election, under the influence of party ideologies. The many conditions under which uncertainty may be high are too complex to analyse here; the situation is easier to look for and check however because it is rather more objective than the other form of uncertainty discussed above.

There are two cases where one can predict differences in uncertainty that we are able, with the data sets used here, to check. One is that it is safe to argue that the more complex the electoral situation the greater the uncertainty. By 'more complex' we mean the complexity of choice presented to the voter. To be precise, where there are more major parties contesting an election, one expects greater uncertainty. This follows from the nature of voting decisions; given only a choice between Labour and Conservative it is going to be safer for the voter to stick to a life-long vote than where he needs to choose between them and the Liberal party.

The second sort of uncertainty must also come under consideration if one thinks in terms of the maturity or age of an electoral environment. From the previous theory that most voters will be perfectly safe in keeping to an original voting choice that was rational and accurate follows the conclusion that the longer a particular set of party choices has been around, the greater the certainty for the voter, and hence the candidates. Thus for a time when one or more of the parties are young and newly arrived on the political scene, one predicts greater uncertainty than at a time, years later, when the young party is now well established and all parties have good reason, from past history, to expect a loyal vote group in any constituency.

The consequences to the parties of uncertainty are likely to be manifold, but at the least one expects competitiveness to be greater. Comparing two situations of differing uncertainty one would predict simply that there will be much greater evidence of candidates' positions being related to both the electoral situation and the opponents' positions in the situation of greater uncertainty.

It is plausible to expect this particularly to show in connection with the impact of one man's political stance on another's. To decide whether one's opponent has provided one with a chance, or a necessity, of taking up a better position, the general problem of taking notice of his effect on the voters, is not to be seen as quite as primary as calculating the safeness of the seat. The prediction then would be that in periods of high uncertainty the relationship between opponents' positions will be more evident than in less uncertain times, while the overall evidence of competitiveness will also be less strong in more certain situations.

We can finish this section then with four specific predictions.

Prediction 1: The position a candidate takes up will be correlated with his electoral strength in a constituency in such a way as to make him more extreme (further from his opponent's end of the spectrum) where his vote is high.

Prediction 2: A candidate's position will be correlated with his opponent's position in such a way that the candidates move in the same direction rather than in opposed directions. (This is in part a strong version; the weaker prediction is really only that there will be a correlation between opponents' positions over and above the effects of the voting on both of them.)

Prediction 3: In situations where there are three major parties campaigning there should be stronger correlations as indicated above than in two-cornered fights.

Prediction 4: In an election where one party is a newcomer, and the voting is less 'frozen' than in later periods, the evidence of competitiveness should be stronger than in later periods, especially with reference to the effects of one party position on another.

2. Some Evidence of Competition: 1955

We shall here consider an analysis of candidates' ideological positions in the election of 1955. Through this, and the analysis of the 1924 election given in Section 3, we hope to confirm the predictions just made.

Before such tests can be carried out we have to decide what is to count as evidence of competitive behaviour. A very simple operational definition presents itself. Inevitably candidate scores will vary; not only is there inherently a great deal of measurement error in the data gathering process, but candidates will, in any case, be bound to display non-significant (from a political viewpoint) differences.

What there should not be, however, is patterned variance, variance which is correlated significantly with the electoral fortunes of the candidate. Nor should the variance in candidates' performance be correlated with the performance of their opposite candidate. In fact no significant relation was found between the political stances of one candidate and his opponent. It is clear, however, that in the case of the Conservative candidates on three of the four, and of the Labour candidates on the fourth dimension, the extremeness of position is significantly related to the electoral strength of the candidates as measured by the votes they eventually gained in that election.

This is not a pattern which is compatible with the 'integrity' theory of propaganda. Whether it can be directly seen as evidence of competitive behaviour is not certain. As with any other observed phenomena it is capable of a certain set of explanations. One can only proceed by inference. However, any offered explanation that is to rival competitiveness has to be compatible with the fact of a relationship between voting strength and ideological position. For instance, one possible alternative is to argue that candidates do voice their own opinions in a perfectly 'sincere' way. To be acceptable this theory has to explain away the coincidence that candidates who are relatively extreme fight constituencies which are relatively safe. Even if a plausible explanation for this can be suggested the explanation might be rejected in favour of the competitive politics hypothesis on grounds of simplicity. It requires an extra set of premises to explain what is then taken as the independent variable to explain ideological positions, while the competitiveness model does not require such extra assumptions.

Again one would be able to argue that candidates please their constituency parties, or are chosen by them to please them. This requires the argument that there is good reason to expect that the extremeness of constituency parties is related to the safeness of seats itself. Why should this be so?

It would be senseless to deny the highly inferential nature of the data used here. Not only is one measure, the election address, used as an indicator of a whole stream of political output by the candidates, but it has the disadvantage of being the starting shot of the campaign. Interaction between candidates as they respond to each other's propaganda initiatives cannot be trapped by this measure—for that one would need (what would be very interesting), a dynamic stimulus response model of the whole of a campaign. Secondly, the independent variable here, the voting, is used to indicate underlying trends that are supposed to have been apparent to the candidates before the actual voting. One way round this might have been to use the results from the past election, but as this was not only four years prior, but also the rather odd election of 1951, there was little point in so doing. Where this was possible, in examining the election of 1924, we have done so.

This election was chosen for several reasons. First that it would be regarded by a large majority of political commentators and historians as the first of the high consensus modern elections. It thus provides an opportunity to investigate party competition at a time which is fairly representative of modern conditions without, however, the complicating factor that would appear in 1964, of the Labour party suffering from the 'thirteen wasted years' out of office. It still represents a time when there were clear and easily perceived differences between the parties in some respects.

Two problems immediately appeared. One, how to rank the candidates on ideological dimensions, and second, what these dimensions were to be. These problems occurred in Chapter 4, where we desired to rank parties at different time points on such directions. The same solution was used, namely a Factor Analysis, which can derive entirely objective dimensions from a series of observations on entities. This still left the problem of how data on a candidate's position is to be found. As indicated earlier, this was done by a content analysis of the election address issued by all candidates. For this study a sample of fifty constituencies was drawn from the total list of constituencies in England, Wales and Scotland. A coding list of all the important issues discussed was derived, and the election address of each candidate from the Conservative and Labour parties was coded from this list.

'Coding' in this context means simply counting the number of times an issue was mentioned in the text of the address. Sentences were used as the basic counting unit on the grounds that they are a natural unit. Though Content Analysts have spent much effort and time on deriving other counting units, the only one which seems to vie with sentences is the word. This is unsatisfactory as it needs to be put into the framework of sentences or paragraphs before it can be coded. In some cases, for instance a category dealing with Nuclear Deterrents (number nine), the code can be positive or negative, indicating support for or opposition to, that position. For the sake of convenience in such cases the position espoused by the Labour party is always coded $(+)$, and that of the Conservatives is coded $(-)$.

In order to produce as exhaustive and as reliable a set of codings as possible it was found necessary to have a rather long list of coding categories (there are thirty-one in all) even though this meant many of them were little used. It is worth stating here that we are fully aware of the crudeness of this data, and of the amount of purely random statistical 'noise' thus generated. This shows up, of course, in the subsequent analysis—the factor solutions are not neat, the relationships tested are not strong. This however does not mitigate against the validity of the conclusions—rather, the mere fact that any meaningful results show through the mess of this data is remarkable. We would be justified in claiming that the real world relationships between these variables are probably rather stronger than the ones that show through our murky measuring instrument.

At this stage we should state precisely what we take the scores of candidates on those categories to be, and what they are used as indicators for.

It is obvious what they are. The list of sources of each candidate on each coding category (henceforth 'variable') when adjusted for relative verbosity produces a matrix 99 (the number of candidates) by 31 (the number of variables). Reading along a row one gets the relative emphasis placed by one candidate on each political issue. Reading down the columns one gets the relative importance to each candidate of one particular issue. What is measured is the stress placed on issues or policies by different men. Because some of the symbols are coded both positive and negative, there can be a contrast where a man stressed two issues equally, one to which he is opposed and one which he favours. One can treat the scores on each variable then in much the same way one would treat survey responses to questions in which someone is asked to react to a statement on a Likert scale—unfavourable responses ranging from, say, -7 to favourable responses going up to $+7$. All we need to remember is that it is relative emphasis that we are measuring.

It is inevitable that we must concentrate on emphasis—not the result of the research instrument. A deliberate choice was made to take account of two factors in the political scene during electoral campaigns.

The first factor is that all candidates very largely reiterate the official party manifesto, but they do this selectively, suppressing some aspects and stressing others. It is here that differences between candidates come out. None of them invent or espouse policies different from others. They do attach different relative weights to various problems. To the extent that party competition, indeed policy making generally, consists in identifying problems and ranking them in urgency, rather than the technical question of finding solutions, this is inevitable.

The second major reason for dealing with relative emphasis is that electoral propaganda and campaigning does not consist in mutual debate and the clash of closely argued positions. It consists rather in constant repetition of simple points, points that slide past one's opponent's points. A candidate does not present to his constituents a technical discourse on how his party will go about doing X. Rather he reiterates the fact that his party has, or will, do X, Y and Z. As each party has to claim they will do a great many things and, in modern British politics at any rate, many of them are of sharply different appeal to various sectors of society, emphasis on issues becomes the medium for competition. The evidence for which we must search in order to test the extent to which candidates do 'compete' is this relative emphasis.

This has a particular relevance to the Factor Analysis undertaken here. In our case the data are measures of emphasis. To say, for instance, that variables 1 and 5 are highly correlated is to say that when a candidate stresses variable one, he is also likely to stress variable 5. Thus the factors extracted will also deal with emphasis. If the first factor was to contrast, say, policies on welfare and education with policies on foreign affairs and military expenditure, it would not be correct to say that a man who scores high on that dimension preferred welfare to foreign affairs, but rather that he stressed issues of welfare to his constituents and neglected issues of foreign affairs. There are here two possible explanations: one that he thought his constituents would be uninterested in foreign affairs and the other that he thought they would dislike his foreign affairs policies but might like his welfare policies. These two explanations can be disentangled, which is as well, or the former explanation would not be evidence for competitiveness. In fact we invented that example and the situation is not ambiguous in this way. It was necessary however to demonstrate precisely what sort of data we are really dealing with. In practice we need to keep in mind that, unlike some studies, this does not concentrate on 'issue' at the expense of policy. What the data is, in fact, is the stressing of a certain policy for a certain issue (for the policy is predetermined by the central party) over another policy for another issue. The situation is one in which a Conservative in a safe seat stresses in his address the Conservative policy of 'free enterprise' as a solution to long term problems of the economy and hardly mentions short term policies of budgetary control for full employment. Or a Labour candidate in a marginal seat makes almost no mention of nationalisation in his desperation to talk about the problems of the unfair budget.

We shall, briefly, describe the factor analysis solutions. One must bear in mind that our interest is not in the nature of the particular dimensions extracted so much as in the scores of the individuals on those objective factors. The factors themselves represent nothing more than numerical relationships between the variables. If they are easily interpretable, so much the better. But if not, and if the scores of the individuals on them display a significant pattern, significant both statistically and in terms of the theory under which we are operating, then the incomprehensibility of the factors themselves does not very much matter.

Because of the essentially 'soggy' nature of the data used, the factor analysis did not produce a classic solution in terms of a very few factors accounting for a very high percentage of the total variance. This is partly the result of a methodological decision not to use the various rotation techniques available to simplify the solution. Strictly speaking no factor analysis was carried, as the only analysis was a Principal Components Analysis. Had we been primarily concerned to produce a neat factor analysis we might have rotated at least for an orthogonal solution. The Principal Components Analysis produces as its first, and most important component, a general one on which many of the variables score highly. This fits our analysis. Intuitively, even if we abandon a simple one-dimensional model of political competition, we think in terms of one basic and crude left–right dimension and one or more secondary dimensions cutting this. These deal with issues that, though important, and not reducible to left–right, are not as near the heart of political analysis, either because they are temporary, or culturally relative. For instance a clericalism dimension, cross cutting the basic left–right dimension, is used by nearly all commentators on French politics. In part it is our decision to see politics in primarily one dimensional terms. In the terms of this analysis it is a decision to produce a basic dimension which simply produces a contrast between Labour and Conservative candidates. The weighting of those variables that reach significance on the first component is given below, using a weighting of $+ \cdot 300$ as significance level. This, though in the end arbitrary, is suggested in most texts. See, for instance, Childs (1970).

Table 23. Dimension No. 1

Variable No.	Loading	Description of Variable
10	$- \cdot 443$	Conservative peace proposals $(-)$ v. Labour peace proposals $(+)$
15	$- \cdot 491$	Socialist economic policy $(+)$ (inc. Controls) v. Free enterprise $(-)$
17	$- \cdot 343$	Prosperity as a value $(-)$ v. Stress on artificiality of Conservative record on prosperity
19	$- \cdot 512$	Stress on fair Tory low tax budget $(-)$ v. Stress on need to use budget for income distribution

In all these tables, a negative variable score is a Conservative one.

All the variables that reach significance on this dimension are amongst those which were coded positively and negatively to identify different positions on the issues. The dimension is clearly a general one of Conservative policy versus Labour policy in the two areas of prime concern in the fifties, foreign policy and economic policy. The picture may become clearer if we calculate what would be necessary for someone to get a very high positive or negative score on this dimension. He would have had to stress the relevant side on each of four issues more or less equally and at the expense of most of the other categories coded. The only unifying theme we need to notice here is that the dimension extracts all the variance which is common to all these policies; it is simply, but usefully, a dimension of 'partyness'. In the same way the first dimension extracted from data which represents children's performances on a battery of different skill tests is one of ability to do different skill tests, i.e., I.Q.

This second dimension is one which represents a conflict stressing immediate economic manipulation through the budget versus the long term debate over the essential nature of the economy. This is represented by the difference in signs between the highest scoring item, No. 19 'The Budget' at $- \cdot 721$ and the cluster of positively loaded items, only one of which reaches significance, No. 15 'The Socialist v. Free enterprise economy' and the related issues of control

Table 24. Dimension No. 2

Variable No.	Weight	Description of Variable
3	+255	Control over monopolies
15	+477	Socialist economy v. Free enterprise
16	+226	Price stability
19	−721	Low tax budget v. Income redistribution
31	+254	Internal democracy and evolution of power

of monopolies and the degree of internal democracy and devolution of power. A Tory with a high positive score would stress the budget item (his budget category scores would be coded negative, and as this item is weighted negatively the resulting multiplication would give a positive score) and would play down the problem of free enterprise.

Table 25. Dimension No. 3

Variable No.	Weight	Description of Variable
8	−·342	Agricultural policy (Two codes [+] and [−])
10	−·490	Peace policy (Two codes [+] and [−])
15	+·631	Socialist economy v. Free enterprise
19	+·214	Budget

Here again we get a split dimension, contrasting stress on long term economic policy versus, in this case, almost anything, but in particular agricultural and general foreign policy. In fact the only other variable to begin to appear significant, though, at +·214, it does not score highly at all, is the other ingredient of economic policy. The dimension reflects basic policy emphasis differences. Here for instance a Labour candidate whose address stressed nationalisation and perhaps income distribution would end up with a high positive score, and one who stressed foreign policy would end up with a high negative score.

It is necessary to bear in mind that because of the positive and negative codings of the categories, a similar score for a Conservative and a Labour candidate may not indicate a similar position. For instance, while as above the Labour candidate who kept off economics ended up with a negative score, it is the Conservative who does stress this issue who scores low or negative. Attention will be drawn to this point later in the analysis.

The final dimension requires no careful interpretation at all: it is weighted by only one variable, No. 9, $+\cdot831$, which is that covering policy towards an independent nuclear deterrent. To lay stress on their necessity is to get a negative score, to stress their undesirability is to get a positive score.

We have extracted only four dimensions, accounting for not quite 60% of the common variance. There are, of course, several more dimensions, but in no case does the latent root reach $1\cdot00$, and thus by Kaiser's criterion they are not to be considered significant. Again, were the primary aim to describe a factor solution we would extend the number of dimensions discussed. But here we are concerned only to set up a simple multi-dimensional model of party competition, and four dimensions are enough in which to do this. We shall now proceed to analyse the factor scores of the candidates on these four dimensions.

The factor scores are used here to examine the hypothesis that candidates moderate their propaganda output, as exemplified in their election addresses, according to the strategic position in which they find themselves. First let us look briefly at Figure 26. This is a map of the positions (in the space described by the first two dimensions) of all the candidates. What we would like to do at this stage is draw attention to four of the positions on this map, to attempt to give confidence, in the most journalistic and intuitive of ways, to anyone who is inclined to assume that this map, and the analysis of the data on which it is based, cannot have much bearing on the interpretation of politics. Let us point out that candidate No. 78, who takes up the most 'right wing' position on the map, is Mr. Enoch Powell, whose inclusion in this random sample of 50 Tory candidates is quite fortuitous. Follow this by noticing that No. 21, the most 'left wing' position (taking a two dimensional view) is that of Mr. Anthony Wedgwood-Benn, a man whose public pronouncements, if not his actions, have always tended to stress the populist-democratic extreme of Labour party politics.

The other two points are relevant because of the constituency the candidates come from. Are we not pleased to have our innate suspicions confirmed in that No. 59, the most right wing of Labour positions, is held by the candidate in Plymouth Sutton, won easily for the Conservatives by J. J. Astor, and that No. 94, the most left of the Conservative positions, is that of the unfortunate Conservative candidate in Battley and Morley?

To test the hypothesis that a candidate's position on a dimension was related either to (i) the position that the opposing candidate took up on that dimension, or (ii) the character of the constituency, and in particular the *a priori* chance, on the basis of past electoral history, of his winning the constituency election, a series of distributions were worked out.

It was immediately clear that hypothesis (i) would not wash. When the average score of candidates whose opponents had high, moderate or low positions on a particular dimension were calculated, it was found that these average scores did not differ significantly. Nor was it the case that a persistent pattern, which failed to reach statistical significance but which was of itself

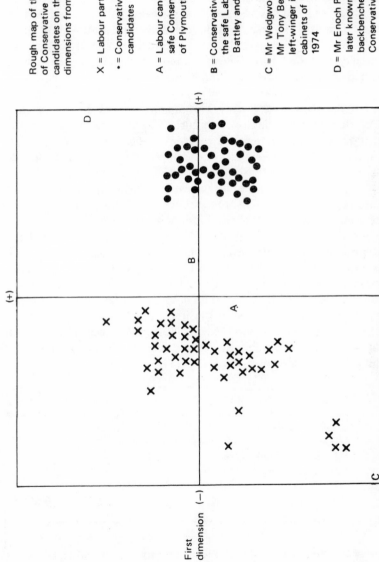

Rough map of the distribution of Conservative and Labour candidates on the first two dimensions from the 1955 election.

X = Labour party candidates

• = Conservative party candidates

A = Labour candidate in the safe Conservative seat of Plymouth Sutton

B = Conservative candidate in the safe Labour seat of Battley and Morley

C = Mr Wedgwood-Benn, later as Mr Tony Benn, to be a noted left-winger in the Labour cabinets of 1964/70 and 1974

D = Mr Enoch Powell, then and later known as a right-wing backbencher in the Conservative party

Figure 26

suggestive, turned up. There was no sign of a correlation between one man's position and his opponent's.

The picture as regards hypothesis (ii) is different, however, and is complicated. Hypothesis two, let us repeat, is the one which says that a candidate's position will be related to the safety or impossibility of the seat from his party's standpoint. It is, of course, the thesis that is indicated as preferable on theoretical grounds in the first part of this chapter.

The data here can be summarised most easily in a series of tables, one for each dimension. The candidates for each party were divided, according to their scores on each dimension in turn, into three groups. The groups were those whose scores were in the top third, the middle third and the bottom third, for the distribution on that dimension. The mean majority gained by each of these groups was then calculated, and the differences between these majorities was tested for significance.

Exactly what the theory we are working under predicts differs for each dimension, of course, depending on its nature. The basic pattern is that the average position for each dimension which is the more extreme, i.e., is calculated to appeal least to the voters of the opposite party, should coincide with the average majority most favourable to the party in question.

Secondly this pattern ought not to be consistent for each party, because we have quite strong theoretical grounds to assume that either the possibility or the need for competitive behaviour will differ across the dimensions for each party.

It is worth pointing out that we have taken, in judging the significance of the following tables, a relatively cavalier approach to statistical significance tables. By which we mean two things. One is that we have not restricted discussion to results technically significant because we do not believe that arbitrary calculations of the probability of an event occurring in vacuum should govern what we find of interest in a table of numbers. More importantly, perhaps, we have on some occasions used the 10% significance level, even though it is so commonly assumed that nothing greater than the 5% level is relevant.

Table 26. Analysis of Positions on 1st Dimension

	Conservative Candidates			Labour Candidates		
	High Scores	Medium Scores	Low Scores	High Scores	Medium Scores	Low Scores
Mean Majorities	+14·11	+2·62	+1·76	−7·59	−9·06	−6·68

In the case of this dimension, where no Conservative or Labour candidate is to be found on the opposing party's side of the zero point, we have taken absolute scores—thus 'High Score' for the Conservative party in fact means a high positive score, and for a Labour candidate means a high negative score. 'High' means 'extreme in the party's own direction'. The interpretation of this table is very clear. For the most extreme third of the Conservative party the average majority indicates a very safe Conservative seat, with a Conservative majority of 14·11% of the vote. The majority decreases as the group gets less extreme, so that the third of the Conservatives with the lower (more moderate or 'left wing') positions have only very low majorities, with a mean of 1·76% of the vote, indicating that the most moderate Tories come from the least safe seats. (Many of them of course come from seats Labour actually won in that election.) In the case of the Labour party, however, the differences in means of majorities are very small, quite random (the medium score majority is higher than either extreme) and not significant at any published level, or by pattern. This dimension is, of course, the one of general policy opposition. The table suggests that, in very general policy terms, the Conservative candidates adjusted the stress they put on Tory plans for Free enterprise, Low tax budgets, and indeed their own peace proposals and their pride in achieving national prosperity. If fighting in seats where prosperity was a stranger, where national-isation was not feared, and where no one much had benefited from the budget, they were distinctly 'moderate'. The difference between the mean majority of High Conservative scores and Low Conservative scores is significant at the 5% level with degrees of freedom of 1 and 33, where the F ratio comes to 4·24 against a necessary level of 4·13. As I have said, no such assertion about Labour candidates' behaviour on this dimension can be made.

Table 27. Analysis of positions on 2nd Dimension

	Conservative Candidates			Labour Candidates		
	High Scores	Medium Scores	Low Scores	High Scores	Medium Scores	Low Scores
Mean Majorities	+14·92	+5·31	−1·69	−10·78	−1·30	−7·31·

For this and subsequent tables scores are not taken as absolute figures.

Here again one gets, for the Conservative party, a situation where one end of the spectrum, the positive end, is associated with safe seats, and the other with seats where in fact the average majority is a Labour party majority. This translates as saying that the stress to the Low tax budget, which is to get a high score for a Conservative, is probably something one only does if fighting a pretty safe seat (mean majority of high scores is +14·92). As the score decreases so the majority decreases, leaving people with low scores (those who in the context of 1955 discussed a controlled economy chiefly in terms of the horrors of war-time regulations and rationing rather than boasting of the Conservative budgetary fairness and incentives) in seats where victory is very much less safe. In this case all the differences between the groups' average majorities are significant at the 10% level (*df* 2, 48, *F* = 3·32) and the difference between the two extreme groups, high scores and low scores, is significant at the $2\frac{1}{2}$% level (*df* 1, 32, *F* = 5·79).

Again the differences between the Labour groups are not significant even at the 10% level, and there is in any case no obvious interpretation for a case in which both high scores, displaying stress on Nationalisation and low scores, stressing budgetary redistribution, occur in pretty well unwinnable seats, while only a medium position shows any difference, there being only a small adverse majority. One could argue that in neither case, of high scores stressing Nationalisation, nor low scores stressing income redistribution, could the Labour candidates try to be competitive, and only by talking about neither and stressing something else could they hope to compete with the opponent. But this cannot account for this medium position being in seats where they have little to fear—rather it should be the medium position that the worse adverse majorities are to be found, as a reflection of the Conservative case of clearly competitive behaviour.

Something like this explanation however appears to be the case for dimension No. 3.

Table 28. Analysis of Positions on 3rd Dimension

	Conservative Candidates			Labour Candidates		
	High Scores	Medium Scores	Low Scores	High Scores	Medium Scores	Low Scores
Mean Majorities	−·34	+10·7	+6·3	−3·2	−2·8	−13·5

There we have a reverse of the case in the first two dimensions. High and medium scores by Labour candidates come from the groups fighting relatively easily winnable seats, while low scores are disproportionately found amongst those fighting hopelessly Conservative seats (where the mean Conservative majority is 13·5%). A low score for a Labour candidate on this dimension involves stressing Agricultural and Foreign affairs issues and making relatively little mention of economic issues at all. To stress the question of economic policy, particularly Nationalisation, is a propaganda position found only amongst those whose seats are, on average, more winnable. (Conservative majorities of 3·2 and 2·8%.) The difference between the smallest mean and the largest is significant to the 10% level (*df* 1, 32, *F* = 3·95). In this case there is no significant difference between any of the three Conservative groups. There is nonetheless a clear pattern of competition, parallel to the Labour case. Here a high score for a Conservative, which involves keeping off economic problems altogether, is to be found amongst the group which has the least safe majority (indeed an average Labour party majority of ·34%). The mean majorities do not show a linear trend, but one can hardly ignore this fact which seems to speak very clearly of competitive behaviour. As with the other two dimensions one can almost see the rule of thumb, 'When in a working class constituency a Tory ought never to mention Economics', directly reflecting the apparent wariness of economic issues amongst Labour candidates in safe Tory seats.

The last dimension is one peculiar to the fifties, but so important then that one would be suspicious had it not appeared. It is, of course, the one characterised solely by the variable dealing with the nuclear deterrent. This was coded both positively and negatively according to whether one had reservations about it, even including believing in unilateral disarmament, or whether one regarded it as vital to national defence and prestige.

Table 29. Analysis of Positions on 4th Dimension

	Conservative Candidates			Labour Candidates		
	High Scores	Medium Scores	Low Scores	High Scores	Medium Scores	Low Scores
Mean Majorities	+3·52	+4·29	+6·7	−1·2	−3·8	−15·58

This for Labour is the equivalent of the first dimension for the Conservatives; they are clearly acting in a definite (and statistically significant) manner, while their opponents scatter their scores at random over the constituencies. High scores, which for Labour candidates indicate propaganda intended to question the need for the bomb, are found amongst the group who have the lowest average Conservative majorities, and this increases linearly to the group with the lowest (least anti-bomb) scores who are to be found in the most heavily Conservative seats. The difference here between the smallest and largest mean majorities for the Labour groups are significant at the $2\frac{1}{2}$% level (df 1, 31, $F = 5\cdot90$). The Conservatives on the other hand display no differences which are significant at any level, although there is a linear trend in the right direction, that is for highest scores in the least safe seats to lowest scores in the most safe.

The overall result of the tests on these four dimensions is encouraging for the theory outlined in this study. Both parties do behave with what seems to be competitive electoral tactics: the Conservatives clearly behave competitively on dimensions 1 and 2, and show some sign of so doing on dimension No. 3. Labour shows no sign of behaving competitively on the first two dimensions but clearly does so on the latter two.

To summarise:

1. That Conservatives will, on the general policy dimension, take up positions, the extremism of which depends on the safety of their seats.

2. That they will avoid talking about such issues as their budgetary policy in working class constituencies and to some extent

3. Will avoid discussing economic policies altogether in these areas.

1. That the Labour party will avoid talking about economic issues in middle class constituencies; and

2. Will take up anti nuclear deterrent positions only in constituencies they are pretty sure to win.

The two points to be stressed here are

1. General evidence for competitive behaviour

2. The selection of dimensions

Thus it can be argued that as dimension No. 2 contrasts long-term with short-term economic policies the Labour party is unable to be competitive. Neither can be attractive to the well off, while the Conservative party can at least hope to direct attention to the long term results of Free enterprise which need not be unattractive to a Labour voter, while long term Nationalisation policies will be disliked by the middle class. Had a welfare policy dimension emerged from this analysis (as it did from an earlier experimental one) one might have found again Conservative competitive behaviour and Labour party stasis, on this occasion because Labour had no need to compete. (This is in fact what the earlier policy dimension analysis showed.) It is then possible to see some dimensions 'owned' by a party as the other one cannot hope to be effective, or 'owned' in the sense that party A can do what it likes because it will be trusted on this issue while the other party is forced to try and compete by dropping its preferred position in unsafe seats. Thus on dimension No. 4 the Conservatives have no need to be competitive as no one is going to lose his seat, in 1955, by being pro-bomb. There is indeed no pattern of significant or obvious behaviour here for the Conservatives, this being the only dimension on which this is entirely true. The Labour party on the other hand is not able to take up anti-bomb positions except in safe seats.

We shall stop considering these general positions now until we have discussed the situation of 1924 when the analysis is enriched, and complicated, by the appearance of third Party candidates.

3. The Election of 1924

We shall not bother describing again the methodology of this piece of analysis, as the content analysis and principal components analyses are substantially the same as in Section 2. The important difference in this section as far as methodology is concerned comes in the use of the principal components. Though one does not want to assume in a facile way a unidimensional universe, it is useful to be able to talk of the overall position a candidate takes up in a constituency, rather than being restricted to making separate points about each of the dimensions. The justification and explanation of such a model was covered in Chapter 3. If one is at all concerned to compare the effects of each of three parties on each other, and of the electoral situation on each, it becomes necessary to have a summary measure of extremism which aggregates all of the dimensions that may have been present at the election.

To achieve this we use in this section not the separate component scores of the candidates, but a single measure, the distance of a candidate from the origin in the space of all the components. This is like the LMOD and CMOD measures in Chapter 4. As the components of a principal components solution are orthogonal there is no difficulty at all in calculating this as a Euclidean distance.

The additional advantage of this is that we waste no information about inter-candidate distances; the principal components solution, carried out on a data matrix of over thirty variables (the symbol counts—this big a list being needed to get anywhere near an exhaustive coding) and 124 observations did not yield a clear and small dimensional solution. Were we to restrict ourselves to the components that are easily interpretable we would be throwing away a great deal of information. As long as there is some way of interpreting the summary measure, we can, by using it, incorporate the information from all the components. The interpretation, or rather the certainty that the distance from the origin is a good summary of the various dimensional distances, is faciliated by the fact that it acts as a Conservative versus a Labour measure, with the Liberals scattered all over it.

This feature is due to the way that on all of the separate dimensions the mean Conservative position is lower (nearer the origin) than the mean Labour position. Necessarily this is mirrored in the total space distance from the origin. Thus from this summary measure an observed move by a Conservative candidate away from the origin can be taken as a move towards the Labour overall position, hence a move towards moderation. A similar move by a Labour candidate would be a move away from the overall Conservative position and thus a move away from moderation. The converse holds, that moves towards the origin are moves towards moderation for Labour and away from it by a Conservative. The Liberals are distributed all over the range, and the actual range of the Liberal positions is much larger than that of either other party. We thus conveniently have a measure of overall 'Toryness' or 'Labourness' for all of the parties, which allows us to compare the various effects easily.

There are four categories of seats included in this sample of fifty constituencies:

1. Three cornered fights, where all major parties stood.
2. Conservative/Labour fights.
3. & 4. A few seats which were either Conservative/Liberal or Labour/Liberal fights.

Most of the analysis is carried out on group 1, the most interesting, with certain comparisons made to group 2. There are so few constituencies in groups 3 and 4 that little can be said about them, though the pattern into which they fall is certainly entirely consistent with any expectations one might draw from a theory of party competition.

While we shall not discuss in any detail at all the distribution of candidates on the individual dimensions, it is just worth describing these distributions in a cursory way for the first two dimensions. These two, which can be interpreted as, respectively, a general left–right dimension, accounting for about 20% of

158

the variance, and a cross-cutting one accounting for roughly another 10% have an interesting feature. The first dimension clearly distinguishes Conservative and Liberal candidates, while the second one, apparently (from looking at the variable loadings) having to do with financial and trade policies, distinguishes the Liberal candidates from both of the others. The dimension is generally loaded by variables on which the Liberal candidates have a high score. This perhaps gives some sense to the way in which a third party can be 'in the middle' of any left–right spectrum on which we conversationally distinguish politicians.

Figure 27 gives a rough representation of the way in which these groups lie in the two-space represented by the first two components.

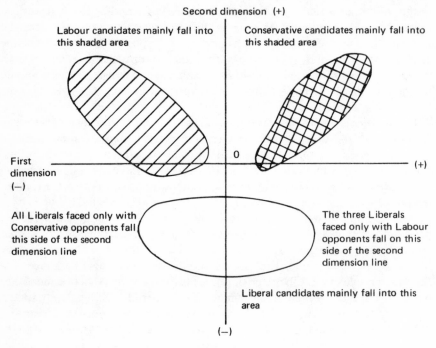

Figure 27

One point here that can be made about the Liberal candidates in two-party constituencies is that, of the seven, they are all distributed in a way clearly consistent with a competitive hypothesis. Three of the seven are in constituencies where their opponents were Labour candidates. All of these three took up positions on the right hand, that is, the Conservative, side of the first dimension. Two of them indeed took up positions indistinguishable from those of Conservative candidates, falling within the cross-hatched ellipse in Figure 27. The other four, faced with Conservative opponents and no Labour rival, took up positions on the left hand (negative, Labour party) side of the first dimension. Clearly nothing can be said with statistical significance from this finding on a total of seven candidates, but it still leads us to suspect that on the whole Liberal candidates do take up positions such as to capitalise the absence of any major party candidate.

As can be seen from the diagram, there is a correlation between the first and second dimension position of both Conservative and Labour candidates; these are respectively $+\cdot622$ and $-\cdot680$, i.e., a Labour candidate who takes up an extreme position as regards the Conservatives on dimension 1 will also take up a position extreme as regards the Liberals on dimension 2. The equivalent is true of the Conservatives, and we thus have evidence of a relationship between ideological positions on two dimensions, despite the fact that, the dimensions being orthogonal, there can be no overall correlation between the positions of candidates on any two components. Two other correlations worth noting here are these: there is a correlation between Labour and Conservative positions on dimension 1, and between Liberal positions on this first dimension and the voting in the constituency. The correlation between Labour and Conservative positions is $+\cdot447$; high positive (extreme) positions for Conservatives are matched by relatively high positions for Labour and vice versa. This is what one is led to expect from the model outlined earlier—where one candidate moves towards his own end of the spectrum, away, presumably, from the vote maximising point, the opposition moves that way as well to grasp the chance of votes of which he would otherwise be deprived.

The other correlation is in keeping with, and strengthens, the impression given by the positioning of the seven Liberal candidates in two-cornered fights. The Liberal position on the first dimension is correlated $-\cdot408$ with the Labour party vote—where the Labour candidate is doing well, the Liberal takes a relatively Labour-like position on the main left–right dimension. There is a smaller and not quite significant correlation of $+\cdot360$ between the Liberal's own vote and the Liberal position on this dimension. The obvious question to ask is where one expects a Liberal to go, on a dimension which basically contrasts Labour and Conservative, when Liberals are doing well. Though a strictly *post hoc* point, one would expect that a Liberal in 1924 would, in preference, take up a position to the right of the Labour party, which conforms with this correlation. What is interesting, and will be clearly shown soon when we look at the three-cornered fights, is that the Conservative voting strength, and for that matter the Conservative positions, have much less effect on the Liberal candidates than do the Labour votes and positions.

The data from this two-space distribution are in no way overwhelming or conclusive, but they do impressionistically point to the predictions made in the model. That the positions of Liberal candidates are clearly related to the electoral situation, and that the Labour and Conservative positions themselves are correlated are both predicted earlier.

We can now turn to the examination of the two major sorts of constituencies, three-cornered and two-cornered Labour/Conservative fights, using the summary measure presented by the calculation of Euclidean distance from the origin in the space of all the components.

We can most usefully start by comparing two intercorrelation matrixes, for the two sorts of constituencies. These are given below in Tables 30 and 31. It is quite clear from them that while there appear to be significant relationships between the variables in the second table, representing three-cornered fights, none of these hold up in the Labour/Conservative straight fights. None of the relationships in Table 30 are significant at the ·05% level, and only the two underlined are significant even at the ·10% level.

Table 30. Intercorrelations in Labour/Conservative Straight Fights

	1	2
1. Labour Position		
2. Conservative Position	·13	
3. Labour Vote	·25	·39
4. Conservative Vote	−·23	−·39

That is, the Conservative position is correlated with their electoral strength—as the Labour vote increases, the Conservative score increases. Remember that a high score is moderate for the Conservatives, extreme for Labour. The same tendency, to moderation where the opponent does well, is shown in the signs of the Labour position/vote correlation, but less strongly.

Table 31. Intercorrelations in Three-Cornered Fights

	1	2	3	4	5
1. Labour Positions					
2. Conservative Positions	·56				
3. Labour Vote	·54	·49			
4. Conservative Vote	−·31	−·58	−·60		
5. Liberal Positions	·56	·40	·27	−·10	
6. Liberal Vote	−·23	·03	−·53	−·35	−·18

All the correlations in Table 31 are significant (at the ·05% level) except for those underlined, which are not significant at any acceptable level. The one exception is the correlation between the Conservative vote and the Liberal vote, which is, here, only significant at the ·10% level. This is irrelevant as it is not conceivable that there was no such relationship, though it does suggest, as do the candidate position patterns, that neither of the old parties was as much affected by each other as by the new challenger.

In comparison with Table 30 one can see that there is, as predicted earlier, a considerably more marked degree of competitive behaviour in the three-cornered fights. There the degree of uncertainty which candidates must feel in deciding their policy statements is greater.

The more interesting comparison between the tables is over correlation between Conservative and Labour positions; the r of $\cdot 13$ is very low indeed from Table 30 compared with the r of $\cdot 56$, easily significant, in Table 31. It was our prediction that relations between positions, rather than between voting strengths, would vanish with lesser degrees of uncertainty. This is borne out by this comparison, as it is by the fact that the 1955 data, also from a situation of greater certainty, shows no relationship between positions, despite a definite relationship between positions and votes.

The matrix in Table 31 presents a more complex situation, of which we have many questions to ask. What the exact strategic connections between each of three parties in the multi member constituency should be is not something that the model can predict; that they will not be all the same would be anyone's guess, as Table 31 would indeed support. The connections between Labour and Liberal, and Labour and Conservative, both in terms of voting and of mutual effect of positions, are stronger than the relations between the two older parties. These need to be looked at in more detail, as do the relative importances of votes versus positions as determinants of each particular party position. As yet the predictions of Section 1 cannot be said to be confirmed, because they call for us to be able to show an effect of positions over and above the effect of the votes. From Table 31, with no evidence of the results that partials might produce, we cannot answer this.

What is called for here is some form of path analysis, or at least regression equations by which we can measure relative importance of influences controlling for others.

Here we come into a problem that has not yet been satisfactorily resolved in the path analysis literature. Most models in the literature that we know how to deal with, and which can be both easily calculated, and given some substantive sense, are recursive models. That is, they all assume unidirectional causation with no feedback chains. They require, at the minimum, that all variables in a path model be allotted some temporal sequence. And yet we cannot here regard the measures of Labour, Conservative, and Liberal positions as so ordered. The election addresses from which the positions are calculated are taken as indexes of the rough positions of the candidates. We expect that these positions will influence one another, but we cannot say that the Labour positions causes the Conservative one, or make any other assumptions about temporal priority. Indeed it is more likely that the candidate of party A, in deciding his approach, takes note of what he expects (or would were he of party B) his opponent to do, rather than waiting to find out during the campaign. It will then be the mutual previous knowledge of each other—and their guesses about the likely vote support, that determine each candidate's position. We end up using the election addresses as indicators in a rather indirect way. There are two ways of dealing with, but by no means solving, this problem in analysis here. Either we can pretend that the two positions to be used as independent variables in explaining the third are not intercorrelated at all, or we can impose some temporal/causal sequence and look only at one rather than both, of the path coefficients. This should be made clearer by the following Figures.

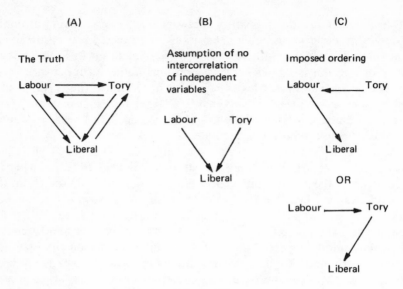

Figure 28

None of these can be regarded as very satisfactory; A is the truth but is non-recursive and therefore out of the scope of path analysis, while B is plainly counter-intuitive. The trouble with C is that we may have few grounds on which to impose such a priority. All we can do is to look at what evidence there is in the data for making such assumptions. We may perhaps be able to show why, although one cannot rule out certain paths, they may be sufficiently weak to be ignored in practice.

The first thing to do is to draw, with values, the pattern as in A, just to see which of these six paths may appear weak. The path coefficients (i.e., the Beta weights from a multiple regression equation) for these are given below.

1. Taking Liberal position as dependent we have:
Lib. = $a + b$ (Cons.) + b (Lab.) = Lib. = $15·2 + ·186$ (Cons.) + $·676$ (Lab.). This gives an R^2 of $·319$, significant at $·05\%$. The Beta weights are, for Cons., $·125$ and for Lab., $·486$.

2. Taking Labour as the dependent variable gives:
Lab. = $a + b$ (Cons.) + b (Lib.) = Lab. = $18·8 + ·426$ (Cons.) + $·287$ (Lib.), with an R^2 of $·442$, significant at the $·01\%$ level. Here the Beta weights are: for Cons., $·397$, and for Lib., $·399$.

3. Taking Conservatives as the dependent variable we get:
Cons. = $a + b$ (Lab.) + b (Lib.) = $22·7 + ·453$ (Lab.) + $·084$ (Lib.), giving an R^2 of $·319$, again significant at the $·05\%$ level, with Beta weights of Lab., $·485$ and Lib., $·125$.

Taking notice at first from this of only the direct path effects, the following illicit non-recursive path diagram could be constructed.

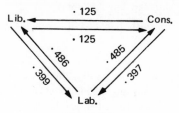

Figure 29

The earlier question about relative effects of each party on the others is quite easily answered from this; the paths joining Liberal and Conservative positions are both extremely low, and the *b* coefficients from which they are ultimately calculated are non significant at any useful level. At the same time as noting this total absence of causal significance between these two variables, one must note the symmetry of the diagram. The paths showing the supposed strength of the Labour influence on each of Conservative and Liberal are virtually equal, as are the effects of both of these two on the Labour party.

If we take the indirect path coefficients here to be, as suggested by Duncan (1972), the product of the relevant direct paths, the tables below allow us to check this claim by comparing direct and indirect effects of the three interrelated variables.

Table 32. The Determinants of the Liberal Positions

	Direct	Indirect	Total
Labour	·486	·060	·546
Conservative	·125	·192	·317

Table 33. The Determinants of the Conservative Positions

	Direct	Indirect	Total
Labour	·485	·060	·545
Liberal	·125	·193	·318

Table 34. The Determinants of the Labour Positions

	Direct	Indirect	Total
Conservative	·397	·049	·446
Liberal	·399	·049	·448

Here the total path coefficients still show Labour clearly the most influential, in both the cases where it is the independent variable, and exceeding, at ·546, the effect of either other party on itself as shown in Table 34. The indirect effects of Conservative on Liberal, and Liberal on Conservative, that is the paths via Labour, are in both cases definitely bigger than the direct path equivalents.

As well as giving valuable information about the symmetry of effects, this exercise makes it slightly easier for us to impose a causal/temporal ordering on the fuller analysis to follow. In one case at least, when we are to have Labour as the independent variable it is safe to follow the strategy depicted in B of Figure 29 and treat both Lib. and Con. as uncorrelated. Given that Labour's influence on the other two is greater than theirs on it, we can also risk enforcing a causal modelling in those cases in which we give priority to Labour over both of the others.

A final problem before the full causal models (which include voting strengths) can be used is this. We have in the correlation matrix of Table 31 given correlations between the three positions and the votes gained by each of the three candidates. This is necessary because we have no way of taking one single voting indicator. It is perfectly sensible, historically, to expect that the position of, say, the Labour candidate, will be influenced both by the votes he expects to get, and what he expects to be the ratio of Liberal support to Conservatives. After all, if one is a Conservative candidate, one would want to produce a different image in a constituency where the Labour candidate is to come a bad third to Liberals, from the one that would be most useful if one was in a red area with the Labour candidate almost bound to win. Thus all three voting figures, Liberal, Labour and Conservative, are relevant, and are to be expected to influence each party differently.

Unfortunately one cannot (though we absent-mindedly did at first) plug all three into a regression equation as independent variables. To do so is, not surprisingly, to produce a nearly singular matrix. Controlling for two votes does not actually allow the third to vary in a three party universe. The solution of estimating the importance of each vote in separate equations, or of each pair in such a series is unsatisfactory because there is great danger then in comparing the different Betas.

A little thought, and a considerable addiction to principal components, suggest that one ought to make up one's mind about what the voting figures are supposed to represent. They are seen here as representing underlying political distributions in the constituencies. That one is committed to a multi-dimensional model of ideological competition, even despite the use for convenience of a summary measure for them, rather implies that the voting loyalties of the constituency should also be multi dimensional. This presupposes that rather than seeing the votes of the three parties as indicating only how radical or conservative the constituency is, one admits that constituencies can be ranked on some other dimension as well. The force of the previous example of a Conservative candidate in a constituency where the Labour candidate is going to do very badly is to suggest that there is some dimension on which voters are loyal either to Conservatives or Liberals without reference to the Labour strength; in other words, a set of orthogonal components should be derivable from the voting. Being orthogonal they can both be used in one regression equation, and, if they account for a sufficiently high proportion of the variance, will do the job that all three single votes would do could one avoid singularity. As one does here in any case wish to use the votes, not as precise event-type data, but as indicators of underlying tendencies, this seems all the more sensible.

Carrying out a principal components solution on the three voting variables produces the following highly satisfactory results.

Table 35.

Variable Name	Loading on Component 1	Loading on Component 2
Labour vote	$-\cdot773$	$+\cdot092$
Conservative vote	$\cdot536$	$\cdot625$
Liberal vote	$\cdot340$	$-\cdot775$
Percentage of the variance accounted for	54·9%	44·8%

One gets in fact what might have been expected, a first dimension representing the general radicalism of the constituency, comparing Labour with Conservative, and with the Liberal party nearly as highly scored as the Conservatives, followed by a dimension on which the Labour weighting is quite insignificant contrasting Liberal and Conservative voting strength. For convenience here we shall from now on refer not to actual votes, but to the 'radicalism' or to the 'Liberalism' of the constituency, and use these as the background electoral strength variables.

The correlation matrix from which the rest of the analysis is done is therefore that given below in Table 36 replacing the individual votes with these two components.

Table 36.

	1	2	3	4
1. Labour Position				
2. Conservative Position	56			
3. Liberal Position	56	·40		
4. Radicalism	−51	−53	−25	
5. Liberalism	03	−29	·09	0·00

Even without regression analysis it is clear that the Liberal party is much less affected by voting strength. Most interesting is the way the 'Liberalism' of the constituency affects only the Conservative party.

The same preliminary position is found in Table 31, of course. The sign changes are due to the fact that the signs of the components are such as to make a highly radical constituency negative; as moving towards the extreme for a Labour candidate is an upwards, positive move, the correlation between radicalism and Labour position is negative.

166

What one needs to do now is to calculate path coefficients for three separate models, taking each party as dependent in turn. These follow, along with tables giving the direct, indirect and total path coefficients for these three models, as well as for certain other ones that are possibly relevant.

Model 1. The Liberal Candidate Position as Dependent

The full model here is based on assuming no direct path between the Conservative and Liberal positions. We assume here also that the causal relationship between Labour and Conservative is given by a recursive influence only of Conservative on Labour. This, despite the evidence earlier that the reverse arrow is stronger, because there is no point in putting in a relation between A and B in a model to explain C if one is to have no path between A and C.

The full set of equations needed for this model is as follows:

1. Lib. = $a + b$ (Lab.) + b (Radicalism) + b (Liberalism
2. Lab. = $a + b$ (Cons.) + b (Radicalism) + b (Liberalism)
3. Cons. = $a + b$ (Radicalism) + b (Liberalism)

1. Lib. = $18 \cdot 1 + \cdot 799$ (Lab.) + $\cdot 556$ (Radicalism) + $1 \cdot 04$ (Liberalism) $R^2 = \cdot 315$ (Significant at $\cdot 10\%$ level) Betas = Lab. = $\cdot 575$, Radicalism $0 \cdot 04$, Liberalism $0 \cdot 07$.

2. Lab. = $24 \cdot 5 + \cdot 494$ (Cons.) $- 2 \cdot 56$ (Radicalism) + $1 \cdot 74$ (Liberalism) $R^2 = \cdot 399$ (significant at $\cdot 05\%$ level) Betas = Cons., $\cdot 461$, Radicalism, $- \cdot 269$, Liberalism, $\cdot 165$.

3. Cons. = $56 \cdot 7 - 4 \cdot 69$ (Radicalism) $- 2 \cdot 86$ (Liberalism) $R^2 = \cdot 362$ (significant at $\cdot 05\%$ level) Betas = Radicalism, $- \cdot 527$, Liberalism, $- \cdot 290$.

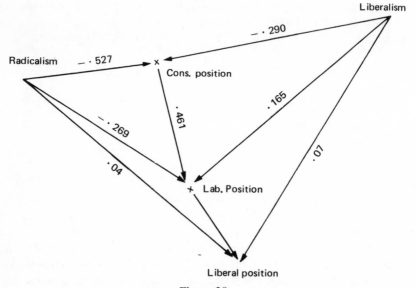

Figure 30

Table 37. The Full Determinants of the Liberal Position

Source	Direct	Indirect	Total
Radicalism	·04	−300	−296
Liberalism	·07	−·01	·06
Conservative Position	None	·267	·267
Labour Position	·575	None	·575

The second model takes the Conservative position as a dependent variable, and again assumes no direct effect between the two older parties. The equations required are:

1. Con. = $a + b$ (Lab.) + b (Radicalism) + b (Liberalism)
2. Lab. = $a + b$ (Lib.) + b (Radicalism) + b (Liberalism)
3. Lib. = $a + b$ (Radicalism) + b (Liberalism)

The correct values for these are:
1. Cons. = $33·4 + ·372$ (Lab.) $- 2·87$ (Radicalism) $- 2·98$ (Liberalism) $R^2 = ·480$ (significant at ·05% level) Betas = Lab. ·399, Radicalism $-·323$, Liberalism $-·303$.
2. Lab. = $40·2 + ·328$ (Lib.) $- 3·78$ (Radicalism) $- 0·09$ (Liberalism) $R^2 = ·456$ (significant at ·05% level) Betas = Lib. ·456, Radicalism $-·398$, Liberalism $-·009$.
3. Lib. = $68·0 - 3·34$ (Radicalism) $+ 1·30$ (Liberalism).
The R^2 is trivial and quite insignificant, as are the Betas here.

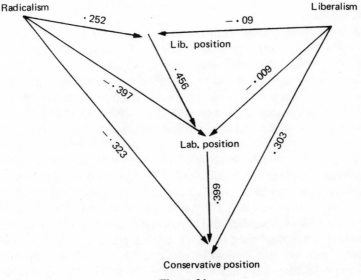

Figure 31

Table 38. Conservative as Dependent

Source	Direct	Indirect	Total
Lab.	·399	None	·399
Lib.	None	·184	·184
Radicalism	−·323	−·210	−·533
Liberalism	−·303	−·024	−·327

The final model is for the Labour position as the dependent variable, and is based, once more, on the assumption of no causal link between Liberals and Conservatives.

The required equations are:

1. Lab. $= 26·6 + ·26$ (Lib.) $+ ·32$ (Cons.) $- 2·51$ (Radicalism) $+ ·89$ (Liberalism) $R^2 = ·505$ (significant at ·05% level) Betas are Lib. ·364, Cons. ·297, Radicalism $-·263$, Liberalism ·085.

2. Lib. $= a + b$ (Radicalism) $+ b$ (Liberalism)

3. Cons. $= a + b$ (Radicalism) $+ b$ (Liberalism)

The values for 2 and 3 have already been given.

Table 39. Labour as Dependent Variable

Source	Direct	Indirect	Total
Lib.	·364	None	·364
Cons.	·297	None	·297
Radicalism	−·263	−·085	−·348
Liberalism	·085	−·065	·020

With these three path diagrams before us we can come much nearer to assessing the predictions suggested earlier, and to getting some idea of the sort of strategic relations that may exist in party competition.

Taking first the determinants of the Liberal position, it is interesting to see how little the voting situation has to do with their positioning; the direct effect of both the voting variables is practically zero, and even when one calculates indirect paths via the Labour position and the Conservative position the effect of the, perhaps not aptly named, 'Liberalism' variable is tiny. The effect of the main 'Radicalism' variable, because of its relatively high effect on both of the other parties, increases with these calculations, but remains very much less than the important effect, which is of the Labour position. As the Labour distance from the origin increases, indicating a movement towards a more extreme left position, the Liberal candidate also moves in this direction. Almost none of this can be put down to the voting variables, and the prediction about the effects of candidates' movements seems to be confirmed here, with the important and interesting rider that only the Labour party affects the Liberals. Indeed were one to look only at the T-tests for significance of the independent variables, in

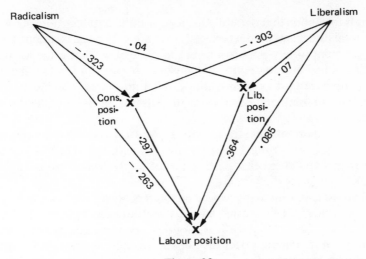

Figure 32

the equation predicting Liberal position from all the other variables, only the Labour position variable is significant even at the ·10% level.

Turning to the figure showing the influences of all other variables on the Conservative position, one finds that in contrast both of the voting variables are important. As the constituency becomes more positive (illiberal) on the Liberalism variable, the candidate moves down, that is, nearer the origin, towards an extreme Conservative position; the effects of the two voting variables are pretty much the same until one looks at the indirect effect. Here, because of the lack of effect of the Liberalism score on the Labour or Liberal parties, the total effect of that variable rises only slightly above the direct effect value, while the total effect of the 'Radicalism' variable, acting through the other party positions, makes it the most important one, overall. The effect of the Labour position is unmistakable, it being the greatest of the direct effects. Even allowing for the indirect effect of the Labour party the Liberal effect is slight. It is true in both these cases that the indirect effects of parties where no direct path is allowed reinforces the main effect from the party that is allowed a direct effect. As the constituency becomes more radical the Liberal party moves towards the Labour end of the spectrum, possibly reinforcing the move of the Labour candidate in that direction, and thus the Conservative moves that way, under the influence of both the other parties and the innate radicalism; only in the case of the constituency being highly 'illiberal' would there be any counter tendency to move back towards a Conservative position. This latter effect, as represented here by the principal components, is, of course, quite uncorrelated with the radicalism of the constituency.

Although this 'Liberalism' effect is not as strong as the other effects, it needs to be taken seriously. Because of the high intercorrelation between the other variables, it, and the Labour position effects, are the only variables to be independently significant according to the T-tests on the b coefficients.

This is information that is useful, but need not stop us taking note of the betas and the total direct and indirect effects, as we are not primarily interested here in extrapolating to any population, but in discussing what evidence there is inside this sample for competitive behaviour. We are not for a moment here trying to advance laws of competition, which must surely be highly context specific, but to find out what sorts of patterns or laws could be at all feasible.

The most important thing to say about the Conservative example here is surely that they are so much more connected with the actual voting in the constituency than either other party, with the total effect of 'radicalism' being the greatest single total effect.

The Labour case is in many ways a medium between the other two. One of the voting variables, 'Liberalism', has, as would be expected from its definition, no effect at all. The fact that it effects Conservatives and Liberals in a different direction from its minute effect on Labour actually means that the indirect effects almost cancel out the direct effects. This is the one case of direct and indirect effects acting in different ways. The other three effects are much more nearly of the same magnitude than has been the case elsewhere. The radicalism of the constituency obviously affects the Labour position, and the total effect, allowing for radicalism to influence the other two parties, makes it the second largest effect. The independent effect of a shift in the Liberal position has the greater effect of the two party paths, and the greatest direct path effect. Yet in this case there must be great doubts about the legitimacy of using a path indicating an effect of the Liberal on the Conservative. It is an unfortunate feature of the summary measure that while it undoubtedly catches some of the Liberal movement, it makes little sense to envisage a voluntary movement of the Liberals towards either end of a dimension that essentially contrasts Labour and Conservative politics. That Liberals may be pulled to the Labour (or Conservative) end of this dimension is perfectly plausible; that they might push either of the other parties there is less so. The problem of dealing with these non recursive situations cannot, as previously mentioned, be settled here very satisfactorily. But if we allow *ad hoc* information and hunches to be brought in it would seem more plausible to set up a slightly different set of models. We still cannot deal effectively with the Labour/Conservative interaction, because this requires really that we should break down the sample in ways that it is too small to bear. Essentially one would want to argue that the direction of influence here depends on what the constituency is like. For a safe Conservative seat it seems sensible to suggest that the Conservative move towards their end of the spectrum pulls Labour along that way, while the reverse applies in a safe Labour seat. Even were the sample good enough to allow of its being split into these two sections, we could not definitely ascribe any particular causal ordering.

Despite these worries and problems it is fairly safe to say that the predictions made in Section 1 are confirmed.

It is true that there is an effect of opposition standpoint on the candidates over and above the electoral effect—indeed only in the case of the Conservative candidates is it absolutely safe to talk of a separate effect of the voting. More generally it is true that there are discernible patterns, both of voting and of position influence on a candidate's standpoint that are not compatible with the notion of 'integrity politics', and are compatible with the notion of 'competitive politics'.

It is true that in the two cases where we can test it, the greater the uncertainty, the greater the evidence of 'competition'. That is true when one compares the situation in 1924, with a new party and an unstable party configuration, with 1955, an election from a very stable and high consensus period of politics. There is much firmer evidence of the effect of voting and of positions in 1924 compared with 1955. In 1955 the competitiveness only shows up given a set of differences of means tests, whereas in 1924 it is sufficiently linear to register through correlation and regression exercises. In 1955 furthermore, we can find no position effect at all.

Secondly, the correlations of the variables in the two- and three-cornered seats are certainly different. In two-cornered seats only the Conservative party can be shown to have set its position in a way that correlates at all strongly with voting strength of the constituencies.

To close we might look very quickly at three simpler models, one for each of the parties, built round the findings above, but using also historical common sense to try to represent as best as possible what the situation of 1924 looks like through this data set.

On the Liberal party, there is really one clear effect, that of the Labour position. The best model seems to be one that argues a causal chain from 'Radicalism' to the Labour standpoint, and from that to the Liberal position. Such an equation, of the form Lib. = $a + b$ (Lab.) $+ b$ (Radicalism) has an R^2 of ·310, significant at the ·05% level, and would attach a beta of ·578 to the path from Labour to Liberal, and of $-·512$ from Radicalism to Labour. We are here leaving out the effect of the Conservatives on the Labour party, and thus explaining only 26% of the variance in the Labour position. As far as explaining the Liberal position goes, however, it seems best to represent the realities of 1924.

To predict the Conservative position one cannot leave out the Labour effect, but one can certainly dispense with the Liberals, and with at least one other path, that from the 'Liberalism' variable to the Labour position; it is, and ought to be, negligible. This model would explain 48% of the variance in the Conservative position, be significant at the ·05% level, and give a beta weight to the paths of ·399 for the Labour/Conservative path, $-·323$ for the Radicalism/Conservative path, and $-·303$ for the 'Liberalism' path.

Finally to explain the Labour position, one would use an equation with only Conservative position and Radicalism in it, explaining 37·5% of the variance, significant at the ·05% level, and attaching a weight of ·395 to the

172

Conservative/Labour path and $-\cdot304$ to the Radicalism/Labour path. These models are all given below in Figure 33.

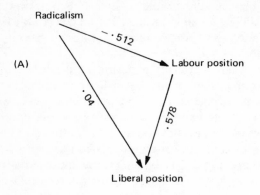

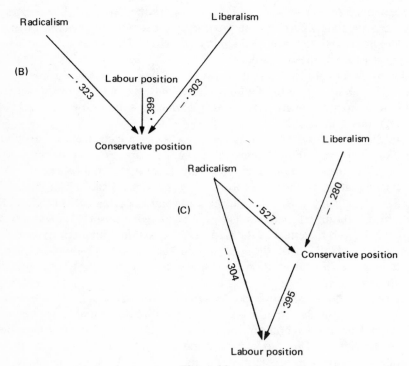

Figure 33

Apart from offering what amounts to very good evidence for the thesis that party ideological competition does exist, and follows certain discernible laws, as is shown by the confirmation of the four predictions of Section 1, this chapter has hopefully helped to suggest deeper points about the nature of such competitive behaviour. One important point is the way in which different aspects of the voting situation influence the various parties differently. Indeed the variance in importance of voting at all as a determinant of parties, even when it is clear that they are behaving competitively, is considerable. Secondly, it is of some importance, and requires further theoretical consideration, that the parties do not influence each other equally. What appears to be the case from this study is that in 1924 both the Conservative and the Liberal party were aware of, and taking strategic action about, the challenge of the Labour party, but were not taking a great deal of notice of each other. Had we enough cases of Liberal/Conservative straight fights, we might well find out that this was not entirely the case. But where all three parties were present there is a definite symmetry to the relationships. Liberal and Conservative influence Labour about equally (as does Labour influence them equally) but have no discernible influence on each other. One would theorise that this is an inevitable occurrence in a situation where a new party appears. It could equally well have been the case that the Liberal and Conservative parties had fought each other, resigning the old left wing entirely to the Labour party. Not that one would wish to suggest that this sort of case study can answer such questions as well as traditional political history. It is not intended to, for we here are using the two elections we have discussed entirely as case studies and theoretical testing grounds. Nonetheless unless they can show that the findings here are meaningless in a way that they are statistically not, it seems that the picture of party competition given in the last page of drawings is something that historians ought not to ignore.

It should finally be remembered that this analysis has been only partial; not only did we not discuss the effects at play in the two-cornered fight situation, when the Conservatives at least can be shown to have been behaving in a way incompatible with the model of 'integrity' politics, but the separate dimensions have been only cursorily discussed. In fact the findings about the Liberal party here are especially important in this case, because the summary measure has dealt less 'kindly' with them than a component by component analysis would have done. There is, as was mentioned briefly at the beginning of Section 3, some evidence that their positions were related to the voting situation there, even though this has not shown up strongly with the summary measure. More importantly, they have in this section been treated as passive partners, influenced but hardly influencing. Had we examined in detail dimensions on which the Liberal party was dominant this might well have been different.

The analysis of this chapter leaves little doubt that a phenomenon of competition does exist, at the constituency level, as we have shown earlier it does at the central party level. Moreover it has been shown to be a very complicated phenomenon, fitting well the theory sketched in Chapter 2 and discussed again at the beginning of this chapter.

The implications of all this, both for the normative and empirical theories of party democracy, are drawn out, and produce tentative conclusions, in the final chapter.

CHAPTER 6

Conclusions

Consider the jury system in English law. It holds a very important position in our esteem, approaching even a basic value in the definition of our society. Why, though, is it thought so well of? The only satisfactory answer is that we believe it to be an efficient machine for deciding questions of legal guilt or responsibility, especially as we insist that the burden of evidence must always lie on the prosecution or the plaintiff. Juries are good things because they will take a common sense approach to evidence, and sympathise with the accused or the defendant. That the ordinary juryman may not have an incisive mind, or any particular quality that will aid in the search for the truth of the matter, that he may not be able to enquire deeply into the true history of the case is not important. In part the jury's talents are unimportant because the Anglo-American mode of trial is not in any case inquisitorial, but accusatory. In this legal tradition reliance is placed on the self interest of the participants in a verbal combat to use every evidential weapon, every factual defence, available to win the minds of the jury. Compared with the Roman law system of the rest of Europe, with its institution of procurator, fiscal, or juge d'instruction, and its aim of discovering the full truth of the case, we can get away with allowing legal outcomes to depend on the random talents of twelve people picked, almost literally, from the street.

It is much the same with our system of electoral democracy. The mass of individual voters are not commonly thought capable, in their private capacities, of solving serious problems of state and economy. Yet collectively we trust them to choose the better of two or three alternative government programmes every four or five years.

Our trust again is placed upon the accusatory nature of the process, and on the competitive element. Only one party (usually, anyway) can win an election. The only way to win an election is to please a majority, or a large plurality, of the voters. Therefore, *quod erat demonstrandum*, the political parties will vie with each other for support of the electorate, by offering such programmes as are likely to command most support, by trenchantly criticising the opponents, and by interpreting the economic and social environment to the electorate. With such fierce competition, surely the electorate will, without great difficulty, be able to choose a government, and will necessarily be offered options very close to those which would be preferred by the largest part of the electorate.

Retaining for the present the jury analogy, consider what the implications would be for justice were some of the facts of political life to extend to the courtroom. The first such fact to be extended would have to be the judicial equivalent of 'party identification'. Suppose that sizeable, and roughly equal groups of jurors were so certain to support one side or another (because they always had and always would, vote for 'their' side, prosecution or defence) that they would not even listen to counsel's argument, would we then have confidence in the courts?

Possibly we still would, because we could rely on the other few percent of jurors to hold the balance, and to hear the case responsibly. All our hopes would then depend on counsel, on the force of forensic battle and the self interest of the adversaries presenting to those few undecided jurors the most persuasive case they could each mount. In this legal analogy hope and faith can also reside in the judge, who should intercede to forbid irrelevant or improper evidence, and will sum up and direct the jury's attention to the most vital points. There is no equivalent to the judge in politics (however hard the editorials of the quality press and the kingpins of current affairs broadcasting may seek that role). Even were there a judge equivalent, his job would be infinitely harder; to complete the legal analogy we would have to apply further behavioural predictions to the prototype court.

It might be that defence and prosecuting counsel always have a choice of strategies—that there are pleas and techniques of witness interrogation or what have you. We might suppose further that different jurors react favourably to different techniques. So those who are already quite determined to convict will be strengthened in this predisposition by counsel dwelling on the accused's criminal background, even though this sort of presentation is unlikely to sway the few undecided jurors. Other strategies, perhaps the calling of many expert psychoanalytic witnesses who will seek to excuse criminals in general, will go down well only with those already likely to acquit. The analogy of electoral politics to the courts would require counsel to decide their strategies according to the prior probability of the jury (whose opinion is largely predetermined and distributed, we must add, in a way at least guessable at) producing a particular verdict. The more likely, *a priori*, a conviction, the more likely both counsel would be to preach to the converted. Only where it seemed likely that an acquittal was possible would we then find counsel presenting cases intended really to convince the undecided.

To make the analogy at all close to the image of competitive politics drawn in Chapters 4 and 5 a host of such behavioural regularities would have to be predicted of the legal actors. There would have to be some equivalent of the finding that short-term economic policy change is related not solely to changes in economic indicators, but to the effect such changes have on the record of the party. We would need a prediction that counsel would seek to describe the crime or tort as worse than it really was, or much slighter than it was, according to whom they were representing; to parallel the tendency for incumbents to be more moderate than oppositions might require the prosecutor, as representative of the State, to stick more nearly to responsible and impartial presentation of the evidence, while the defence could never do so, for fear of seeming to support the current authorities.

All told, the jury and counsel we would get, were our judicial institutions to operate like our electoral machinery, would be described by a set of behavioural laws and safe predictions tending all to produce a systematic distortion of information and argument, presenting the jury with choices that seldom reflected the needs of the public interest.

This extended analogy serves to highlight what is at stake. For it would be hard to defend a jury system like that implied by the analogy. It might still be defended, either on some deontological grounds or by the 'all alternatives are unthinkably worse' option. It could not be held up as a technically efficient way of producing the 'correct answer' on questions of law. Those who do support jury trials must have, and offer publicly, a theory of small group behaviour which predicts that the jury is precisely what it could not be were their theory like the one invented above. We return to our starting point in asserting that the social sciences must always combine three elements. There has to be an intention or purpose behind the institutions studied—to secure justice, or to select the best government. This intention must be fairly well articulated, so it is possible to know when it fails—justice has to be defined, there have to be criteria for a properly-made electoral decision. Note that in neither of our examples need the *actual* outcome be stipulated by the prescriptive aspect of the social science. Justice is compatible with any verdict, democracy with the election of any party, providing only that we have reason to think the jurymen or voters reached their decisions in a suitable way, and were presented with adequate choices.

The prescriptive theory then postulates a goal or valued condition of life, and we can turn to the institutional arrangement prescribed. There must be good reasons for assuming that a particular institution will provide the desired goal. We do not lightly or capriciously opt for competitive political parties or twelve-man juries. Rather the prescriptive theory leads to another form of theory; call it empirical to symbolise its concern with action rather than ideals. That theory must predict how ordinary men, placed in certain situations, will act. It must show how those situations can be structured to lead to behaviour required to achieve the ideal.

So we rely on competitive drives in men who are attracted to the bar or the hustings, and the interaction of rivalry between such men when contending, to produce a set of alternative 'cases' or arguments for voters or jurors to select. We rely, in our predictive theories of forensics and politics, also on the average man to listen, ratiocinate, and decide.

Societies can rig the balance, if they have good predictive theories, to get better performance. Offer the prosecuting counsel a share of any fines levied, and conviction rates may well go up; imprison any jury whose decision is later overturned by an appelate court, and they should all think much more deeply and weigh evidence more carefully. What is indispensible is a detailed and serious empirical theory, and one capable of refutation, or society is designing its institutions in the dark. Both jury rooms and ballot boxes are secret, but at least we have some survey research and some capacity to measure party propaganda and policy change.

In this book we have tried to do three things. First to state a fairly orthodox prescriptive theory of democracy. This boils down to democracy being a system of free competitive electoral politics aimed at allowing the voters to select a government. We characterise government, and therefore party policy, and therefore the information a voter needs to make his decision, in terms of solving problems in a *status quo* defined by consensual values, where change, other than remedying the problem situation, is to be minimised.

Next, arguing that democratic faith does rest on the problem-solving efficacy of party competition, we have constructed a model or empirical theory of the party competitive process. The questions here are twofold. Does the model predict behaviour compatible with democratic faith? Does it predict accurately?

Answering these questions was our third task. As things have turned out, all three sections cannot be right. If the data analysis is accepted, the predictive theory is successful, but democratic theory needs some other justification. There is an asymmetry, though. Reject the data analysis, and you do not justify democracy, for the predictive theory still has to be replaced. This is the rub; a constitution cannot be satisfactory that works well by accident! The point of an institutional prescription is that the values behind the prescription have to be guaranteed by the behaviour predicted by the empirical model. Yet despite the long history of democracy-as-competitive elections (since Schumpeter (1950) at the latest), the only well-defined models of how this competitive process works out in practice are incompatible with the requirements of democracy. There are two broad categories of these models; those produced by survey researchers, who are principally interested in explaining the voter's behaviour, form one. With a few exceptions, notably Key's *The Responsible Electorate* [1966], most follow the pattern set by Berelson in his famous study, *Voting* [1954].

The other, smaller category, of which this book forms a part and which Downs' *Economic Theory of Democracy* instigated, focuses on the parties and their behaviour. There are strains and contradictions between works of the two categories. More importantly, however, this book, no more than the works of the other approach, upholds democratic faith in competitive party politics.

The almost infamous fourteenth chapter of Berelson's book (sometimes one wonders if the other chapters have ever been read) sets up a picture of the 'classic' democratic voter, and proceeds to shoot it down by portraying the 'real' voter from survey evidence. Here begins the general survey research conception of the voter. He has three chief characteristics: ignorance of politics, lack of interest and concern for politics, and a psychological attachment for 'his' party which prompts his vote far more than any rational calculus of self interest, or any general preference issues. Other characteristics are found by some, rejected by other, studies. Most American authors wish to add that these voters who do not have strong party identifications still cannot be taken as the ideal democratic voter because they are more ignorant and even less stable in belief structures than the strong identifiers. This, which clashes with assumptions we make in Chapter 3 and Appendix 3, is controverted by other evidence from Europe (Särlvik, 1975).

Survey researchers themselves frequently set up a distinction between people who vote from party identification (or associated background variables) and those apparently influenced by 'issues'. Budge and Farlie, in a recent paper (1975), use this dichotomy, in a survey of the main predictor variables of voting choice in nine democracies. Although 'issue' variables have some predictive power in most countries, only in a few cases do they appear anywhere in the top ten predictors for each country.

One may well wish to argue that the dichotomy is a false one, or that 'issue' as operationalised by researchers is a very poor way of tapping informed rational voting. Certainly many of the questionnaires would defeat the most rational and thoughtful of respondents at times. The average reader of this book, for example, might find inordinate difficulty in answering the following question:

'There has been a lot of talk recently about nationalisation, that is, the Government owning and running industries like steel and electricity. Which of these statements comes closest to what you yourself feel should be done?'

(A) A lot more industries should be nationalised
(B) Only a few more industries should be nationalised
(C) No more industries should be nationalised, but industries that are now nationalised should stay nationalised
(D) Some of the industries that are now nationalised should become private companies.

There is, in fact for the Englishman a delightful verbal ambiguity in the definition of nationalisation as 'the Government . . . running industries like steel and electricity'. Many rampant socialists would shudder at *anything ever* being run 'like' the British Steel Corporation. More seriously, the chopping of policy alternatives into these four categories (why cannot one sensibly opt for A *and* D?) and the ambiguity of 'A lot' or 'Only a few' may well defeat a thinking voter.

When it comes to analysis of survey data, the standards of rationality or consistency are often idiosyncratically high. We would not wish, overall, to dispute much of what the party-identifier/ignorant voter school says. But one example of analysis helps to set them in context. Butler and Stokes found a depressing instability of issue opinion over time in their 1963 and 1964 panel study. On the nationalisation question quoted above, only 39% of the sample expressed the same opinion on both occasions. The table of data below comes from their analysis in Chapter 8 of *Political Change in Britain*.

Table 40.

		Autumn 1964				
		Lot more	Few more	No more	Less	No Opinion
	Lot More	3	3	3	1	1
	Few more	1	6	6	1	1
Summer 1963	No more	1	5	21	6	3
	Less	1	1	10	9	1
	No opinion	1	2	5	2	6

Quite fairly, they claim that only those falling in the diagonal elements, therefore producing the same response each time, have consistent issue beliefs—39%. Let us quickly demonstrate how, by lowering one's standards, the figure can be radically increased.

(i) Lot more/Few more are too ambiguous, and in any case the important distinction is just between those who do, and those who do not, on the whole, support nationalisation.

(ii) Any respondent, surprised in his house by an interviewer, may be panicked into expressing an opinion when he really does not have one. Reading the total responses to questions one is struck by the effort people make to cover up uncertainty or indifference to the issues. 'That's all I can think of now, but there's lots more I could tell you, etc., etc.' is a very common response. Surely safer to concentrate on those who do, in both waves of the survey, have *some* opinion—sliding in and out of no opinion probably does mean that the respondent is unstable in his attitude.

So, remaking the table according to the dichotomy 'Pro/anti nationalisation of some sort', on those who expressed some opinion on both occasions produces the following two-by-two table.

Table 41.

		1964		
		Pro	Con	
1963	Pro	13	11	
	Con	5	46	
				75

The two consistent cells, Pro/Pro, Con/Con, now total 59 out of 75, giving 79%, with a stable set of nationalisation attitudes over time.

Now the point is not that Butler and Stokes were wrong, and we have analysed correctly, but that neither of us are quite clear on either what standards we should demand of voters, or whether or not 'issue' questions of this type are in any case relevant measures of voter competence. For the 'classical' democratic theory that Berelson attacked in *Voting* was probably a straw man—there is no well worked-out set of democracy's requirements on the part of the voter. We can only guess that much of the evidence from survey research, which cannot be argued away as we have the nationalisation example above, forms a *prima facie* case against the feasibility of competitive democracy. The inability of a sizeable portion of the American electorate to tell an interviewer the party affiliation of their Congressman cannot be lightly dismissed. Nor can we seriously pretend that the Michigan finding of a simple affective link between a party as a social object and a voter's behaviour (which alone has good predictive power in elections), which appears unconnected with any serious policy or ideological beliefs, is entirely compatible with the existence of many rational voters. Though some writers, notably Key (1966) have argued plausibly for a more favourable interpretation of the electorate's general competence.

How serious the situation is defies calculation. It may well be that party identification as such has outlived its utility. A recent conference on this question in Strasbourg (under the auspices of the European Consortium for Political Research) which brought together both American and European researchers produced a somewhat varied set of interpretations and views of the concept's validity outside America (Budge, 1975).

It is probably true that too much effort for too long has been given to predicting rather than explaining voting choice. It is ironic that a strong recent criticism of party identification as a separate explanatory variable has been precisely that it is *too* good a predictor. The correlation between actual vote and partisan self identification in many countries is so high that it is doubtful that we are getting anything more than a tautology. It is precisely in America, where party identification is an a-rational psychological attachment seems most credible that it has the lowest prediction (Budge and Farlie, 1975). One recently noted phenomenon that may lead us back towards a picture of the voter more nearly suitable for competitive democracy is the increasing 'volatility' of the vote and of public opinion polls in Britain. Crewe (1974) has argued plausibly that a complex of signs, by-election reverses, falling electoral turn out, increasing electoral swings, wildly fluctuating opinion poll results, lead to the conclusion that we may no longer unquestioningly rely on a very large 'safe' party vote. 'Volatility' begs too many questions unfortunately. We as yet have little reason to believe that strong party identification (if it ever existed) has been replaced (if it has gone) by thoughtful, informed 'instrumental' voting. We do provide some very slim evidence in Appendix 3 for the thesis that voters (some, anyway) are aware of and respond to, candidates' ideological positions.

In the current state of uncertainty the safer course is to accept that most voters anyway are probably not possessed of, or motivated by, a sufficient awareness of policy to make them suitable actors for a party competitive model of democracy.

The only alternative is to hope that the facts of ignorance and party pre-disposition can be more compatible with rational choice models. The Downsian style model is attractive principally because, as a spelling out of the faith in party democracy, it seems to guarantee that the public interest will emerge from the invisible guiding hand of electoral competition. To be sure, this is a notion of the public interest that is overly naive, a direct distribution of utility to voters in such a way that a plurality of voters cannot find a preferable distribution. Apart from the possible moral criticisms of such an ideal (it invites much the same sort of criticism as utilitarian theories do in general, of excessive penalties on those outside the plurality) it does not really make sense in the bewildering world of real policy problems. One difference between our theory and Downs', which may have deserved more serious treatment than we have given, is that we see parties as offering 'solutions to problems' rather than 'utility streams'. Nonetheless a rational choice model, if it can be made to work, offers more hope than any work in the Berelson tradition.

Just how fatal to rational choice models are the survey based descriptions of the voter? Ignorance and party predisposition are the two primary elements, and both can, with sufficient effort, be redescribed in a way that is not apparently fatal. Ignorance, leading to restricted-information models, is not too difficult to encompass, and in fact leads to a redefinition of party identification in terms of a broad 'ideology'. The need for parties to produce general and rather vague 'ideologies' is derived by Downs actually from the difficulty and cost to the voter of having precise information on policy stands. Something rather like party identification is then incorporated in the model as an information-economising strategy on the part of the voter, pandered to by the parties because it improves their strategic situation by allowing fuzziness of policy stand. Detailed information on policy is difficult to come by and unreliable, but a rough picture of what the party stands for, and a long term attachment to the party on the basis of the similarity between the voter's own 'ideology' and the party's serves instead.

On the basis of this reinterpretation of the requirements of rationality a lot can be done. First, there are rather few irrational voters, because strong party identifiers are seldom attached to the 'wrong' party in terms of social class. Second, it is shown from social mobility data that usually the party identification of a socially mobile voter adjusts to fit his new position (Goldberg, 1969). It must be stressed however that an ideology or voting predisposition as an information economising device is not the same as party identification, and that the latter, used by scholars properly grounded in social psychology, is still incompatible in a serious way with rational choice theory. Ignorance, discovered by survey research, can be fitted into rational choice models, because it is a purely negative finding; voters do not seem capable of high level ratiocination. The same could have been deduced from that great taboo of social science research today, the known distribution of I.Q. in the population.

Accepting this ignorance, an information (and calculation) economising device is forced upon us, and it may look like party identification. Going beyond the symptoms, it clearly is not very like it. The researchers who use party identification have a plausible and deliberate theory of affective psychological links (Miller, 1975); they do not explain party identification in terms of political complexity, or as the result of a calculus that goes something like 'Labour was good enough for Dad, it suits my neighbours, the Tories are too posh for me, I may as well just stick to Labour'. Such might be compatible, as a rational short cut, with Downs, but it is not the same as the ideas of Converse, Campbell, Miller, Stokes, Butler, Valen, or whomever from Michigan.

Nor is the difference trivial. It follows, as we have argued, from the information economising approach to the survey data, that the likelihood of a voter paying careful attention to party policy, rather than voting from habit, is a function of the general ideological positions of the parties. The more probable it is that a shift in party ideology could lead one, by rational calculation, to vote in a way other than that prompted by simple information economising cues, the more probable it is that one will vote from a rational calculus. The party-identification surrogate in rational choice theory is dependent on the ideological preferences of the voter and his interpretation of what the parties stand for.

In contrast to this the party identification school usually argues that party identification is the source of either the respondent's own views, or his perception of party stands. Two quotations from Butler and Stokes serve to demonstrate:

> Since most electors have partisan dispositions and since the parties themselves offer a lead on most issues, it would be surprising if the parties did not assume a special status in giving structure to attitudes. When they do so, the flow of cause and effect is not from issue to party preference but the other way round, from party preference to belief on the issue. Attitudes towards issues have only a conserving or reinforcing influence on party choice and not a formative one.
>
> [*Political Change in Britain* (Pelican ed., 1971), p. 240]

Again, in trying to explain why some people think of themselves in terms of 'left or right', yet do not use these labels to characterise the parties, they say (p. 260):

> ... who have learned a set of ideological labels for the parties have also come to think of themselves, in a wholly nominal way, as being left or right according to their party persuasion. To such people, being asked whether they think of *themselves* as left or right means nothing more than being asked whether they have a preference for one of the

leading parties . . . he has stood on its head the basis of political choice which it assumes—his 'ideology' follows his partisanship, not his partisanship his ideology.

There is sometimes, in the spirit of intellectual pluralism, a demand for 'mixed mode' models of party competition. Unfortunately one cannot mix directly incompatible theories. Either one is a social psychologist of voting, in which case one believes the two quotations above, or one is not. Those two quotations, harmless though they may seem, and true though they may be, are death to the party competitive version of democracy. One cannot rely on competition for the vote maximising spot on the ideological dimension to produce a government satisfactory to the plurality, if the voter's preference depends on 'his' party's position.

We do not think that the party identification theorist's model of political life, as opposed to the raw data they provide us, is in any way yet proven, and may, as we suggested earlier, become ever less plausible. What we have to do now is to decide whether rational choice, with information economising aspects that make the raw data innocuous, will sustain a faith in competitive democracy. It is our feeling that previous models have not taken sufficient care about the implications of this 'predisposition to vote without calculation'. For our theory allows a loyal-vote that each party can expect, regardless of detailed policy. It allows generally that the outcome of an election may depend only marginally, or not at all, on exactly what policies are espoused. This leads us to derive a general logic of party competition which is not always consistent with a democracy that relies on the force of this competition.

The economic analogy we have drawn is with super-normal profits, that breakdown in perfect market conditions where the profit maximising drive of entrepreneurs, insufficiently restrained by competition, acts against the public interest. Stated briefly, the model we have developed requires vote maximising by the party only when this is either necessary or advantageous. At other times the parties have a limited freedom to adopt those policies nearer to the hearts of their supporters. We have recognised that the vote potential of a party position is not determined only by the distribution of voters' ideal preferences but also by the plausibility of the party advocating that policy. This plausibility can produce very serious limitations on a party's ideological movement. An example of this is the empirically observed tendency for the opposition party at election time to be more extreme than the incumbent party, or the way a policy appropriate to an economic boom may be enunciated where an incumbent party has presided over a deterioration in the economy.

Although there is a considerable danger in spurious rigour, it is useful at this stage to restate the argument of the previous chapters in a set of assumptions and propositions. Amongst other advantages, this allows for easier comparison with rival theories, and is the most economical way of summarising the research.

Assume:

1. Political parties consist of (a) leaders; (b) members.

2. (A) Leaders stand to gain directly if their party is elected, regardless of the policy it is dedicated to;

(B) Members stand only to gain by the policy outputs of the party if it is elected;

(C) Leaders depend on the members to help them get elected; they need to satisfy the members where possible.

3. Voters have ideological preferences for government policy output. They vote for that party whose ideology in general, or specific policies in particular, are nearest the voter's preference.

4. (Heuristic and operational assumption that could be avoided were it seriously embarrassing to the theory.) Party ideologies, party policies, and ideological and policy preferences of voters (and party members who are a subset of voters) can be represented in a space of some determinate dimensionality.

5. Preferences of voters are sufficiently varied and collectively incompatible that there is no single policy that perfectly satisfies all voters.

From these first assumptions it follows that:

(A) If two or more parties offer policies at an election, the number of votes they will each obtain is predictable: each voter will support the party whose position is nearest to his own.

(B) Parties can alter the number of votes they get by changing their positions.

(C) Party leaders will attempt to maximise their chances of getting elected by moving to a position that will be nearest to the largest numbers of voters possible subject to the restraining influence of the desires of their members who will cease to support the party actively if it moves too far from their preferred position.

So far the theory is more or less compatible with Downs, and does not obviously cause any problems for democratic faith. Assume further:

6. There is a certain cost and difficulty to voters in gaining and evaluating detailed information about party policy, which they will avoid if possible.

7. Each party has a crude ideology (which may be no more than the general principles its members (and possibly leaders) would prefer were they to be free of competitive forces). Voters have a rough recognition of these.

8. There are limits beyond which a party cannot easily move, at least in the short run. This assumption requires a different explication and justification in various contexts. For now, treat it as given.

It now follows that:

(D) Those voters whose preferred positions lie outside the area of likely change in the policies of a party will not have or require detailed knowledge. They will associate themselves fairly securely with the party whose general ideology is nearest their preferred position.

(E) No party can hope (or fear) to change its vote more than marginally by policy change—for the rest it can rely on a solid loyal vote which it will get whatever it promises to do when elected.

These two deductions take the place in our model of party identification; for us they are essentially rational, instrumental, and *learned* predispositions to vote for a party. Note that:

(F) The size of the loyal vote is dependent on the range of likely policy change.

So, unlike party identification, we do not assume that predispositions are independent of issue preferences, still less that they cause them. The model now fits observable facts of voting behaviour better than Downs, without changing the basic assumptions about voter behaviour on which his, and other, rational choice models rest. As yet it does not carry any anti-democratic implications (unlike party identification theories, which present the voter as the intellectual and moral captive of the party). One further assumption is needed to complete the simplest statement of the theory.

9. Conditions may arise in which the fixed loyal vote of one party is greater than that of its opponent's loyal vote *plus* the total number of voters whose preferences, lying inside the likely area of change in party policy, do not give them a safe ideologically determined, voting predisposition.

It now follows that, where (9) applies:

(G) One party can now win the election even if it adopts a policy that is less than vote maximising, because it does not need the extra voters it could attract.

(H) Where this happens other factors will determine the policy, the simplest of which will be the tug from the members to adopt a policy more attractive to them; this will lead to the fortunate party taking up a relatively extreme position.

Generally it seems most sensible to keep the formal statements of theory as rigorous and unspecific in terms of context as possible. When it comes to applying the theory in a particular context, flesh has to be put on the bones, explanations and justifications given for why some requirement of the theory can be expected to hold. The requirements themselves should be, as they are above, as parsimonious as possible. Otherwise one has not a theory, not an abstract model, but a unique description.

Let us show what we mean by this in pointing out how we have applied this abstract model to the context of British election campaigns *in the constituencies.* All the assumptions of the model are in fact general and do not require contextual amplification except for two. These are numbers eight and nine. Assumption eight requires that there be limits beyond which the party policy cannot easily change, so that (a) most voters need only know the general ideology of the party; and (b) only a few voters can be expected to react to detailed policy positions.

Applied to individual party candidates in the several constituencies, this is easily shown to be true. No political party can allow very much latitude to its candidates in interpreting its official policy, for fear that it cannot present itself as united and responsible. Hence there are limits on the policy a party's candidates can vary between, as required by assumption eight.

Assumption nine requires that situations occur where the expected loyal vote (as defined by the limits imposed by assumption eight) of one party is, by itself, enough to ensure election. This often happens at constituency level, because the policy of the party, to which the candidate is at least loosely tied, has to be aimed to maximise votes over the country as a whole. Any constituency that is very much different in distribution of preferences from the total national distribution (i.e., is a skewed example) is probably one in which assumption nine applies.

If these two assumptions do apply, then we should find, as we did in Chapter 5, in accordance with deduction (H), that as the probability of one party winning the election increases, it takes up a relatively extreme position. As could have been further deduced in these straightforward conditions, the opposition party follows it; the positions of both parties in constituencies where our model applies are pulled towards the ideological position of the dominant party.

In this microcosm, what does this do for democracy? It seems to hint that when one introduces an ersatz party identification into a rational choice model, there is a systematic distortion of policy offerings by parties. First, voters are offered policy positions that differ somewhat over the country, making the rational selection of a government difficult. This is particularly important given all the recent indications in Britain of the reduced importance or effectiveness of parliamentary party discipline. More important, particularly if transferred from this microcosm to the entire electoral scene, the forces of competition when mixed with voting predispositions independent of actual policy, make it likely that voters will not get the choice of two alternatives pitched near the majority *policy* preference position. They will instead get a relatively extreme policy set that will win, as it were, despite itself, and a policy (that loses) that is some way from being the rival moderate position that it should be.

When we transfer this theory to the general context of the national electorate as a whole, and talk about whole parties rather than candidates, the explanation of the assumptions changes and gets more complex. In fact it is useful, though not strictly necessary, to add two extra assumptions:

10. When political parties compete they will be judged partly in terms of the records they have established in office.

11. Government actually consists of trying to solve social problems that voters are aware of:

We can deduce that:

(I) A party's policy will be bound to change as socio-economic conditions and problems vary.

(J) Parties will present themselves, and will interpret the state of society, in the most favourable light.

(K) Apart from the loyal vote, there will be a probable shift of support towards or away from a party at any election depending on its record, and how plausible this makes its policies.

(L) Because problem solving is extremely difficult and major policy innovations very risky, parties will not be able or willing to deviate very far or very rapidly from the *status quo*. Policy making will be highly 'incremental', the more when current policies are highly successful.

This last deduction serves in place of the formal restriction on rapid policy change in assumption eight, and replaces the explanation for this in terms of party discipline on the candidates given earlier.

Unfortunately the richer and more complex the context the harder it is to make a theory produce obvious deductions without adding extra *ad hoc* assumptions that are hard to justify as being permanent additions to the theory. Rather, a simplifying abstract theory becomes, when applied to a context as complex as British electoral politics at the national level, more of an interpretive device. If it points to areas that seem interesting, suggest hypotheses, and is compatible with a still fairly parsimonious explanation, it is certainly better than no theory at all.

It is in this way that we used the theory in the second half of Chapter 4, to help account for observed correlations in policy change. All the theory can technically be said to predict, unless one makes the assumptions on voters' use of the 'record' much fuller, is that an equivalent to super-normal profits may obtain through a form of broad loyalty. As large numbers of people have loyal vote predispositions, and others vote on grounds of competence and record, situations will obtain where one party is freed of the need to be competitive, and the parties will then *not* set policies that give the voter the best chance of rationally choosing optimum policies for society or himself. What precisely the party thus freed will do cannot be predicted, precisely because the mainspring of the theory, force of competition, is relaxed, and this has to lead to indeterminacy. The obvious prediction from our assumptions about party members is that the fortunate party will retreat to its own ideological home, which is what we find the Conservative party doing in such situations.

Similarly the theory does predict both of our findings about the relationship between socio-economic change and party policy.

Economic policy for both parties does change to be more appropriate with changed economic conditions (deduction (I)). But at the same time there is a tendency to set both short and long term economic policy to reflect not 'real' economic conditions, but the strategic value of good conditions for a governing or opposing party and vice versa (deduction (J)).

Whether or not they are actually predicted, the findings that, allowing for other factors, governments are always more moderate than oppositions (less tied to actual current incrementalist policies) and that both parties converge on a moderate position when the economy is doing well (and presumably incrementalist policies are working) is entirely compatible with and suggested by deduction (L).

The only area of serious indeterminacy where another *ad hoc* assumption has to be brought in is, as we have just admitted, where one tries to predict what the general tendency will be where one party is likely to win whatever policy it adopts, and the other to lose whatever it does. The constituency data is not replicated here; although a favourable electoral or strategic situation does indeed, as it did in the constituencies, cause the Conservative party to go to its own extreme, and again likely defeat causes the Conservatives into moderation, the Labour party's behaviour is not symmetrical. For it is where the Labour party has a good chance of winning that it is relatively moderate, and where it is likely to lose that it retreats to the extreme. So the basic empirical 'law' is—'the probability of Conservatives winning is directly correlated with extremism by *both* parties'. (Or, if one thinks of a naive one dimensional left–right spectrum going from far left = zero to far right = 100, the Conservative probability of winning is directly related to Conservative ideological score and negatively related to Labour's score.) As this finding holds not just for the probability of a Conservative win in terms of the vote they got, but also in terms of what we have called 'strategic' economic conditions, it is very important for the relevance of competitive forces to democratic policy setting. It is therefore the more unfortunate that the theory should be indeterminate here.

The *ad hoc* assumption necessary to yield a prediction is neither complicated nor one that strains the model. It is also easy to see why it is needed, why the assumption related to party members and their 'pull' is not apparently applicable to the Labour party. The trouble is, as we have argued before and consider briefly in Appendix 1, the theory as it rests so far is static, and assumes an essential identity in the strategic conditions governing any two parties. If this is not so, if in fact one party has a much greater chance of winning elections just because it has been around longer and is more likely to be accepted as a 'natural' ruler because its own ideology is more closely related to the incrementalist policies and the *status quo*, then we have to expect that the effects of the competitive force being lifted at times will not be the same for both parties.

We have stressed elsewhere that in any election one party, the incumbents, are challenged for office by the 'outs', resulting in our successful prediction of the greater moderation, *ceteris paribus*, of the governing party.

This should alert us to an obvious and well accepted 'fact' of any political system—rival ideologies are not equally 'at home' or natural in the prevailing consensus. However moderate, a party that is relatively new and represents 'loyal voters' previously disenfranchised is always the 'challenger'.

What we need is an extra assumption that says, briefly, that one party, in our case the Conservatives, are in the position of having, sometimes, to defend themselves against a challenge by being moderate, but can afford the rest of the time to be relatively extreme because they have the benefit of the doubt as the party of the consensus. The rival party can *only* hope to win by being moderate, can never afford to be extreme *if there is a chance of winning*. On the other hand they have a harder job of keeping a loyal vote and a mass membership, and need, where there is little to be gained by competitive moderation in the face of a likely victory for the established party, to retreat to ideological purity.

All this demonstrates perhaps, is that the competitive theory of democracy *is* highly indeterminate when something, loyal vote groups (or party identification) removes the mainspring. That is enough to create severe problems for competitive democracy, as our data in Chapter 4 shows. The *ad hoc* assumption suggested here cannot be built into the theory because it is too historically specific to be worthwhile in a general theory. But it is entirely compatible with the theory, which indeed was necessary to point out where to look for an explanation of data that could not even have been discovered without it. It is common in all the sciences, social or otherwise, to find that theory building in any rigorous or abstract way is only really possible when the theory is a static one—introducing dynamics makes the problems increase exponentially.

To wind up, there are six broad empirical 'laws' we have discovered because of, in most cases deducible from, our effort to take seriously and develop the almost instinctive faith in competitive parties that lies at the heart of modern democratic theory. They are not, most of them, exactly conducive to that democratic theory's prime values or expectations. They are:

1. As the Conservative vote increases, both parties tend to their own extreme.

2. As the strategic economic situation brightens for the Conservatives, both parties tend to their own extreme.

3. As the strategic economic situation worsens, the parties tend to adopt an 'inappropriate' economic policy.

4. As the economy worsens, both parties tend to their own extremes.

5. *Ceteris paribus*, incumbents are more moderate than opposition parties.

6. At the constituency level, as the chance of one party winning increases, both parties move towards the ideological 'home' of that party.

How much does all this matter? Are the consequences for democratic theory at all serious? The temptation is to say that the argument and evidence in this book amount to a serious threat to the faith we can put in democracy, as long as that form of government is defined round the competition of parties. This cannot be sustained, if only because the model of democracy it attacks never had much chance anyway.

Nothing we have said seriously challenges the minimum defence of competitive democracy. The minimum is that competing political parties will not be able to consistently and flagrantly flout the electorate's will. This remains true, for all that we have said refers to policy setting at the margin. Despite our six 'empirical laws', no candidate can win his own constituency by extensively deviating from central party policy—only at the margin may he modify party policy, only the marginal votes can be won by his competitiveness. When separate constituencies vote, the resulting government is supported by a parliamentary party that is, very roughly, agreed on policy. So no very serious collective inconsistencies are involved.

Though there is a tendency to interpret the economic climate to one's best advantage, resulting in the selection of party policies that may be out of keeping with the times, this cannot go too far—economic reality cannot be ignored for very long. So only a marginal variation of policy, only a marginal misinformation of the electorate is possible there.

The tendency for a losing Labour party or a victorious Conservative party to be more extreme than the probable vote maximising policy, with the result that there can be times when no party offers the vote maximising policy is, again, only marginal. It is dependent on both parties having a large block of loyal votes, and it is dependent on one of them being pretty sure to win because of its record whatever the exact policies are. If any party goes too far, passes the threshold where it forces the party's faithful voters to think twice, it will lose.

Incumbents may be forced to stick close to a moderate position, in defence of their incrementalism, while their opponents may have to be extreme, disowning the current policies whether or not they are successful, but this again has sharp natural limits. A very successful incumbent party will find its rivals having to admit that existing policies are worth following, while a party that has presided over disaster will have to risk unlining this rather than offer the electorate a second dose.

There is no danger of the forces of competition failing so badly that extreme policies, policies that a sizeable majority of the population dislike, are chosen because there is no consensual choice available, any more than there is a danger of highly dubious and economically irrelevant reactions to the economy being enshrined in party policy. The collective choice of the several constituency elections will not be seriously inconsistent as a result of local competitive forces. To repeat, everything happens at the margin.

But the margin is important. Lenin says somewhere that the trouble with people is that 'they think theoretical systems can be played on like a flute'. Which we take to mean that one cannot ignore small scale theoretical predictions because they are small scale. In this case, of the selecting of governmental policy, largely economic policy, by party competition, margins, so vital to economic theory, are vital also for us. Policies do not have to be very far out of kilter, after all, to cause quite enough trouble.

In the end the utility of this book depends entirely on what one hopes competitive politics will ensure. As a protective mechanism, to ensure that the people are not forced to take policies they are strongly opposed to, it works. It has usually been put in this light, because of the stress on satisfying people's wants as though this were a purely distributive question, and because the principal value of democracy has been the right of the voter to be the sole moral judge.

We have right through this book being addressing a secondary problem, another task that the electorate might be thought to play, which has less to do with distributive questions, and more with technical questions. What we have worried about is the chance of competitive democracy ensuring that the correct policies are applied to solve problems. This is what policy making, as contrasted with the making of general moral commitments, is about. And this is where the margin comes into play. If, at the margin, policies are determined by competitive forces so that they are unlikely to be particularly close to a vote maximising point, and if the choice of alternative solutions is, even at the margin, competitively determined rather than technically or ideologically determined then we can hardly rely on the voter to select wisely.

It may be argued here that the voter has never been capable of resolving details of policy, so that it hardly matters that political parties will not be likely to offer him the choice from which some hypothetically competent voter could choose correctly. We think this argument is false for two reasons. The first is simply that, if the voter cannot make decisions, even in the limited sense of choosing between two or three broad alternatives, who is there to choose? Who, indeed, could we trust to do the choosing? The electorate may be incompetent, but the electorate, particularly if aided by the arguments of responsible parties, is the only tribunal open to democratic theory.

The main reason for rejecting this argument however is that even if voters are too stupid or ignorant to be relied on to come to the correct answer, matters can only be made worse by competitive forces that seem to ensure that the correct alternatives will probably not even be offered.

That is where we must leave the matter. We have tried to show that the very invisible guiding hand of party competition on which democratic hopes rest can be shown, theoretically and empirically, to be less than adequate. Of course we have studied only a limited area. Many other aspects of the interaction between party and voter are cloaked in appalling ignorance. At least two stand out. We know very little about the extent to which political parties are able, or even forced, to change public opinion itself, to create a market for their goods. Above all, we have very little idea about the definitions of social problems, about how something comes to be seen as a problem by party or voter, about the setting of the political agenda against which the process of party competition works. These should be investigated, and theorists ought to come to grips with the underpinning of a democratic theory orientated to modern complexities of social problem solving. It is more than likely that the fears that seem here to be sustained will be shown to be chimerical. But we are sure that the work that does that will have to be the sort of mixture of normative, prescription, abstract modelling, and empirical analysis that we have feebly attempted here. Perhaps the only virtue of this book is as a methodological exercise, an attempt to decompartmentalise political science, to study a problem for good theoretical reasons, where 'theory' means neither exclusively 'prediction' nor prescription, but both.

Party Systems: Development

Disraeli is credited with seeing the expansion of the electorate in 1868 as holding out the promise of millions of working class Conservative votes. His colleagues were truer to Downsian theory, assuming that to enlarge the franchise was to open up the political spectrum and shift the policy required for election sharply to the left. In time the enlargement did do this, and a new Labour party, as we show in Chapter 4, converged on the Conservatives, presumable squeezing out the Liberals.

Two facts are significant. One is that it took a great deal of time for manhood suffrage to produce even a minority Labour government. Indeed since its birth in 1900 the Labour party has only twice won firm electoral victories. The other is that, as we show in Chapter 4, while the Conservative party has moved left over time, the Labour party has had to move as firmly rightwards. What we want to do in this note is to comment on two aspects of the development of party competitive systems. It seems clear that perfectly competitive parties do not spring up overnight, and that the relationships between parties in the competitive arena are not static. It is equally obvious that if politics has to do with problem solving according to some paradigm, the paradigms change at times, the dimensions of competition change.

As Downs would have it, changes in party systems come about by changes in the suffrage, or by cataclysmic social shocks like wars that shift the beliefs of voters dramatically. Party systems change with an expansion of the franchise because the new voters shift the distribution of opinion; this must lead either to one or more of the existing parties benefiting, or to the creation of a new party, taking advantage of the new voters. Figure A.1 displays this.

When one concentrates on politics as the satisfaction of demands, or the distribution of utility this is plausible. Where governments can act in this way, then a rational voter in the new segment of the electorate can have no reason for not preferring the new party. Furthermore, as franchise extension usually means the gradual enfranchising of lower and lower social statuses, it is more than plausible to see an enlargement of the franchise as meaning an extension of the spectrum. This though is not inevitable. Franchise extension could leave the distribution outline unchanged, where the vote has been withheld on some criterion that is uncorrelated with economic interests, or ideological

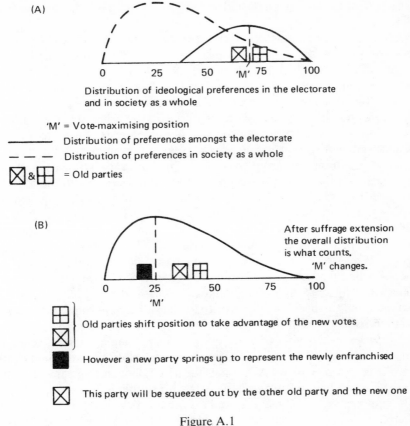

Figure A.1

preference. Thus the 1928 enfranchisement of the 'flapper' might have led to no change in the distribution profile at all.

We, on the other hand, have consistently argued that governing, and hence competition for office, cannot be seen in such simple want distribution terms. The identification of problems, and the discovery of solutions to them provides dimensions of party competition where it is by no means clear that adding a poorer stratum of society extends the area of competition. The new voters may have very different interests, but they have to be persuaded that these are capable of solution outside the existing paradigm. Furthermore, as a large element in competitive success must be the reputation for competence of the party, a new party, necessarily starting small and building up its resources and membership, with political solutions of some novelty, will by no means be a rational choice, for even the poorest voter.

One can possibly hold that a millworker who votes Conservative in 1970 because he believes they are Britain's natural rulers is irrational. It is somewhat harder to maintain the same of his father who votes Liberal in 1924 because he does not trust the new and untested ideas of a leadership who have never held office.

We have already stressed the incrementalist nature of democratic government selection by the voters, the idea that democracy is not a method for radical social change. Elections do not, usually, change social paradigms. This does not mean, however, that extremist parties (where by extremist we mean no more than that a party has a set of policies outside the social paradigm) can never have effects. As a party advocates, over and over, a new set of priorities, a new set of methods, which may be more in the interests of a more recently enfranchised or organised class, one would expect the number prepared to risk them to go up. It is in this way, and gradually, that one expects social paradigms to change, with the old party accepting bit by bit policies and attitudes of the newcomer to fend off defeat. At the same time the newcomer, having made its mark on the scene, changes its character. At first it could not compete, because, as it were, it did not speak the language, and had no natural voting support. It could not hope to compete on the old terms, and if it tried would fail to attract support. Why bother voting for a Labour party that offers the same as the Liberals, when they have never been put to the test? That would be no more rational than to accept an untried, nonparadigmatic ideology.

So we would expect a new party to remain in a noncompetitive stance, effectively isolated from the rewards and constraints of competitive strategy until its presence begins to shift the paradigm, making it feasible to be competitive. Such a sequence of events consequent on the extension of the franchise is shown in Figure A.2. It must be noted, though, that paradigms, the accepted definition of problems and criteria for solutions, are not apolitical.

By apolitical here we mean to indicate that a paradigm, or part of one, belongs, in a sense, to the party that first thought of it or introduced it. In the British case, there is little that is basic to the definition of political reality that is the work of the Labour party alone. Only the nationalisation of industry is solely theirs amongst the stock in trade of policy makers; even the welfare state owes as much to the other members of the wartime coalition. For this reason political parties are not to be seen as equally competitive. One, the older, the one that remains from an earlier time, which is traditionally associated with most elements of the paradigm has an edge. It cannot be sure of election, but is probably the fail–safe choice for anyone who does not wish the *status quo* to be seriously changed. The rivals, whose heart lay, if it does not still lie, outside that paradigm, can still win elections, but its job is harder; it has either to compete against the accepted managers on their own terms, which will be difficult, or trust to a strong desire to change it. One way of putting this is to say that, in our case, the Conservatives sometimes need fear losing, Labour only occasionally can hope to win.

We cannot begin to prove this contention, and it is offered only as speculation that seems to follow from the theory of the rational voter and the competitive party, and which explains both facts of our electoral history and the evidence we adduce in Chapter 4.

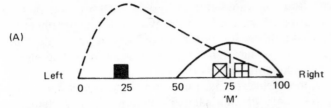

(A)

The ideological preferences may be extended, perhaps by the enfranchisement of voters with new class interests, without this leading to the victory of the new party ■ . For these new interests still have to be mapped on to a 'policy-method' space as in (B) below, which may not shift the vote-maximising point much, as the traditional policy method paradigm remains dominant.

'M' = Vote-maximisation point   ■ = New party

⊠ & ⊞ = Old parties

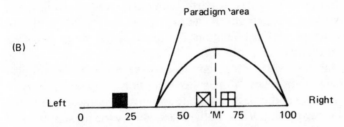

In this case 'M' indicates not only the vote-maximising point but the basic social consensus. As this changes, partly because of the policies advocated by the new party and as the new party itself moves right to attract votes, it comes into the area of real electoral competition (As in (C) below)

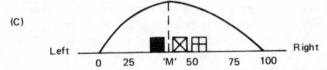

Now one old party ⊠ is in danger of being squeezed out. The other old party ⊞ remains dominant as the 'natural' governing party of the modified paradigm.

Figure A.2

Certainly it is necessary that a theory of party competition have a dynamic element. Much of what we have said above is similar, in implication if not basis, to Key's theory of the critical election (Key, 1966), and we do need some systematic explanation of the changes in paradigms. There is no case in the western democracies of frequent changes of governmental control. Everywhere, at any time, one party or group seems dominant. *Ad hoc* explanations abound, and are doubtless true in their limited aims. The New Deal clearly shifted registration to make the Democrats the natural rulers of America since the early thirties, religious cleavage clearly explains protestant dominance in Ulster. Those cases are significantly different however in that the latter is not an example of competitive politics. Why, given an instrumental, pragmatic, political tradition, as for instance in Australia, New Zealand, non-French Canada, Britain, America north of the Mason-Dixon line, should competitive parties not frequently alternate?

It is not because voters dislike the idea in principle, as Butler and Stokes show, when they report 54% of their samples favouring regular change of governments.

Why has suffrage not usually led, with any speed, to the importance of new parties, or radical shifts in the position of old ones? In Britain, in 1868, 1928, 1970, no working class, no women's rights, no youth-oriented, policies or parties came into sudden strength. This has to be a problem for a rational voting theory, for obvious reasons. But it is no less a problem for any other social science explanation of voting and party competition. Perhaps the idea of a 'natural' ruling party sounds insufficiently value free, because it is so often the arrogant claim of a country's right wing party, with aristocratic overtones. Yet if we call it a 'dominant' party, as political scientists are prone to, and still do not have some non-instrumental explanation in terms of religious or other cleavage, we do not remove the problem.

It would take another work altogether to analyse the idea of political paradigms, and their relation both to party competition and to the theory of policy making, yet it seems the best candidate we have. Taking seriously the idea that a party's record is important both in fact, and by the prescriptions of rational voting theory, and the 'problem and solution' concept of governing used here, makes the concept of ownership of a paradigm the most obvious candidate, to solve many of our problems. In its turn it focuses our attention on the need for dynamic, developmental theorising on party competition, as a vital part of democratic theory in general. For democracy's greatest weakness is probably in the handling of change, and the adopting, when necessary, of new assumptions of how society must be moulded. If we are right about the primacy of party competition as the driving mechanism in representative democracy, the nature of the paradigm, and its setting are urgent questions for political theory.

APPENDIX 2

Rationality

It might be argued that our treatment of party competition rests heavily on an implausible belief in the rationality of the voter and the party activist.

While we have discussed shortly the problem of voter rationality, the activist we have not considered. Yet he is vital, because the need of the party for activists, and their having ideological preferences which act as a brake on the party's mobility, is our principal alteration to Downs.

It might be said, of the activist, that our portrayal of him as ideologically committed and calculating is untrue or unlikely. He will work, not because of any precise commitment to a policy or ideology, but because he enjoys partisan canvassing, because his family has traditionally worked for the party, because it is expected of him by his social circle, or to oblige a friend.

We do not wish to deny any of this. Nor do we deny that a man thus motivated may have only a very loose idea of what the ideology of the party is, and no clearer set of views of his own. We accept the suggestion that a man is motivated generally, in his political activity, by the intrinsic value an action has for him. It is doubtful that an activist's time is not wasted by the expectation of his activity gaining him rewards. This we see as a necessary assumption, because without it the theory of party competition comes across a very serious problem.

As this problem has so far been presented, it refers to the decision to vote. If voting is to be seen as the action of choosing a government, the greatest danger to the assumption of voter rationality comes not from data explaining voting, but from the fact that people vote at all. For the chances of any individual's vote affecting the outcome of an election are minute. Voting as a rational action has been seen to imply that to vote is to carry out an act with the intention of producing an effect on the world, that of getting one's favourite party elected. If the probability of one's action affecting the result approaches zero, the action itself is irrational. It is irrational to do something that has virtually no connection with the goal one seeks, because 'rationality' when used by social scientists is usually defined as 'choosing and implementing the most efficient means to achieve a goal', or 'maximising utility and minimising costs'. The rational man does not vote.

Downs and his followers have sought to escape this paradox by falling back on a sense of 'citizen duty', or an allegiance to democratic ways. The destruction of democracy is seen as likely if turnout falls badly in an election.

The former escape is giving up the attempt to produce a theory based on the assumption of rationality. 'Citizen duty' is clearly a motive for an action that breaks down the teleological nature of the standard definition of rationality. The second escape, via the dangers to democracy of abstention, has rightly been shown to be not an escape at all, because it meets the same charge as voting to select a party—one's own vote is not going to make the slightest difference.

The same charge could be made were we to insist that the party activist is a man motivated by a desire to change political reality. It is not true that one activist by himself can produce no change, admittedly. The size of his contribution to the total effort needed here is big enough to escape the exact charge put in the voting case. But we are too well aware that people do work very hard for candidates who have not the slightest chance of getting elected. Such action, because the connection between the activist's effort and his desired result is virtually nil, must again be judged irrational.

We have no desire to engage in the rather empty game of debating exact definitions of 'rationality'. It is clear that (i) the definition of rational behaviour which makes it a teleological relation between effort and achieving a goal is one of the meanings we give the phrase, and (ii) that in this case much political behaviour is irrational. At the same time we cannot escape the facts of ordinary language. We would not call a man who goes out to vote and votes for A, when he knows A is nearer to his preferences than B, irrational. We might call him irrational had he voted for B. Not necessarily, for there are excuses he could make. We would certainly regard his behaviour as 'odd', or 'inconsistent', and even as 'surprising', unless he did make an excuse. The excuse might be that his wife would be unhappy that he voted for A, or that in this particular case he preferred the B party candidate although generally A's candidates were nearer his desires. It does not matter what we would expect of him by way of an excuse. What does matter is that they would probably be forthcoming, that we would, ordinarily and not just as social scientists, see a *prima facie* case of 'oddness' about voting for B when one's beliefs were closer to A. Let us be clear about some of the things we would not see as odd. We would not regard it as odd or irrational to stay at home and not vote, though we might regard it as bad or lacking in civil duty. One reason we would not regard staying at home as odd is that we would expect to be given as an excuse, that the man's vote would not achieve anything. This is the point the critics of Downs make, but it should be clear that it is only a very partial account of rationality. It is rational to refrain from voting because of that probability calculation, but it is not irrational not to refrain from voting.

To carry out an action is not irrational because it is unlikely to achieve a certain end; it is only irrational if the achievement of that end is the only, or the main, reason given. The heart of rational action is that it is consistent action, consistent with any fact or desire that is relevant. Hence it is inconsistent, and thus irrational, to vote for B while desiring A, unless one provides an excuse. What the excuse is doing is saying, for instance, that in this case the voter's preference is judged, by him, less relevant than his wife's. Under the 'consistent action' definition of rationality it is rational to vote when this is unlikely to produce any effect, in all cases except the one where producing the effect is the necessary cause. It is rational to work hard for a political party which is bound to lose as long as getting the party elected is not cited as the only relevant 'fact'.

It should be said that this accords with usage, for it avoids a mistake often made when talking about the irrationality of political action. Everyone who uses such language would agree that goals themselves are not subject to judgement as rational or irrational. A man may seek any end he chooses, and he may be judged for this according to the language of morality. A goal may be noble, evil, less than worthy, degrading. It cannot be irrational. The only grounds we would have for describing a goal as irrational are these: that a man is known to desire more something else, that this something else is incompatible with the goal, and that he knows this. Once again we use 'irrational' to mean that pursuit of a goal is inconsistent with a consideration the subject in question regards as relevant.

It is also true, though sometimes not noticed, that motives are not subject to the epithets 'rational' and 'irrational'. A man is not irrational (or rational) in voting either out of self interest, or because of the intrinsic satisfaction of voting. Again, motives, like the goals they are ontologically related to, may be good or bad or base or noble, but not rational or irrational. For rationality is a concept that refers to a connection or a relationship, and if it does not mean precisely 'consistent', it means something rather close to it.

Now there would be little point in saying all this if the result were to establish that voting or working for a party is not irrational, and that the concept of rationality could have nothing to do with such activity. We have tried to show something rather different, that such political activity, like any activity, is *non*-rational as far as motivation goes, but is subject to judgement in terms of rationality (or consistency) *in its details*. This is far more useful. By and large we can expect political activity to be rational in this sense: we expect that a man's actions will not be inconsistent with facts, values, desires, that appear relevant to him. It is an open and empirical question how much one man's estimation of what is relevant in an action situation will accord with the estimation of others, and of the social scientist in general. In the end the sociologists may rule that even in this sense man is not rational, because he is inconsistent, or that he cannot be known to be rational because we cannot know his estimation of relevance. As yet, however, this point has not been argued, and we know of very little evidence for it.

The value for social theorising of this 'consistency' version of rationality is great. It ought, in the end, to allow for better prediction than the definition of rationality previously used which succeeded simply in ruling much activity irrational. For that which is irrational is in some ways inherently unpredictable, because random.

The way we use the assumption of consistency can be demonstrated schematically.

1. X finds action A intrinsically valuable.
2. X is aware of the following facts: f_1, f_2, f_n.
3. X is consistent in doing A, given $f_1 \ldots f_n$.
4. 'The fact that $\ldots f_1$' ceases to be true.
5. X stops doing A.
6. X retains consistency, as would be predicted given the statements: 'X is a consistent (rational) man'. 'A is only consistent action, given $f_2 \ldots f_n$ if also given f_1'.

To demonstrate: X finds it intrinsically valuable to work for party A, because he is committed to the principles A espouses. In X's cognitive environment there is no 'fact' 'f_n' such as to make him find that the 'fact' (f_1) (that he believes in the policies of A) is irrelevant.

Party A changes its policies considerably to try to attract more votes. X begins to see an inconsistency between working for party A and his own espousal of the policies A formerly, but no longer, stood for.

No one would deny that the 'facts' (in the odd way we use the word here) that X may judge relevant can be enormously varied. We do not insist that X's working for A is always dependent on the motivation we mentioned in the example, that he was committed to the policies of A.

Our argument is this: whatever the motivation X has for working for party A, it is very hard to think of a case where the ideology of A is not in some direct or indirect way, a relevant fact. Thus if the policy of A changes at any time, the cognitive background against which X's support for A was rational is going to change, and this may well, but not certainly, cause X to see continued support for A as irrational, and give up. If our argument is correct, we should be able to predict changes in political activity which arise from a much wider range of motivations than under the teleological conception of rationality. Before, any action not teleologically motivated was ruled as irrational, and hence not predictable, nor subject to theoretical calculation.

The examples of motivations given earlier seem to accord with this. Support out of a simple desire to take part in political activity still poses the question, 'Why choose that particular party?'

Any answers to this question must take account of the fact that the ideology of a party is so basic in defining it, that a change in ideology is bound to be relevant.

Supporting a party to please a peer group, a friend, a social caste, or to keep up with a family tradition may all, in themselves, be motives for which ideology is not a significant fact. But we still, obviously, need to ask the further questions—why is there that family tradition, why did your friend, peer group, social caste or whatever, wish you to support A? Indeed to be part of a caste, a peer group, to have that particular friend, involves values that are likely to make the ideology relevant.

The argument amounts to this. Human behaviour is predictable, if it is, because of an interlocking web of social 'facts' which produce for any man a limited set of actions which are internally consistent. The rationality judgements on which the theory of party competition, and democratic theory generally, rest, are usually presented as a form of 'teleological rationality'. Because this assumes a particular motivation, one in which men desire to see particular changes in the world come about from their actions, there is considerable doubt about the veracity of the assumptions.

However an alternative definition of rationality, as 'consistent' behaviour, serves all the needs our theory has, and is much more immune to criticism.

In fact it is not clear that the stronger version of rationality is untrue. There is considerable evidence now that party identification is not only usually perfectly 'rational', but changes, as social status changes, to preserve 'rationality' (Goldberg, 1969).

There are also research reports demonstrating a close connection between governmental popularity, and the efficiency of the government in controlling the economy. This is evidence not only of the form of rationality we require, but of a degree of knowledge that is hard to square with the ignorance of the voter presented to us by survey research (Goodhart, 1970; Kramer, 1971).

APPENDIX 3

Ideological Competition: Does it Work?

Throughout this book we have endeavoured to theorise and measure the changing ideological message of politicians. It has been assumed that at least some voters do vote in accordance with the policies adopted by candidates and parties. There is little direct evidence on this point. The most that can be squeezed out of survey research is that some voters are potentially 'issue voters'. Examinations of aggregate voting statistics concentrate on demographic values, and again show evidence that is compatible with voters' being influenced by policy positions, but cannot demonstrate, for lack of data about ideological stands, that they actually do vote partially as a result of ideological competition.

We feel that Chapters 4 and 5 of this book establish safely that ideological competition is engaged in by politicians, and show this particularly clearly at the constituency level. Unfortunately not only is there little direct evidence of competition affecting the vote, but there exists an accepted view, about British electioneering, that no candidate can ever hope to influence his vote very much. From somewhere a figure has even been put on this; it is now a common wisdom that no candidate is worth more than about five hundred votes over or below the national swings.

The previous homogeneity of electoral swing in Britain is mentioned for example in Stokes (1967) as a reason why the local candidate effect he finds over and against both the statewide and national swings in American politics cannot be expected to have an analogy in Britain. All of the Nuffield election studies since 1950 stress this, usually to the point that even rival organisational strengths and relative campaign efficiency are dismissed as not being important factors in deciding elections.

Some counter evidence is accumulating. Whatever may have been true in the past, regional swings are no longer entirely homogenous, as is witnessed by the results of the (perhaps unusual) general elections of 1974. Increasing fluidity of electoral loyalties, termed 'volatility' in the press shows up here as much as in other indicators (Crewe, 1974), and there are some reports of the difference that can be made in turnout at least by canvassing (Bochel, 1971).

It is not likely that candidates, organisations, or any purely local forces have a major effect on the constituency results. Indeed it is part of our theory that they should not do so, for the ideological positions of candidates are assumed (and shown) to be dependent on the size of the loyal vote for the candidates. How much do local forces have to affect votes to be important, however? If only a few percent of the voters change, a large number of constituencies are lost. In 1955, the year our data for the first part of Chapter 5 comes from, there were 42 seats in which the majority was less than a thousand, 22 less than five hundred. Had the swing to the Conservative party varied even slightly from its national average of 1·6% many of these seats would have been different. One example will suffice; Ealing North was won in 1955 by the Conservatives with a majority of only 246, and, much more significantly, on a swing of only ·3% to Labour.

Obviously then any statistically significant effect of the candidate's ideology on the swing to his party in his constituency has a decided political significance. As Table A.1 shows, there was a group of candidates for the Conservative party in 1955 whose average swing, ·73, was so much lower than the national swing that, had it been repeated over the whole country, the party would have won hardly any seats. These candidates have only one thing in common—on the straightforward left–right dimension that we describe as the first to be extracted from our data on this election (Chapter 5), they are all relatively 'right' wing even for their own party.

In this way we can go a little towards testing the hypothesis that the relative positions of the candidates in an election can marginally affect their vote, a *sine qua non* of our whole theory. We carry out two separate tests. First, we look just at the Conservative candidates on the first, general, left–right, dimension that we claim characterised the policy measures of candidates as indicated by their election addresses. This we do only for the Conservatives, because we have good evidence that they are acting competitively on this dimension, whereas we showed in Chapter 5 that the pattern of ideological positions for the Labour party over the four dimensions was somewhat more complex. In our second test however we use three measures of ideology, the Conservative positions on two dimensions and the Labour party position on one.

For the first test we set up the simple hypothesis that the more extreme a candidate is, the lower should be the swing to his party. As far as we are concerned, the swing represents those voters who are in a sufficiently marginal position socially to need to take note of changing party policy. The grounds for our hypothesis are spelled out in detail in Chapter 3 and in a more rigorous way in Chapter 6 and need not be repeated here.

Unfortunately the election of 1955 followed a widespread change of constituency boundaries, so that only in a sub-sample of 28 constituencies are we able to calculate the swing, based as it is on the change between two elections in similar constituencies. Table A.1 shows how, if one split the sample of 28 Conservative candidates into two, according to how far they are from their own end of the left–right dimension, the more extreme have a decidedly lower swing to their party than the less extreme.

Table A.1. Differences in Swing to the Conservative Party
Enjoyed by Two Groups of Conservative Candidates

Relatively Extreme Candidates	Relatively Moderate Candidates	
0·73	1·67	Mean Conservative Swing
N = 13	N = 15	

The difference here is statistically significant, despite the very small sample size, at the 10% level, with a 't' score of 1·50 and 26 degrees of freedom. The difference therefore upholds our theory, and goes some way to redressing the balance of importance to the candidate. Before we turn to the second type of test, it is worthwhile examining these data in slightly more detail, for the value of social science hypotheses rests perhaps more on their specificity than on their statistical significance, and it is interesting to consider the interaction between both candidates in the light of the test just demonstrated.

The swing to a candidate should clearly depend not only on his own position, but on how extreme or moderate his rival is. The most successful candidate should be the one who, though moderate himself, is opposed by an unusually extreme rival, and vice versa.

By scaling both Conservative and Labour candidates we end up with four possible constituency types: Conservative extreme, Labour moderate; Conservative moderate, Labour extreme; both moderate; both extreme. From common sense we can predict a pattern here; the highest Conservative swing should come in the constituency where most of the possible marginal voters will be nearer the Conservative than the Labour candidate, that is, where a moderate Conservative faces an extreme Labour party candidate. The lowest Conservative swing will therefore be in the opposite case. The other two cases should be intermediate, but we can perhaps be a little more precise here as well. Where both candidates are either unusually extreme for their party, or unusually moderate, there is in a sense nothing for the marginal voters to base a choice on. Where both are extreme, neither party is trying to maximise its vote, neither is trying for the middle ground of the marginal voters, and it seems likely that they will split more or less equally, producing a rather low swing for the Conservatives. Where on the other hand, by being both rather moderate, they are trying to vote maximise, local strategy may well cancel out, leaving the swing to be decided by national forces alone. If this is so, one would expect a swing to the Conservatives rather closer to the national average.

Obviously with a sample of only 28, these four categories will not be large enough for serious significance testing, but the pattern alone, if it conforms to our predictions, carries some weight. Table A.2 shows that the pattern indeed does so conform.

Table A.2. Average Conservative Swing According to Interaction Pattern Between Candidates' Ideological Positions

Extreme Cons. Moderate Lab.	Extreme Cons. Extreme Lab.	Moderate Cons. Moderate Lab.	Extreme Lab. Moderate Cons.
0·75 N = 6	0·83 N = 6	1·25 N = 6	2·25 N = 6

The largest discrepancy is, as expected, between the seats with an extreme Conservative fighting a moderate Labour candidate, and its opposite, and the difference in mean swing there is, in fact, mildly significant at the 10% level ('t' = 1·46, df = 10). The other predicted difference, that the intermediate seats would have intermediate scores, and that seats with two moderates would be nearer the national swing than those with two extreme candidates is also borne out, though not at any significant level.

So far we have not done much to show the direct effect of the ideology of the Labour party on the swing away from them and towards the Conservatives. There is no reason at all to suppose that the measurement difficulties that precluded this in the first test mean that there is no such effect.

Indeed the second test shows that they can be. This is more complex (slightly) because we wanted to produce a full path diagram of effects, and have thus used a regression equation. It was also done using a slightly different set of dimensions derived, as the others were, but using only a subset of the original variables. In this case two out of the three dimensions used apply only to Conservative candidates, and the third only to Labour candidates. Other sets of dimensions could have been used, and these are chosen only for display purposes as they have a certain intuitive appeal.

The test takes the form of regressing swing to Conservatives against:
(a) The position of the Conservative candidate on a dimension which stresses faith in private enterprise, and puts the benefits of economic growth above welfare matters. A high score indicates a great stress on the Conservative end of this spectrum.
(b) The Conservative position on a dimension stressing the party's record as international peacemakers. (This election was, after all, the first one after Korea, and one when the Conservatives feared the label of warmongers.)
(c) A dimension on which Labour candidates are arrayed according to the extent they emphasised the need for redistribution of wealth. Positive scores indicate great stress on this aspect.

The path diagram below demonstrates the various effects. The equation as a whole is significant at the 1% level with an R^2 = ·394.

There is clear evidence here for both competitive behaviour and its effectiveness. Briefly, as the Conservative expected vote goes up, they take a more extreme position on private enterprise, and make less play of their peacemaking role. However, to stress the virtues of *laissez-faire* depresses their

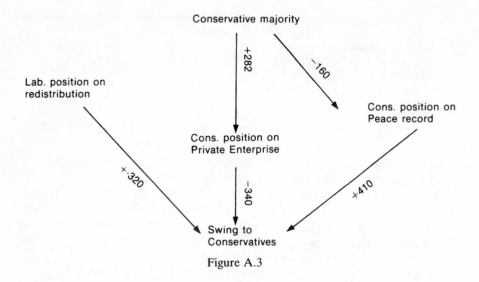

Figure A.3

swing, while to talk about peace making boosts it. The Labour candidates, who are not significantly affected by the voting on this model, nonetheless affect the swing, for as they emphasise redistribution, they boost the Conservative swing, making their own position less good. All of these effects work in reverse as well of course. The basic lesson seems to be that playing down one's own economic philosophy is the best way to capture votes one needs in a marginal constituency. All the paths shown in this model (they are of course standardised beta weights) are significant at, at least, the 5% level. Slim though the overall effect of the equation is, explaining only 39% of the variance in swing, it is notable.

Though they have never put it in those terms, it is doubtful that the political experts who discount the worth of the candidate, would allow them to explain as much as 39% of the variance even were they able to point to some other powerful explanatory variable that accounted for all the remaining 61%. In fact there must be so much random 'noise' in our measures of ideological position that the estimate of variance explained is surely lower than the truth.

Why should this evidence be so unusual? Why, if there is evidence for the effect of ideology, should it be so disregarded? There are two reasons at least. One is that the total size of this effect is very small (though enough to change political futures), and is only going to be discovered by someone looking in precisely the right way. Unless one has, as we had, good theoretical reasons to expect such an effect, such very marginal phenomena, vastly more significant than obvious, will not be observed.

The other reason though is that overall we do not expect that even this marginal effect will occur in such a way as to cause any thing so dramatic as an electoral defeat for a candidate otherwise likely to win. After all the situations where ideological position will lead to a local swing being far from the national one are precisely those where the strength of competition is weak. In any seat which is at all marginal, we expect that candidates will both be moderate, both be trying to maximise votes. The seats where the two parties interact in such a way as to give one party a sizeable divergence from national results are those where at least one party is being unusually extreme—and this will not happen, says our theory and its supporting data, unless that party is sure of winning the election anyway.

It is part of the logic of the situation that makes it so hard to find evidence in general for party competition/rational vote theories. As long as competition is working, and both parties are fixed firmly as near as possible to a vote maximising position, party loyalties will predict the vote both in rational choice and in party identification theories. One has to look at extreme cases to get a chance of clearly refuting one or other. So nationally one needs an election with a Goldwater or McGovern, at the constituency level one needs to look, as we do here, at those constituencies only where theory tells one the candidate should matter. He seems definitely to do so.

Bibliography

There are unusually few references in this book. We assume that readers are familiar with both the traditional writings on democratic theory, and modern survey research on voting. To summarise and discuss this is unnecessary here. The ever increasing literature on rational choice and spatial models of party competition is surveyed and criticised admirably in the three books mentioned below. To include yet another discussion would be otiose. For the rest, the argument in this book falls into a little-researched field; where our contentions can be backed up with references to other writers, we have done so. But we have not bothered to scan reading lists for marginal support, or to reference books and articles simply because they consider related fields or problems.

Three essential books:

Brian Barry (1970), *Sociologists, Economists and Democracy* (London: Collier-Macmillan). This is the best critical analysis of the conflict within the discipline between rational-choice and party-identification approaches to voting and party competition. It includes an excellent annotated bibliography.

William Riker and Peter C. Ordeshook (1973), *An Introduction to Positive Political Theory* (Englewood Cliffs: Prentice-Hall). Written by two of the major exponents of the rational choice approach, it contains the best statements of the faith, and basic coverage of most of the problems.

Ian Budge and Dennis Farlie (forthcoming), *Voting and Party Competition* (London: Wiley). This is an attempt to synthesise party identification theory and spatial modelling. It contains an extended discussion of the existing spatial and rational choice models. While we do not agree in detail with the authors, both our books have benefited from conversation and from attempts to bring the two works closer together. Our summary statement of the predictive theory in Chapter 6 can be set easily against the similar format of Budge and Farlie's discussion of other models.

There is one other forthcoming book of importance. Ordeshook, Budge and Farlie, and the author of this book were amongst the participants at a recent conference on Voting, Turnout and Party Competition held in Strasbourg under the auspices of the European Consortium for Political Research. The papers from this conference which brought together scholars from most European countries as well as North America, and from both sides of the methodological division we have written about, are to be published soon. They will be edited by Ian Budge, Ivor Crewe and Dennis Farlie, under the title *Party Competition and Beyond*, Wiley (1976).

One general reference book that may be useful is the only complete compilation of British party manifestos, on which the data for Chapter 4 is based. Had this been published when we collected the data, life would have been much easier. They can now be found in F. W. S. Craig (1972), *British General Election Manifestos 1918–1966* (Chichester: Political Reference Publications).

Adorno, T. W. (1964). *The Authoritarian Personality* (New York: Harper and Rowe).

Barry, B. M. (1965). *Political Argument* (London: Routledge and Kegan Paul).

Barry, B. M. (1970). *Sociologists, Economists and Democracy* (London: Collier-Macmillan).

Beer, S. H. (1965). *Modern British Politics* (London: Faber and Faber).

Berelson, B. R., Lazarsfeld, P., and Mcphee, W. N. (1954). *Voting: A Study of Opinion Forming in a Presidential Campaign* (Chicago: University of Chicago Press).

Berelson, B. R. (1971). *Content Analysis in Communications Research* (New York: Hafner).

Berlin, Sir Isaiah (1969). *Four Essays on Liberty* (London).

Bochel, J. M. and Denver D. T. (1971). Canvassing, Turnout, and Party Support; an Experiment, *British Journal of Political Science*, I, pp. 257–69.

Brittan, S. (1968). *Left or Right; The Bogus Dilemma* (London).

Budge, I. (1970). *Agreement and the Stability of Democracy* (Chicago: Markham).

Budge, I., and Farlie, D. (1975). *Factors Correlating with Voting in Nine Democracies*. Paper given at conference on Voting, Turout and Party Competition, Strasbourg, April 1974. *See also* Budge, Crewe and Farlie.

Budge, I., and Farlie, D. (forthcoming). *Voting and Party Competition* (London: Wiley).

Budge, I., Crewe, I., and Farlie, D. (1976). *Party Identification and Beyond* (London: Wiley),

Burns, J. M. (1963). *Deadlock of Democracy* (Englewood Cliffs: Prentice-Hall).

Butler, D. E., and Stokes, D. E. (1969). *Electoral Change in Britain* (London: The Macmillan Co.).

Butler, D. E., and Pinto-Duschinski, M. (1971). *The British General Election of 1970* (London: Macmillan).

Campbell, A., Converse, P. E., Miller, W. E., and Stokes, D. E. (1960). *The American Voter* (New York: Wiley).

Campbell, A., Converse, P. E., Miller, W. E., and Stokes, D. E. (1966). *Elections and the Political Order* (New York: Wiley).

Converse, P. E. (1966). The Problem of Party Distances in Models of Voting Change, in Jennings, M. K., and Zeigler, L. H., (eds.), *The Electoral Process* (Englewood Cliffs: Prentice-Hall), pp. 175–207.

Charlot, J. (1971). *The Gaullist Phenomenon; the Gaullist movement in the Fifth Republic* (London).

Childs, D. (1970). *The Essentials of Factor Analysis* (London: Holt, Rinehart and Winston).

Crewe, I. (1973). The Politics of 'Affluent' and 'Traditional' Workers in Britain: An Aggregate Data Analysis, *British Journal of Political Science*, III, pp. 29–52.

Crewe, I. (1974). Do Butler and Stokes really explain political change in Britain?, *European Journal of Political Research*, II, pp. 47–92.

Crossman, R. (1975). *The Diaries of a Cabinet Minister* (London: Hamilton & Cape).

Dahl, R. A. (1956). *A Preface to Democratic Theory* (Chicago: University of Chicago Press).

Dahl, R. A. (1972). *Democracy in the United States: Promise and Performance* (Chicago: Rand McNally and Co.).

Downs, A. (1957). *An Economic Theory of Democracy* (New York: Harper).

Duncan, O. D. (1972). 'Path Analysis: Socialogical Examples', *American Journal of Socialogy*, 1972, pp. 1–16.

Duvergar, M. (1959). *Political Parties* 2nd ed. (London: O.U.P.).

Eysenck, H. J. (1951). *The Pyschology of Politics* (London: Routledge and Kegan Paul).

Goldberg, A. S. (1969). Social Determinism and Rationality as Bases of Party Identification, *American Political Science Review*, **63**, pp. 5–25.

Goldthorpe, J. H., and Lockwood, D., et al. (1968). *The Affluent Worker: Political Attitudes and Behaviour* (Cambridge Studies in Sociology 2, Cambridge University Press).

Goodhart, C. N. E., and Bhansali, R. J. (1970). *Political Economy*, Political Studies, 18, pp. 43–106.

Harmon, H. (1967). *Modern Factor Analysis* (Chicago: University of Chicago Press).

Herig, S., and Pinder, J., (1969) (eds.) *European Political Parties* (London: P.E.P.).

Henkel, R. E., and Morrison, D. E. (1970). *The Significance Test Controversy* (London: Butterworth).

Hope, K. (1968). *Methods of Multivariate Analysis* (London: University of London Press).

Key, V. O., Jr. (1966). *The Responsible Electorate: Rationality in Presidential Voting* (Cambridge, Mass.: Belknap Press of Harvard University Press).

Kornhauser, W. (1959). *The Politics of Mass Society* (Glencoe, Ill.: The Free Press).

Kramer, G. H. (1971). Short Term Fluctuations in US Voting Behaviour, 1896–1964, *American Political Science Review*, **65**, pp. 131–143.

Lindblom, C., and Braybrooke, D. (1963). *A Strategy of Decision: Policy Evaluation as a Social Process* (Glencoe, Ill.: The Free Press).

Macdonald, K. I. (1973). *Causal Modelling in Politics and Sociology*, paper for SSRC Seminar in Quantitative Social Science, 1973.

Michels, R. (1966). *Political Parties* trans. E. and C. Paul (New York: The Free Press).

Miliband, R. (1972). *Parliamentary Socialism* 2nd ed. (London: Weidenfeld and Nicolson).

Middlemas, K., and Barnes, J. (1972). *Baldwin* (London: Weidenfeld and Nicolson).

Miller, W. E. (1975). Party Identification in Retrospect, in Budge, I., and Crewe, I. (1975).

North, R. (1963). *Content Analysis, A Handbook* (Evanston: Northwestern University Press).

Riker, W., and Ordeshook, P. (1973). *An Introduction to Positive Political Theory* (Englewood Cliffs: Prentice-Hall).

Robertson, D. B. *Surrogates for Party Identification in a Rational Choice Framework*, in Budge, I., Crewe, I., and Farlie, D. (1976).

Rose, R. (1962). The Political Ideas of English Party Activists, *American Political Science Review*, **56**, pp. 369–375.

Rose, R. (1967). *Influencing Voters* (London: Faber and Faber).

Särlvik, B. (1975). Stable Voters and Party Changers, Mimeo, Institute of Political Science, University of Göteborg.

Schubert, G. (1965). *The Judicial Mind: The Attitudes and Ideologies of Supreme Court Justices, 1946–1963* (Evanston: Northwestern University Press).

Schubert, G. (1965). *Quantitative Analysis of Judicial Behaviour* (Glencoe, Ill.: The Free Press).

Schumpeter, J. (1950). *Capitalism, Socialism and Democracy* (New York: Harper and Row).

Stokes, D. E. (1966). Dimensional Models of Party Competition, in Campbell, A. (1966).

Stokes, D. E. (1967). Parties and the Nationalisation of Electoral Forces, in *The American Party System: Stages of Political Development*, Chambers, W. D., Burnham, W. D., (eds.), (New York: Oxford University Press).

Strauss, L. (1959). What is Political Philosophy? and other studies (New York).

Williams, P. (1970). *French Politics and Elections, 1951–1969* (Cambridge: Cambridge University Press).